BOT PROGRAMMING:
INTELLIGENT AUTOMATION FOR WINDOWS APPLICATIONS AND GAMES

Steven C. Miller Jr.

North Iowa Area Community College

BOT PROGRAMMING: INTELLIGENT AUTOMATION FOR WINDOWS APPLICATIONS AND GAMES

International Standard Book Number (ISBN): 978-1-453-85596-6

First Printing: November 2010

Credits

Editoral Manager: Judith Ann W. Miller
Proof Readers: Jeff Brandt, Daniel Thomas, Stefan Sliger, Adam Seiler and Scott Sonberg.
Cover Design: Norb Thomes
Cover Photos: ©iStockphoto.com Members: Omergenc(Robot), Sorbetto(Pinball Machine)

Trademarks

All terms mentioned in this book that are known to be trademarks or service marks have been appropriately capitalized. However, use of a term in this book should not be regarded as affecting the validity of any trademark or service mark.

Windows, Visual Basic, Visual Studio, 3D Pinball for Windows, Microsoft Notepad, Windows Internet Explorer are registered trademarks of Microsoft Corporation in the United States and/or other countries.

Warning and Disclaimer

Every effort has been made to make this book as complete and as accurate as possible, but no warranty or fitness is implied. The information provided is on as "as-is" basis. The author and the publisher shall have neither liability nor responsibility to any person or entity with respect to any loss or damages arising from the information contained in this book. No patent liability is assumed with respect to the use of the information contained herein.

Acknowledgment

I would like to start by thanking you for taking the time and energy to learn more about Bot programming. It will give you personal gratification to create bots that perform automations that typical automation programs cannot. The fact that you are reading this book proves you are ready to take automation to the next level when it comes to software development and testing. I am sure you have envisioned the benefits of automating software, but quickly realized the difficulty and limitations of off the shelf automated software. If you take the time to learn and practice the automation techniques in this book, your automating skills will increase greatly and save you an immense amount of time.

All of these Bot techniques have been refined over the past four years while I was teaching the Bot Programming class at North Iowa Area Community College (NIACC).

I would like to thank NIACC for giving me the opportunity to teach the Bot Programming class. I would like to thank all the NIACC students that helped shape the Bot Programming class.

Huge thanks to Idle_Mind and other geniuses on experts-exchange.com for taking the time to help me on my quest to learn botting, one question at a time.

I wish to thank my beautiful wife, Judith Ann. Because of her dedication to editing and her support of my dreams, this book quickly became a reality to share with you.

I wish to thank my small army of proof readers: Jeff Brandt, Daniel Thomas, Stefan Slinger, Adam Seiler and Scott Sonberg.

I would like to thank my partner in crime, Norb Thomes, for creating the art work for my awesome book cover. Also, thanks to Tracy Purchase, for the idea of a command line Bot.

I would like to thank the loving God that created all things, and who made this book possible.

Finally, I would like to thank my youngest daughter, Stevie Jo (pictured below), for helping daddy type his book.

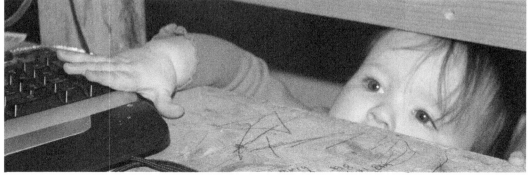

BOT PROGRAMMING: INTELLIGENT AUTOMATION FOR WINDOWS APPLICATIONS AND GAMES
Please Check Out The Other Formats:

eBook

Description: Enjoy the same content the book version has to offer with full color images and all the benefits of the ebook format.

Where to purchase:
http://stores.lulu.com/faintinggoat

Instructional DVD

Description: My extensive teaching over the last ten years has enabled me to produce instructional videos which are easy to understand. Enjoy the same content the book version has with step-by-step video instructions that will ensure your success.

Where to purchase:
https://www.createspace.com/296499

College Credit

Description: For those interested in getting a college credit. I teach CIS-620 Bot Programming for Game and Application (1 Credit Hour) in class at North Iowa Area Community College (http://www.niacc.edu). The course is offered face-to-face in the spring, or anytime as a directed study online with instructional videos.

How to register: If you decide to take the class on campus, simply register for the course in the spring. If you would like to take it as an online directed study, please contact me at milleste@niacc.edu and include "Need help registering for Bot Programming" in the title. I will work with the Registrator directly to ensure a speedy registration.

Table of Contents

Chapter 1:
Introduction

In 2005, I began teaching a new degree at North Iowa Area Community College called Video Game and Software Testing (Quality Assurance), in addition to the two year transferable Computer Science Degree. The Quality Assurance (QA) degree focuses on testing, programming, networking, pc technician, and database.

The Advanced Testing Concepts course started with a section on automation. I quickly realized that off-the-shelf automation tools work great for applications and web browsers. But fail miserably when trying to automate games such as 3D Pinball for Windows, as shown in Figure 1-1. I spent the next four years developing a section for the class that would teach students how to create custom automation applications (Bots) that would work on games as well as applications and web browsers. The book you are about to read has been refined numerous times in the lab of the classroom with students that have only basic programming skills. In 2009, I received numerous requests from the Computer Science students to be able to take a Bot Programming section in the Advanced Testing Concepts class. I split the course up into two courses in 2010 after receiving approval from NIACC. The new one credit course title Game Automation Bot Programming, was created.

It is my hope that you come to enjoy Bot programming as much as I have, and that this book will help you down the path of learning techniques in order to create custom automation Bots.

Here's a suggestion to get the most out of this book: Practice, Practice, and Practice. After reading the book and doing all the examples, find ways in which to apply it in your life. If you can't think of any applications at first, try creating bots for free games, apps, and websites.

Figure 1-1 | 3D Pinball for Windows – Space Cadet

2

A Collage Of Bots, Applications And Games In This Book

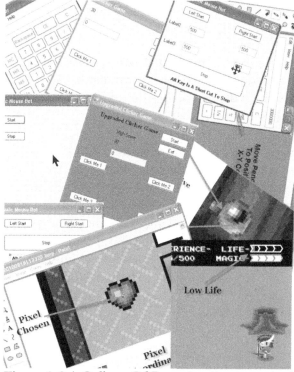

Figure 1-2 | Collage Of Bots, Applications, And Games Used In Book

Conventions Used In This Book

New code that needs to be inserted appears with a bold font throughout the book, as the example in Figure 1-3. Design View Properties to be updated appear in bold font.

Existing Code
> **New Code To Be Entered In Bold**

Existing Code

Figure 1-3 | Form1_load Configuration

Buttons, menus, and items that need to be clicked, double click, selected, highlighted, and moved are *italicized* to assist with readability.

Downloading This Book's Code

The code for the projects can be downloaded from Lulu website at:
http://www.lulu.com/commerce/index.php?fBuyContent=9367801

How To Reach The Author

A valiant effort was made to make this book free of errors. Rest assured any problems you find or I discover, will be given prompt attention to fix. Any revised updates can be downloaded from the Lulu website at:

http://www.lulu.com/commerce/index.php?fBuyContent=9367846

If you find any problems with the text or code examples in this book, you can contact me at steven.c.miller.jr@gmail.com. I cannot promise to answer every question, but I will correct any problems in the book and provide free access to the updates at the above URL. I am always interested in improving my ability to teach effectively and would like to hear any comments on what you liked and did not like with this book.

Ethics Of Using Bots For Automation

The definition of ethics can be defined as consciously making decisions based on ideas of what is right and wrong. The reason you write bots is to save time, increase performance, create virtual cloned players, and more. All of these are great reasons to Bot, but just remember to only Bot when the rules of the site or game or situation allow you to do so. The ramifications of botting on software that strictly bans it can include confiscation on your account and all of its real or virtual items. So please, think twice before using this book in unethical ways.

Introduction To Visual Studio .NET IDE Windows

All of the code provided in the book has been complied in Visual Basic 2010. Visual Basic comes in multiple editions, but I will be programming the below examples using Visual Basic 2010 Express.

Microsoft Visual Basic 2010 (VB 2010) Express can be downloaded at: http://www.microsoft.com/express/downloads/.

Always check the latest system requirements to ensure VB 2010 will run on your system.

Starting Up Visual Basic 2010 Express

For those of you with little, or no, Visual Basic (VB) experience, I have included an overview of using Visual Basic.

Please start up *Visual Basic 2010 Express,* as shown in Figure 1-4.

Figure 1-4 | Launches VB 2010

4

Now click *New Project* located in the upper left of the screen, as shown below in Figure 1-5.

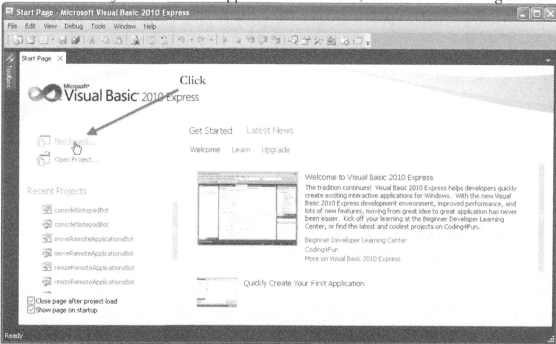

Figure 1-5 | Start New Project

Most of the projects will be created using Windows Forms Application template. Make sure to click on *Windows Forms Application* selection, as shown below in the example in Figure 1-6.

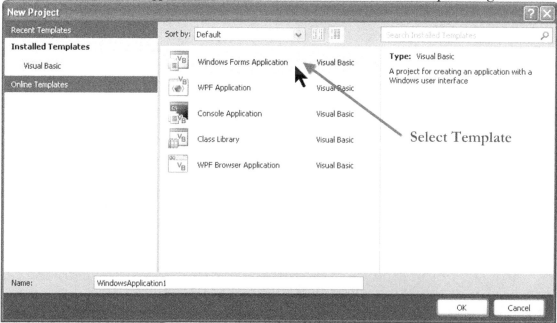

Figure 1-6 | Windows Forms Application

Highlight the *default name* in the Name box and rename the applications before clicking *OK*, as shown in Figure 1-7.

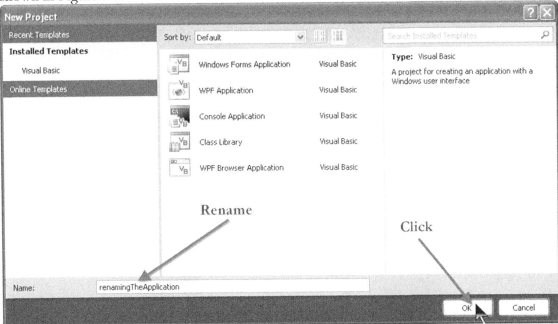

Figure 1-7 | Renaming The Application

After clicking *OK*, the Visual Studio Editor will then appear, as shown below in Figure 1-8.

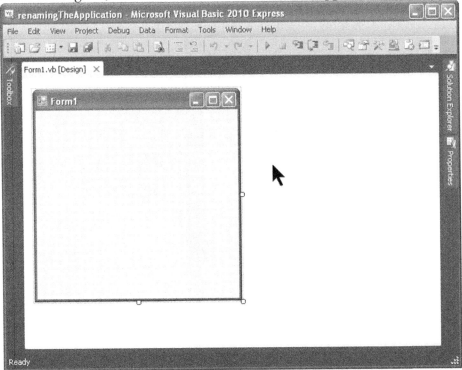

Figure 1-8 | Microsoft Visual Basic 2010 Express Editor

The Toolbox will be heavily used throughout the book for laying out the interface to your Bot application. To access the Toolbox, simply move the mouse over the top of the *Toolbox* icon and it will automatically expand out for viewing, as shown below in Figure 1-9.

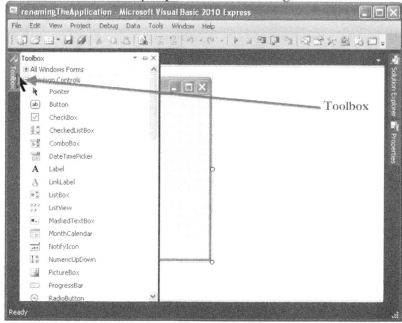

Figure 1-9 | Toolbox

To hide it, simply move the mouse off of the *Toolbox*. To lock the Toolbox in place, move the mouse over to the *left facing pin* and click on it, as shown in Figure 1-10.

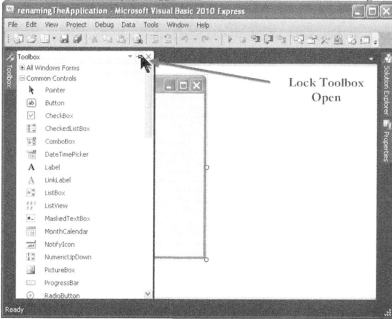

Figure 1-10 | Lock Toolbox

The Solution Explorer allows for switching between the View Designer and View Code. The View Designer allows for editing the Graphic User Interface (GUI) while View Code allows for editing and writiong the Visual Basic code. To access the Solution Explorer, move the mouse above the Solution Explorer tab, as shown below in Figure 1-11.

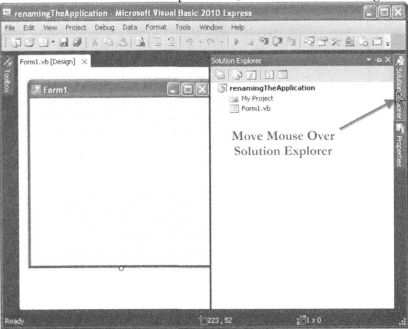

Figure 1-11 | Solution Explorer

To switch to View Code, click on the *View code* Icon, as show below in Figure 1-12.

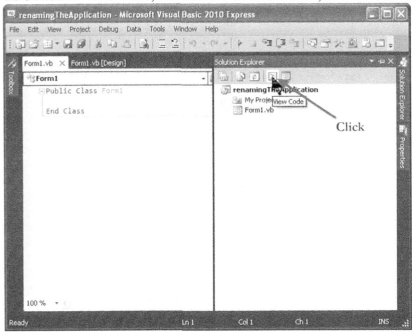

Figure 1-12 | Selecting View Code

To switch back to the View Designer, click on the *View Designer* Icon as in Fig 1-13.

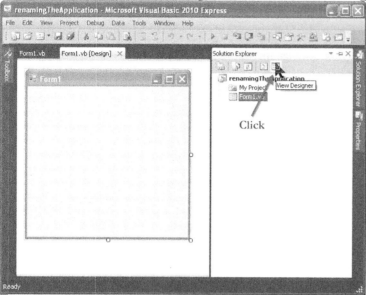

Figure 1-13 | Selecting View Designer

The *Properties* tab will give the ability to configure and set the properties for items in the View Designer, as shown below in Figure 1-14.

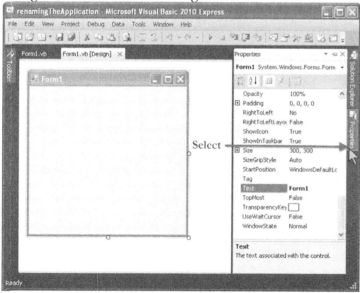

Figure 1-14 | Accessing Properties

Summary

In the next chapter, "Designing a Simple Clicker Game", you will get a hands-on introduction to creating a project in Visual Basic.

Chapter 2:
Designing A Simple Clicker Game

The goal of this chapter is to review the basics of creating a program in Visual Basic. If you are comformatable with Visual Basic you many skip this chapter.

Implementation Overview

The Clicker Game basics start with four buttons, of which only one is active at any given time. The goal of the game is to get a high score by clicking the most buttons within the allotted 30 seconds.

There are two other buttons: a Start Game and an Exit, which start the game and exit the game respectively. You will be using a Label to show the current time and a Textbox to display the current score.

Setting Up The Project

Start a new project and choose *Windows Form Application* and name it: **clickerGame,** as shown below in the example in Figure 2-1.

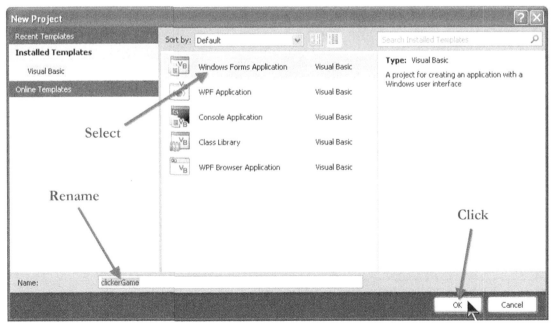

Figure 2-1 | Create clickerGame using Windows Form Application template

After clicking *OK,* there should be a blank form, as shown in Figure 2-2.

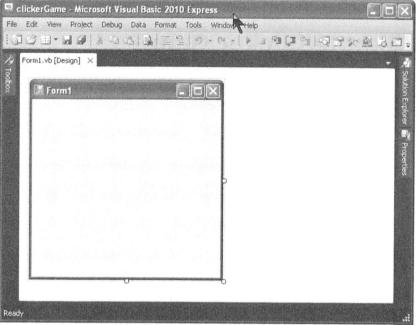

Figure 2-2 | Blank Form

Click the *Save All* button, as in Figure 2-3, below.

Figure 2-3 | Save All

Click *Save* to create a directory structure for **clickerGame** project, as in Figure 2-4.

Save Project			
Name:	clickerGame		
Location:	C:\Documents and Settings\Steven Miller\my documents\visual studio 2010\Projects		Browse...
Solution Name:	clickerGame	☑ Create directory for solution	
		Save	Cancel

Figure 2-4 | Saving And Creating Directory For Project

Rename the Text of the Title bar of the Clicker Game. Make sure *Form1* is selected, and then click on the *Properties* tab. Page down until the Text property is visible, as in Figure 2-5.

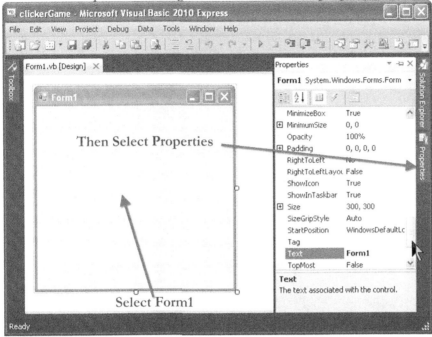

Figure 2-5 | Text Property

Change the form title by clicking in the cell to the right and changing it to **Clicker Game,** as shown in the example in Figure 2-6.

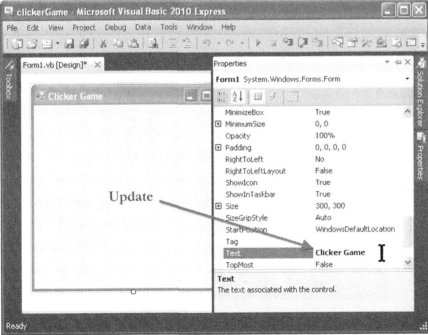

Figure 2-6 | Rename Form Title Bar

Click anywhere to view that the form's title bar is updated, as in Figure 2-7.

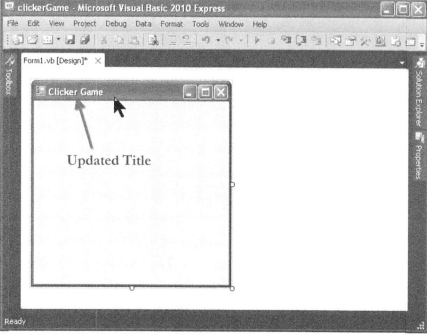

Figure 2-7 | Updated Form Title Bar

Laying Out The Form

Add the Countdown Label to the upper left hand corner to help keep track of the countdown timer. Highlight or click the *Toolbox* to select/click and hold the *Label*, shown in Figure 2-8.

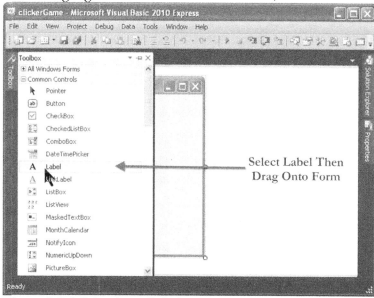

Figure 2-8 | Selecting a Label

While still holding down the left mouse button, drag the *Label* to the upper left hand corner of the form. Use the blue guide lines to help place it in the upper left hand corner. Release the mouse and a default label will appear in the chosen location, as in Figure 2-9.

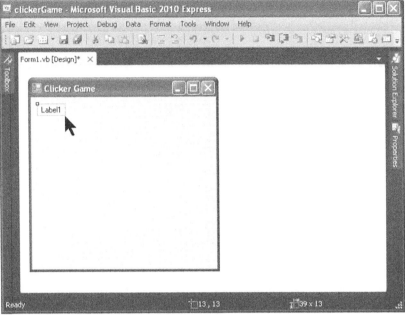

Figure 2-9 | Dragging A Label Onto The Form

To move Label1, move the mouse above the label until the cross appears. Then click and hold in order to move the *label* to the desired location, as in Figure 2-10.

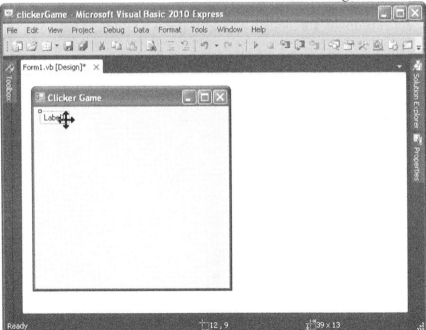

Figure 2-10 | Release Mouse To Place Label

14

Make sure the *Label1* is highlighted. If not, click on the label to highlight it. Click on the *Properties* tab and page down to the Text property and update it to **30,** as in Figure 2-11.

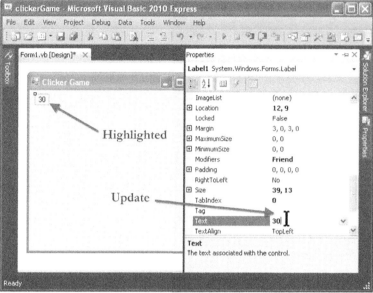

Figure 2-11 | Label Text Property

Use 30 seconds as the duration of the Clicker Game count down. The default name of the Label is Label1. Each time a new Label is added, it increases the default name by incrementing the number by one.

Now rename the Label1 so it will be easier to identify and update later. Click on the *Properties tab* and page down to the (Name) property and update it to **countDownTimer,** as seen in Figure 2-12.

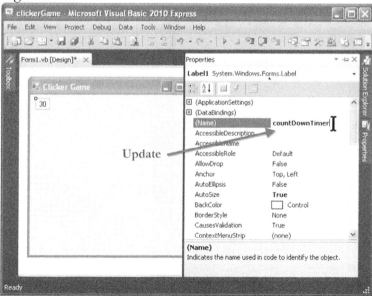

Figure 2-12 | Update Name Property

Add the Score Box TextBox to capture the score of the current game. Click on the *Toolbox* to select and drag the *Textbox* into the upper left hand corner under the countdown timer, as shown in the example below in Figure 2-13.

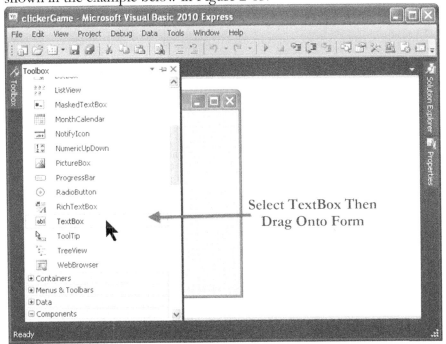

Figure 2-13 | Select TextBox From ToolBox

Use the guidelines to align the TextBox directly below the countdown timer, as in Figure 2-14.

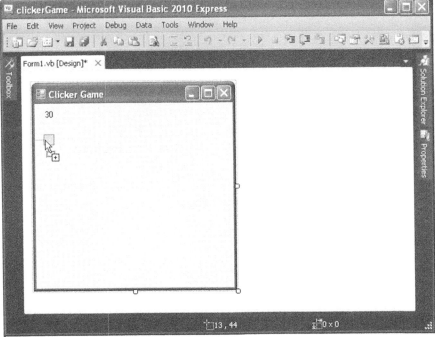

Figure 2-14 | Place TextBox

Resize the TextBox as needed by moving the mouse over the end of the box until the double headed arror appears, then click and drag to resize, as in Figure 2-15.

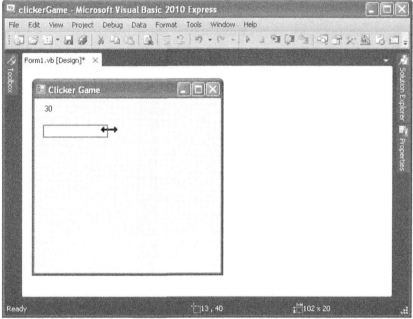

Figure 2-15 | Resize TextBox

Highlight the *TextBox* and then change the (Name) property to **scoreBox,** as in Figure 2-16, and set Text property to **0,** as shown in Figure 2-17.

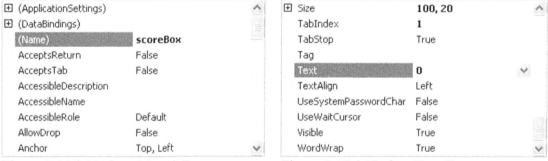

Figure 2-16 | Update (Name) Property   Figure 2-17 | Update Text Property

Add the Start button to the upper-right corner. Click on *Button*, select and hold, and then drag the *Button* into the upper-right corner, as shown in Figure 2-18.

Figure 2-18 | Add Button

Use the guidelines to help align the Button1, as in Figure 2-19.

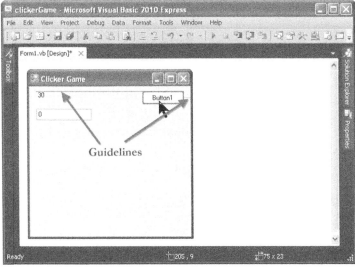

Figure 2-19 | Place Button

Highlight *Button1* and change the (Name) property to **startButton**, shown in Figure 2-20, and set Text property to **Start**, as in Figure 2-21.

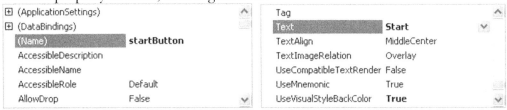

Figure 2-20 | Update (Name) Property   Figure 2-21 | Update Text Property

Add the Exit button below the Start button, as shown in Figure 2-22.

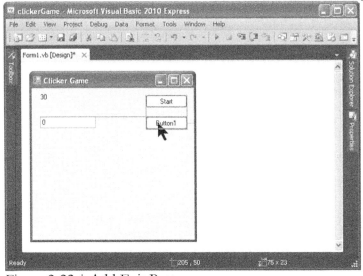

Figure 2-22 | Add Exit Button

18

Highlight *Button1* then change the (Name) property to **exitButton**, as in Figure 2-23; and set Text property to **Exit**, in Figure 2-24.

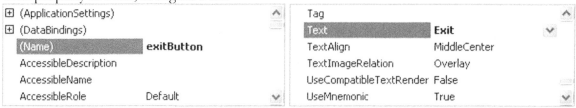

Figure 2-23 | Update (Name) Property   Figure 2-24 | Update Text Property

Add the four Click Me buttons to the remaining area of the form. Drag four *buttons* and place them as shown in Figure 2-25, below.

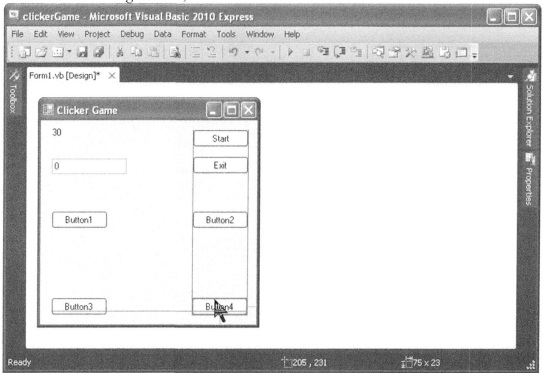

Figure 2-25 | Adding Click Me Buttons

Highlight the *Button1*. Change the (Name) property to **clickMe1**, shown in Figure 2-26; and set the Text property to **Click Me 1**, as shown in Figure 2-27.

Figure 2-26 | Update (Name) Property   Figure 2-27 | Update Text Property

Highlight the *Button2*. Change the (Name) property to **clickMe2** and set the Text property to **Click Me 2**.

Highlight the *Button3*. Change the (Name) property to **clickMe3** and set the Text property to **Click Me 3**.

Highlight the *Button4*. Change the (Name) property to **clickMe4** and set the Text property to **Click Me 4**.

The Design view is now complete and should look like Figure 2-28.

Figure 2-28 | Completed Design View

Coding The Project

The game starts up with the Click Me buttons disabled. To disable the Click Me buttons double-click anyplace on the *Form* where there is no a button, label, or text box. I would suggest double-clicking in the middle, as shown in Figure 2-29.

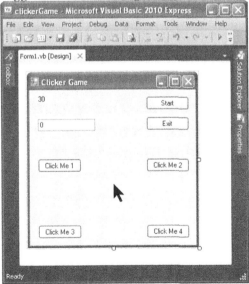

Figure 2-29 | Double Click To Enter Form1_load

This gives access to the Form1_Load subroutine, as shown in Figure 2-30. The load subroutine allows for adding code that will be run once at startup. This is the typical location for initialization settings.

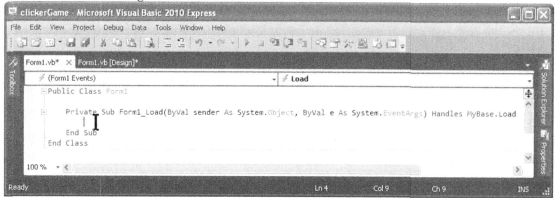

Figure 2-30 | Form1_load Subroutine

Take advantage of using the auto complete by hitting the space bar or tab key after choosing the correct option, as shown in Figure 2-31.

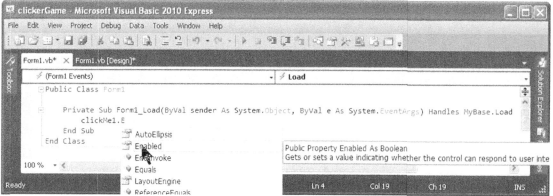

Figure 2-31 | Use Auto Complete To Assist Your Coding

To help with code visibility I will need to use multiple lines to display a single line of code, throughout the book. To separate a single line of code into multiple displayed lines, I will place an underscore _ at the end of the line, as shown in Figure 2-32.

The clickMe1.Enabled = ? indicates whether the control is enabled or disabled. Code from Figure 2-32 results in all of the Click Me buttons being disabled and becoming transparent in appearance. Enter the following code shown in **bold** into the Form1_load subroutine:

```
Private Sub Form1_Load(ByVal sender As System.Object, _
    ByVal e As System.EventArgs)  Handles MyBase.Load

    clickMe1.Enabled = False
    clickMe2.Enabled = False
    clickMe3.Enabled = False
    clickMe4.Enabled = False

End Sub
```

Figure 2-32 | Form1_load Configuration

Save the project by clicking on the *Save All* icon on the toolbar, as shown in Figure 2-33.

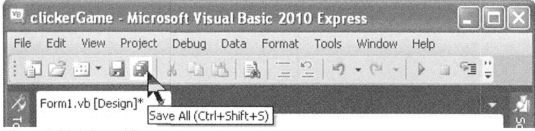

Figure 2-33 | Save All

The next step is to test the code from above by debugging the code. There are three easy ways to start debugging the code. The first is to click on the *Debug* menu and choose *Start Debugging*, as shown in Figure 2-34. The second is to click on the *right pointing green arrow* on the toolbar, as in Figure 2-35. The third way is to simply use the short cut key of (*F5*).

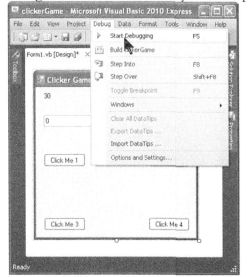

Figure 2-34 | Menu Start Debugging

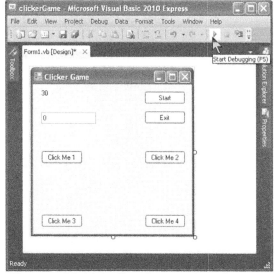

Figure 2-35 | Toolbar Start Debugging

Start Debugging will build the Clicker Game windows application, as shown in Figure 2-36. Notice how the Click Me buttons are transparent and completely disabled from receiving any clicks from the user. The Start button is enabled but clicking on it does nothing. The Exit button is enabled but clicking on it does nothing. The label called countDownTimer appears with the default number of 30 and cannot be changed. The textbox called scoreBox starts out as zero but can be overwritten.

Figure 2-36 | Clicker Game Application

It is very important to remember to close the application that spawned when Start Debugging was clicked before making any additional changes to the Design View or the Code View, as shown in Figure 2-37.

Figure 2-37 | Closing Application

The countdown timer is the next item to create. A variable is needed to store the value of the countdown timer. Double-click in the *middle of the design view* or click *view code*. Create global variables of the type Integer called gameTimerLimit and intTimerCount so that it can be accessed anywhere in the program, as in Figure 2-38. The variable gameTimerLimit will be assigned a value of **30**. This matches the value of the text that was set in the label countDownTimer. The variable intTimerCount will be assigned a value of **0**.

```
Public Class Form1

    Dim gameTimerLimit As Integer = 30
    Dim intTimerCount As Integer = 0

    Private Sub Form1_Load(ByVal sender As System.Object, _
        ByVal e As System.EventArgs) Handles MyBase.Load

        clickMe1.Enabled = False
        clickMe2.Enabled = False
        clickMe3.Enabled = False
        clickMe4.Enabled = False


    End Sub
End Class
```

Figure 2-38 | Form1_load Configuration

The intTimerCount is reset to zero every time you click the Start button. This is important because when restarting the game, the timer count also needs to restart.

Double-click on the *Start* button in the design view, as shown in Figure 2-39.

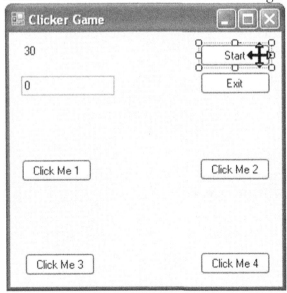

Figure 2-39 | Enter Start Button Subroutine

The cursor will appear in the startButton subroutine, as shown in the example in Figure 2-40.

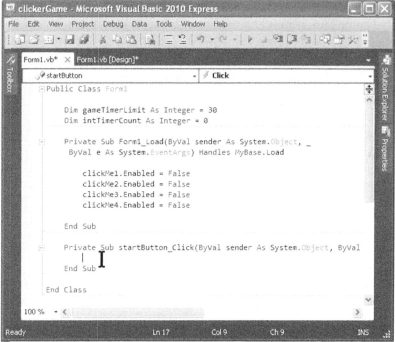

Figure 2-40 | Inside startButton Subroutine

Now insert **intTimerCount = 0** into startButton_Click, as in Figure 2-41. This will ensure that when starting a new game the countdown time will be reset.

```
Public Class Form1
    Dim gameTimerLimit As Integer = 30
    Dim intTimerCount As Integer = 0

    Private Sub Form1_Load(ByVal sender As System.Object, _
        ByVal e As System.EventArgs) Handles MyBase.Load
        clickMe1.Enabled = False
        clickMe2.Enabled = False
        clickMe3.Enabled = False
        clickMe4.Enabled = False
    End Sub

    Private Sub startButton_Click(ByVal sender As System.Object, _
        ByVal e As System.EventArgs) Handles startButton.Click

        intTimerCount = 0

    End Sub
End Class
```

Figure 2-41 | Insert intTimerCount = 0

Once every second, the application needs to update the label countDownTimer by reducing it by one. To accomplish this, add a Timer from the Toolbox. Drag a *Timer* to any place on the application form, shown in Figure 2-42 and Figure 2-43. To resize the *Timer display area* move the mouse to the separation, as shown in Figure 2-43, and resize as desired, as in Figure 2-44.

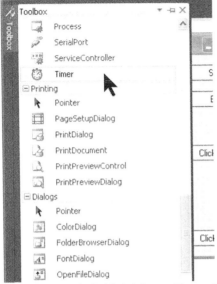

Figure 2-42 | Add A Timer From Toolbox

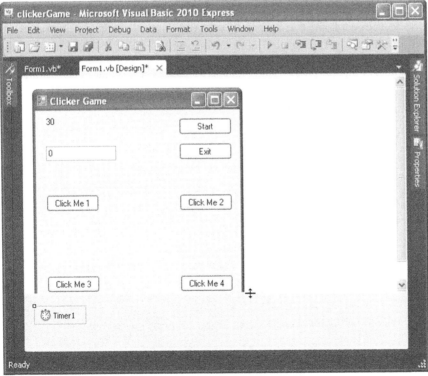

Figure 2-43 | Resize Timer Area

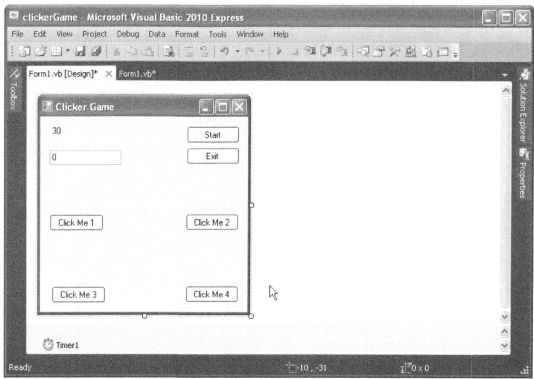

Figure 2-44 | Resized Timer Area

Just as with the Start button, double-click on the *Timer1* to edit the Timer1 code, as shown in Figure 2-45. The cursor will be placed in the Timer1 subroutine, as in Figure 2-46.

Figure 2-45 | Double Click Timer1

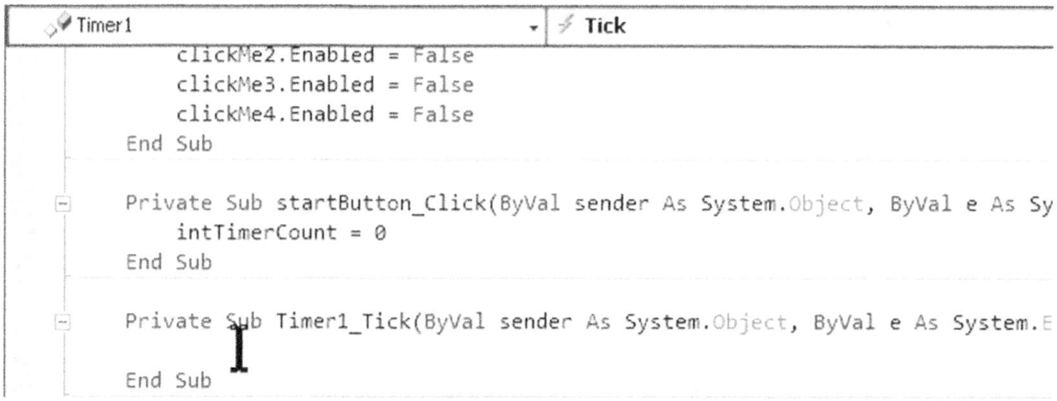

```
Timer1                                    ⚡ Tick
            clickMe2.Enabled = False
            clickMe3.Enabled = False
            clickMe4.Enabled = False
      End Sub

      Private Sub startButton_Click(ByVal sender As System.Object, ByVal e As Sy
            intTimerCount = 0
      End Sub

      Private Sub Timer1_Tick(ByVal sender As System.Object, ByVal e As System.E

      End Sub
```

Figure 2-46 | Inside Timer1_Tick Subroutine

Now insert the code in **bold** into the Timer1_Tick subroutine, as shown in Figure 2-47.

```
Private Sub Timer1_Tick(ByVal sender As System.Object, _
    ByVal e As System.EventArgs) Handles Timer1.Tick

    Dim timeValue As Integer
    intTimerCount = intTimerCount + 1

    If (intTimerCount <= gameTimerLimit) Then
       timeValue = gameTimerLimit - intTimerCount
    Else
       clickMe1.Enabled = False
       clickMe2.Enabled = False
       clickMe3.Enabled = False
       clickMe4.Enabled = False
       startButton.Enabled = True
       exitButton.Enabled = True
    End If

    countDownTimer.Text = timeValue.ToString
End Sub
```

Figure 2-47 | Timer1_Tick Code

The code is broken down here line by line:

Code (C): Dim timeValue As Integer
Description (D): Declare a local integer variable to be used in keeping track of the count.

C: intTimerCount = intTimerCount + 1
D: Increment global timer count.

C: If (intTimerCount <= gameTimerLimit) Then
D: Check to see if you are equal to or below the timer limit.

C: timeValue = gameTimerLimit - intTimerCount
D: If still equal or below, then subtract the intTimerCount from the gameTimerLimit.

C: Else
D: The time is no longer below or equal, so the game session is done

C: clickMe1.Enabled = False
    clickMe2.Enabled = False
    clickMe3.Enabled = False
    clickMe4.Enabled = False
D: Disable all the Click Me buttons.

28

C: startButton.Enabled = True
    exitButton.Enabled = True
D: Enable Start and Exit buttons when game session is done.

C: End If
D: End If/Else Statement

C: countDownTimer.Text = timeValue.ToString
D: Update the countDownTimer label. It is important to know you need to reference: countDownTimer.Text not just: countDownTimer to update the text of the label. Also, it is important to make sure to convert the integer timeValue to a string before assigning it to: countDownTimer.Text.

Now, configure the timer to fire or act once every second. The time interval for the timer is measured in milliseconds. Select/click on *Timer1*, as shown in Figure 2-48. To have the timer fire once a second, update the property *Interval* to **1000**, as shown in Figure 2-49.

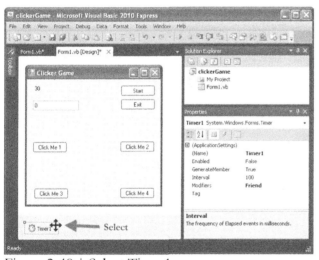

Figure 2-48 | Select Timer1

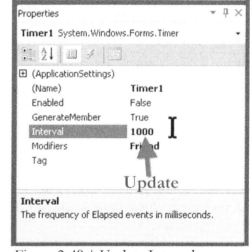

Figure 2-49 | Update Interval

Now test what you have. Click the *Save All* button, as in Figure 2-50. Click either *Start Debugging* or (*F5*), as in Figure 2-51.

Figure 2-50 | Save All

Figure 2-51 | Start Debugging

29

When the application appears, click the *Start* button to see what happens, as shown in Figure 2-52. Nothing happens yet when the Start button is pushed. Close the Clicker Game application.

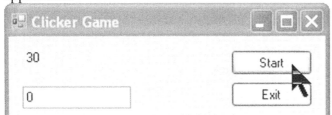

Figure 2-52 | Testing Clicker Me Application

A timer was added, but before it can be used it must be enabled in the code. Before exiting the subroutine startButton, Timer1 needs to be enabled by adding the code **Timer1.Enabled = True**, as shown in Figure 2-53.

Insert the code to enable the Timer1 inside of the startButton subroutine.

```
Private Sub startButton_Click(ByVal sender As System.Object, _
        ByVal e As System.EventArgs) Handles startButton.Click

    intTimerCount = 0
    Timer1.Enabled = True
End Sub
```

Figure 2-53 | Enabling Timer1 inside of the startButton subroutine

Now test what you have. Click the *Save All* button. Click either *Start Debugging* or (*F5*). When your application appears, click the *Start* button to see what happens. The countDownTimer label is updated once every second by being decremented by one, as shown in Figure 2-54.

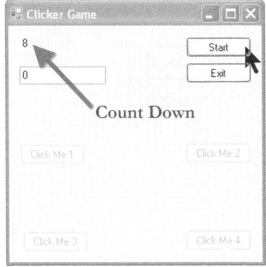

Figure 2-54 | countDownTimer Decrementing

30

When testing has finished, but before editing the code, close the application.

This is how to get the Exit button working. Double-click the *Exit* button and add the following code **Application.Exit(),** as shown in Figure 2-55.

```
Private Sub exitButton_Click(ByVal sender As System.Object, _
    ByVal e As System.EventArgs) Handles exitButton.Click

    Application.Exit()

End Sub
```
Figure 2-55 | Exiting the application using the Exit button

Now test what you have. Click the *Save All* button. Click either *Start Debugging* or (*F5*). Now click on the *Exit* button to close the Clicker Game application, as shown in Figure 2-56.

Figure 2-56 | Close Using Exit Button

After clicking the *Start* button once, the count down timer begins. If it is pressed a second time prior to reaching zero, it will restart. If the Exit button is accidently hit while playing the game, it shuts down. To prevent both of these issues, disable both the Start and Exit button after the Start button is pressed by inserting the code shown in Figure 2-57.

```
Private Sub startButton_Click(ByVal sender As System.Object, _
    ByVal e As System.EventArgs) Handles startButton.Click

    intTimerCount = 0
    startButton.Enabled = False
    exitButton.Enabled = False
    Timer1.Enabled = True

End Sub
```
Figure 2-57| Disable Start And Exit Button Inside Of The startButton Subroutine

Now test what you have. Click the *Save All* button. Click either *Start Debugging* or (*F5*). Notice that both the Start and the Exit buttons were disabled until the counter finished, as in Figure 2-58. After the countdown is complete, the Start and Exit buttons are enabled, as shown in the previous code, in Figure 2-47. The result of enabling theStart and Exit buttons is shown in Figure 2-59. When finished testing click the *Exit* button.

Figure 2-58 | Disabled Start Exit button

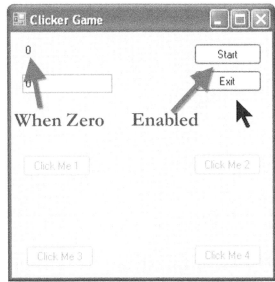
Figure 2-59 | Enabled Start Exit Button

One of the Click Me buttons needs to be enabled when the Start button is clicked. To keep it simple, enable the clickMe1 button in the startButton subroutine, as shown in Figure 2-60.

```
Private Sub startButton_Click(ByVal sender As System.Object, _
        ByVal e As System.EventArgs) Handles startButton.Click

    intTimerCount = 0
    startButton.Enabled = False
    exitButton.Enabled = False
    clickMe1.Enabled = True
    Timer1.Enabled = True


End Sub
```

Figure 2-60 | Enable Click Me 1 Button In The startButton Subroutine.

Now test what you have. Click the *Save All* button. Click either *Start Debugging* or (*F5*). First click on the *Start* button then click on the *Click Me 1* button, as shown in Figure 2-61. When the timer has completed counting down and the testing is finished, click the *Exit* button. The foundation has now been laid for starting and exiting the game.

Next, add the mechanics for the game play itself.

Figure 2-61 | Click Me 1 Button Enabled

To keep track of the score, add another global variable of type integer called gameScore, as shown in Figure 2-62.

```
Public Class clickerGame
    Dim gameTimerLimit As Integer = 30
    Dim intTimerCount As Integer = 0
    Dim gameScore As Integer = 0
```

Figure 2-62 | Adding Variable gameScore

The gameScore also need to be rest to zero for every new game that is started. Set the variable gameScore inside the startButton subroutine to zero, as shown in Figure 2-63.

```
Private Sub startButton_Click(ByVal sender As System.Object, _
        ByVal e As System.EventArgs) Handles startButton.Click
    intTimerCount = 0
    gameScore = 0
    startButton.Enabled = False
    exitButton.Enabled = False
    clickMe1.Enabled = True
    Timer1.Enabled = True
End Sub
```

Figure 2-63| Enable Click Me 1 Button In The startButton Subroutine.

When the Start button is clicked, the game begins with the Click Me 1 button enabled. The clicks on each of the other Click Me buttons need to be processed and randomized in the order in which each of the next buttons appear. Start with Click Me 1 button and copy the same code into each of the other Click Me buttons. The code to insert into the Click Me 1 button is shown below in Figure 2-64.

```
Private Sub clickMe1_Click(ByVal sender As System.Object, _
    ByVal e As System.EventArgs) Handles clickMe1.Click

    gameScore = gameScore + 1
    scoreBox.Text = gameScore.ToString
    Dim randomNumber As Integer
    randomNumber = Int(Rnd() * 4) + 1

    If (randomNumber = 1) Then
       clickMe1.Enabled = True
       clickMe2.Enabled = False
       clickMe3.Enabled = False
       clickMe4.Enabled = False
    ElseIf (randomNumber = 2) Then
       clickMe1.Enabled = False
       clickMe2.Enabled = True
       clickMe3.Enabled = False
       clickMe4.Enabled = False
    ElseIf (randomNumber = 3) Then
       clickMe1.Enabled = False
       clickMe2.Enabled = False
       clickMe3.Enabled = True
       clickMe4.Enabled = False
    ElseIf (randomNumber = 4) Then
       clickMe1.Enabled = False
       clickMe2.Enabled = False
       clickMe3.Enabled = False
       clickMe4.Enabled = True
    End If
End Sub
```

Figure 2-64| Click Me Button Code.

Use the same code for all four of the buttons.

The code is broken down here line by line:

Code (C): gameScore = gameScore + 1
Description (D): Increment the game score by one, since you have clicked on a Click Me button.

C: scoreBox.Text = gameScore.ToString

D: Update the scoreBox with the new game score. It's important to remember you need to assign the scoreBox.Text the new gameScore and not scoreBox directly.

C: Dim randomNumber As Integer

D: Create a local variable of type Integer to store a random number.

C: randomNumber = Int(Rnd() * 4) + 1

D: Int(Rnd() * 4) will create a whole number between 0 – 3. You add +1 to give a range of 1 - 4.

C: If (randomNumber = 1) Then
      clickMe1.Enabled = True
      clickMe2.Enabled = False
      clickMe3.Enabled = False
      clickMe4.Enabled = False

D: If the randomNumber is equal 1 then you will enable Click Me 1 and disable the remaining Click Me buttons.

C: ElseIf (randomNumber = 2) Then
      clickMe1.Enabled = False
      clickMe2.Enabled = True
      clickMe3.Enabled = False
      clickMe4.Enabled = False

D: If the randomNumber is equal 2 then you will enable Click Me 2 and disable the remaining Click Me buttons.

C: ElseIf (randomNumber = 3) Then
      clickMe1.Enabled = False
      clickMe2.Enabled = False
      clickMe3.Enabled = True
      clickMe4.Enabled = False

D: If the randomNumber is equal 3 then you will enable Click Me 3 and disable the remaining Click Me buttons.

C: ElseIf (randomNumber = 4) Then
      clickMe1.Enabled = False
      clickMe2.Enabled = False
      clickMe3.Enabled = False
      clickMe4.Enabled = True
    End If

D: If the randomNumber is equal 4 then you will enable Click Me 4 and disable the remaining Click Me buttons.

Now double-click on *Click Me buttons 2, 3, and 4.* Add the corresponding code for the Click Me 2, 3, and 4 buttons, the code is shown in Figure 2-65.

```vb
Private Sub clickMe2_Click(ByVal sender As System.Object, _
    ByVal e As System.EventArgs) Handles clickMe2.Click

    gameScore = gameScore + 1
    scoreBox.Text = gameScore.ToString

    Dim randomNumber As Integer
    randomNumber = Int(Rnd() * 4) + 1

    If (randomNumber = 1) Then
        clickMe1.Enabled = True
        clickMe2.Enabled = False
        clickMe3.Enabled = False
        clickMe4.Enabled = False
    ElseIf (randomNumber = 2) Then
        clickMe1.Enabled = False
        clickMe2.Enabled = True
        clickMe3.Enabled = False
        clickMe4.Enabled = False
    ElseIf (randomNumber = 3) Then
        clickMe1.Enabled = False
        clickMe2.Enabled = False
        clickMe3.Enabled = True
        clickMe4.Enabled = False
    ElseIf (randomNumber = 4) Then
        clickMe1.Enabled = False
        clickMe2.Enabled = False
        clickMe3.Enabled = False
        clickMe4.Enabled = True
    End If
End Sub

Private Sub clickMe3_Click(ByVal sender As System.Object, _
    ByVal e As System.EventArgs) Handles clickMe3.Click

    gameScore = gameScore + 1
    scoreBox.Text = gameScore.ToString

    Dim randomNumber As Integer
    randomNumber = Int(Rnd() * 4) + 1

    If (randomNumber = 1) Then
```

```
         clickMe1.Enabled = True
         clickMe2.Enabled = False
         clickMe3.Enabled = False
         clickMe4.Enabled = False
      ElseIf (randomNumber = 2) Then
         clickMe1.Enabled = False
         clickMe2.Enabled = True
         clickMe3.Enabled = False
         clickMe4.Enabled = False
      ElseIf (randomNumber = 3) Then
         clickMe1.Enabled = False
         clickMe2.Enabled = False
         clickMe3.Enabled = True
         clickMe4.Enabled = False
      ElseIf (randomNumber = 4) Then
         clickMe1.Enabled = False
         clickMe2.Enabled = False
         clickMe3.Enabled = False
         clickMe4.Enabled = True
      End If
End Sub

Private Sub clickMe4_Click(ByVal sender As System.Object, _
   ByVal e As System.EventArgs) Handles clickMe4.Click

   gameScore = gameScore + 1
   scoreBox.Text = gameScore.ToString

   Dim randomNumber As Integer
   randomNumber = Int(Rnd() * 4) + 1

   If (randomNumber = 1) Then
      clickMe1.Enabled = True
      clickMe2.Enabled = False
      clickMe3.Enabled = False
      clickMe4.Enabled = False
   ElseIf (randomNumber = 2) Then
      clickMe1.Enabled = False
      clickMe2.Enabled = True
      clickMe3.Enabled = False
      clickMe4.Enabled = False
   ElseIf (randomNumber = 3) Then
      clickMe1.Enabled = False
      clickMe2.Enabled = False
```

```
        clickMe3.Enabled = True
        clickMe4.Enabled = False
    ElseIf (randomNumber = 4) Then
        clickMe1.Enabled = False
        clickMe2.Enabled = False
        clickMe3.Enabled = False
        clickMe4.Enabled = True
    End If
  End Sub
```

Figure 2-65 | Click Me Buttons Code

Now test what you have. Click the *Save All* button. Click either *Start Debugging* or (*F5*). Now click on the *Start* button and play the game, as shown in Figure 2-66. When finished testing click the *Exit* button.

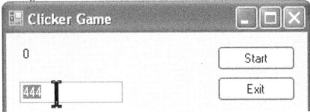

Figure 2-66 | Playing The Clicker Game

One issue is that the scoreBox TextBox can be highlight and the score overwritten, as shown in Figure 2-67.

Figure 2-67 | Overwrite scoreBox

In Design View select the *scoreBox* TextBox. Find the property ReadOnly and then change it from False to **True**, as shown in Figure 2-68.

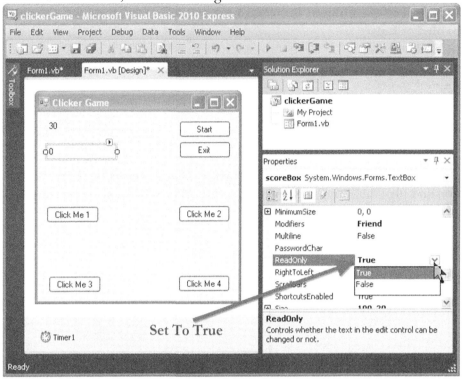

Figure 2-68 | Change scoreBox ReadOnly Property To True

Now test what you have. Click the *Save All* button. Click either *Start Debugging* or *(F5)*. Now click on the *Start* button and play the game, as shown in Figure 2-69. When finished testing click the *Exit* button.

Figure 2-69 | Updated With ReadOnly scoreBox

Summary

The goal of the Clicker Game was to review Visual Basic skills and bring you up to speed on the basic components used throughout this book. VB .NET is a very useful and exciting language. I hope you continue to explore all of the potental that VB .NET has to offer in this book and beyond.

Chapter 3:
Upgrade The Clicker Game To Have A High Score Piece And Color

Implementation Overview

Upgrades are going to be added to the Clicker Game. The goal here is to practice going back to use existing Bot applications, and then making upgrades as needed.

Version Control

Version control, in its most basic form, is making copies of the code at different times in development so a programmer can go back, if needed. To keep things simple here, I will create a copy of the code directory of the clickerGame. In Visual Basic it will be necessary to create a copy of the whole project.

This can be done in multiple ways, but this one is simple. First, go to the menu and select *File*. Then select *Open Project*, as shown in Figure 3-1.

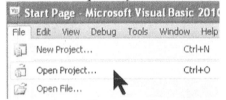

Figure 3-1 | Choosing Open Project

Select the folder/directory *clickerGame* as shown in Figure 3-2.

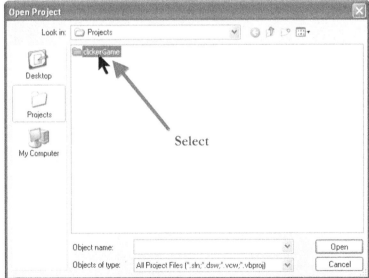

Figure 3-2 | Selecting The clickerGame Folder

Next, right mouse click on the *Copy* option from the menu, as shown in Figure 3-3.

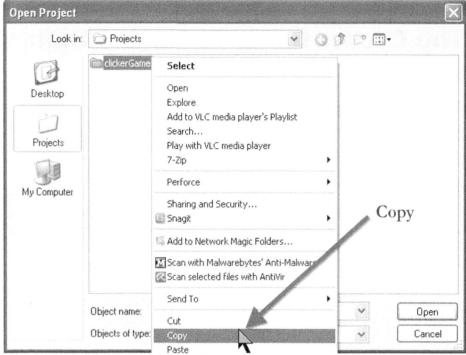

Figure 3-3 | Copy clickerGame Directory

Right mouse click, but this time choose the *Paste* option, as in Figure 3-4.

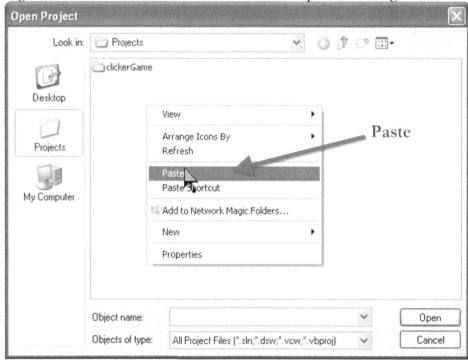

Figure 3-4 | Paste A Copy Of clickerGame Folder

Select the folder/directory *Copy of clickerGame*, as shown below in Figure 3-5.

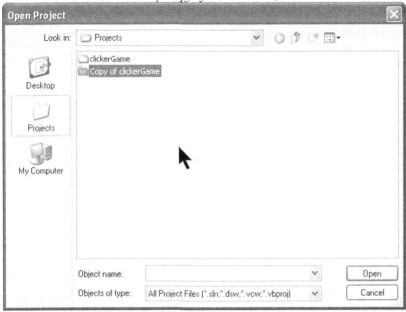

Figure 3-5 | Select Copy of clickerGame Directory

Right mouse click and then select *Rename* option, as in Figure 3-6.

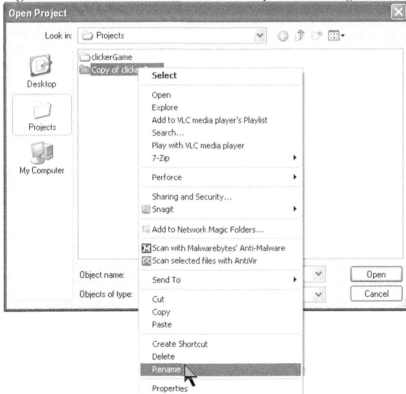

Figure 3-6| Select Rename Option

44

Change the name **Copy of clickerGame** to **clickerGameUpgrade,** as in Figure 3-7 and Figure 3-8.

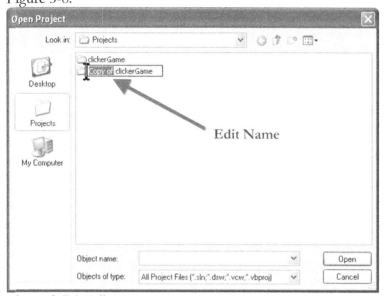

Figure 3-7 | Edit Name

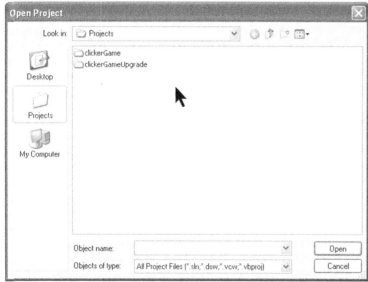

Figure 3-8 | A New Version To Do Upgrade On

When creating multiple versions of code it is helpful to include a date stamp in the name. Examples:

- clickerGame
- clickerGame04July2010
- clickerGame17July2010
- clickerGame21December2012

Setting Up The Project

Open the project called clickerGameUpgrade. Choose *File -> Open Project* or *Ctrl + O.*
Double-click on *clickerGameUpgrade* Folder, as in Figure 3-9.

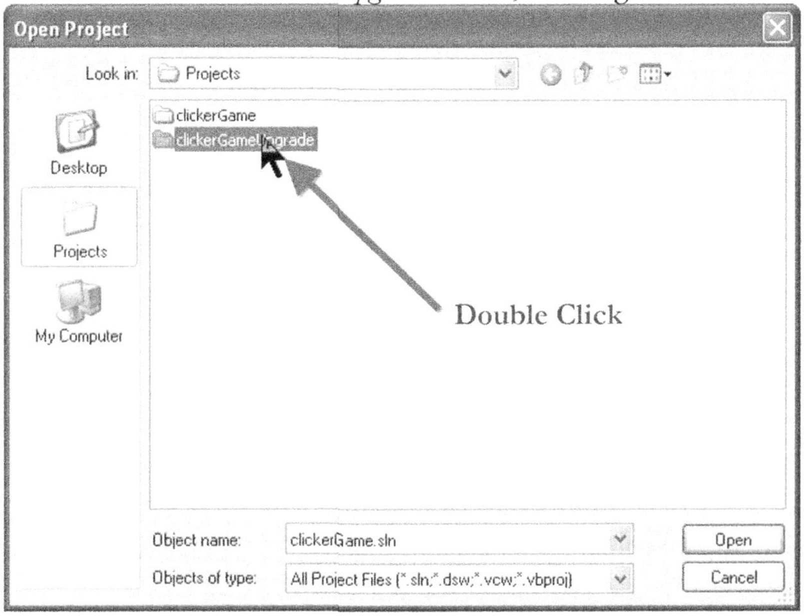

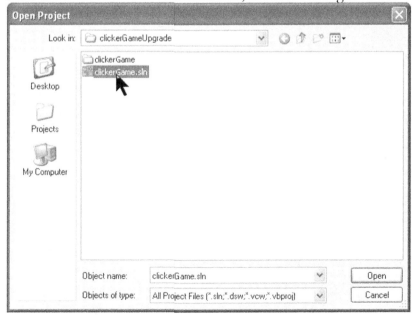

Figure 3-9 | Double Click clickerGameUpgrade Folder

Now select *clickerGame.sln* Solution File, as shown in Figure 3-10.

Figure 3-10 | Select clickerGame Solution File

Finally, click on the *Open* button, as shown below in Figure 3-11.

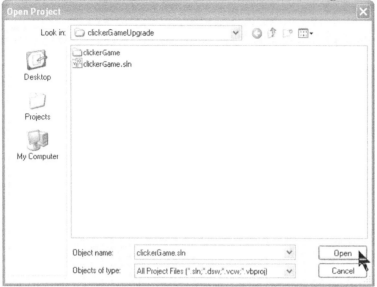

Figure 3-11 | Open clickerGameUpgrade Project

If the project opens without Design or Code View double-click on *Form1.vb*, as shown below in the example in Figure 3-12.

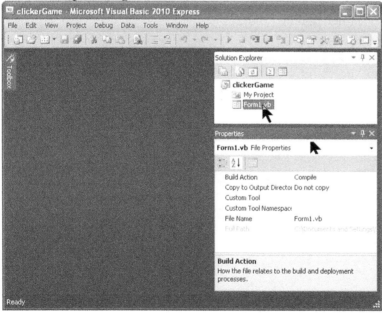

Figure 3-12 | clickerGameUpgrade Project Open

Notice that the folder contains exactly the same contents as the original clickerGame folder. It is helpful to include some identification in the Design View that distinguishes the difference between versions.

Laying Out The Form

To quickly identify the upgraded Clicker Game, add a Label titled Upgraded Clicker Game. Open the *ToolBox* to click and drag a *Label* to the top center of the Form, as in Figure 3-13 and Figure 3-14.

Toolbox
Pointer
Button
CheckBox
CheckedListBox
ComboBox
DateTimePicker
Label
LinkLabel

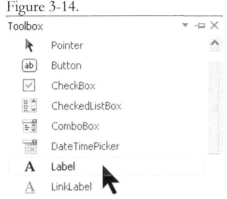

Figure 3-13 | Select And Drag A Label

Clicker Game
30
Label1
Start
0
Exit

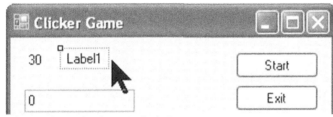

Figure 3-14 | Place Label On Form

With *Label1* selected go to the *Properties* tab. Select the *Text* property and change the value to **Upgraded Clicker Game**, as in Figure 3-15.

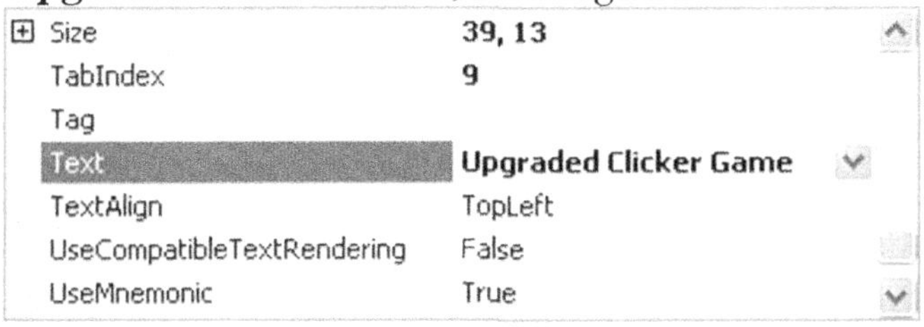

Size
39, 13
TabIndex
9
Tag
Text
Upgraded Clicker Game
TextAlign
TopLeft
UseCompatibleTextRendering
False
UseMnemonic
True

Figure 3-15 | Change Label1 Text

Select the *Font* property and then click on the *trip dots* on the right, as shown in Figure 3-16.

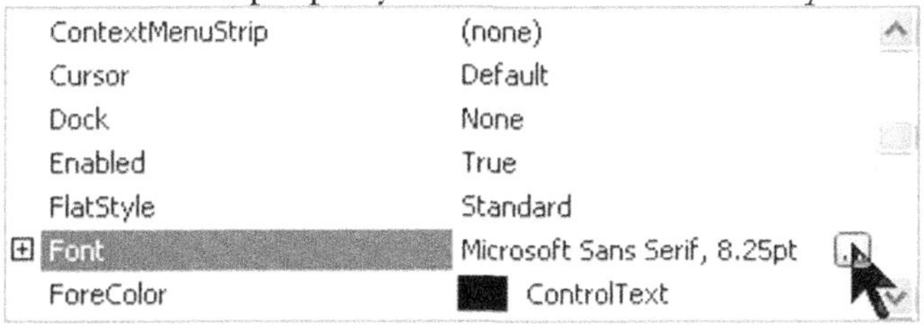

ContextMenuStrip
(none)
Cursor
Default
Dock
None
Enabled
True
FlatStyle
Standard
Font
Microsoft Sans Serif, 8.25pt
ForeColor
ControlText

Figure 3-16 | Click To Change Font

48

Update the Font to **Times New Roman**, Font style to **Bold**, and Size to **12,** as shown in Figure 3-17.

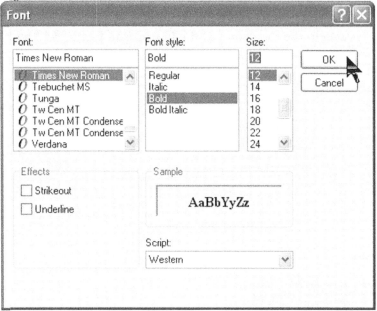

Figure 3-17 | Update Font of Label

Move the updated *Label* near the top, as can be seen below in Figure 3-18.

Figure 3-18 | Move Labels Location

Make room on the form for the *High Score Label.* Move the *Label countDowntimer* and the *scoreBox TextBox* down, as shown in Figure 3-19.

Figure 3-19 | Move Label and TextBox

Click and drag a new *Label* and place it just above the countDownTimer. Update the *Text* property to **High Score,** as in Figure 3-20.

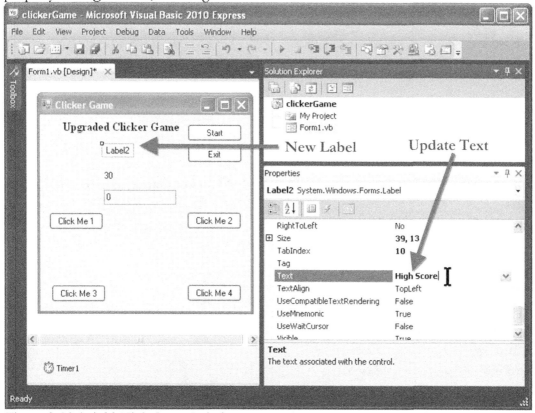

Figure 3-20 | Add High Score Label

50

Change the High Score Label (Name) to **highScoreLabel,** as in Figure 3-21.

Figure 3-21 | Update The Labels Name To highScore

Now change the title of the Form. Click in the *center of the form* away from any buttons, labels, etc, as shown in Figure 3-22.

Figure 3-22 | Select The Form

Select the *Text* property and update the value to **Upgraded Clicker Game,** as shown in Figure 3-23.

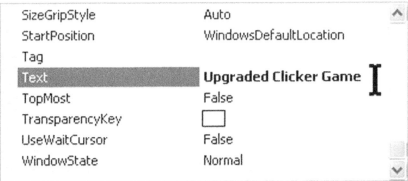

Figure 3-23 | Update Form Title

Now make the Upgraded Clicker Game a little more colorful. With the *form* still selected, find the *BackColor* property and select the *down arrow*, as in Figure 3-24.

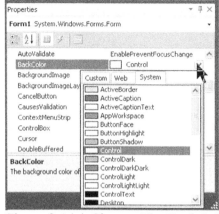

Figure 3-24 | Choose The BackColor Property

Click on the *Web* tab and choose the color **Olive** (or any color you prefer), as in Figure 3-25.

Figure 3-25 | Choosing Olive Color

The final layout should look similar to Figure 3-26, as shown below.

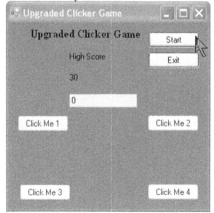

Figure 3-26 | Updated Upgraded Clicker Game Layout

Coding The Project

To keep track of the high score add another global variable of type integer called highScore, as shown in Figure 3-27.

```
Public Class clickerGame

    Dim gameTimerLimit As Integer = 30
    Dim intTimerCount As Integer = 0
    Dim gameScore As Integer = 0
    Dim highScore As Integer = 0
```

Figure 3-27 | Adding Variable highScore

The calculation of the high score is done within the code of Timer1. After the completion of each game, verify whether the gameScore is greater than that of the current highScore. If it is, update the highScore to be that of the gameScore.

Double-click on *Timer1* to enter the new code, as in Figure 3-28.

```
Private Sub Timer1_Tick(ByVal sender As System.Object, _
    ByVal e As System.EventArgs) Handles Timer1.Tick
    Dim timeValue As Integer

    intTimerCount = intTimerCount + 1

    If (intTimerCount <= gameTimerLimit) Then
        timeValue = gameTimerLimit - intTimerCount
    Else
        clickMe1.Enabled = False
        clickMe2.Enabled = False
        clickMe3.Enabled = False
        clickMe4.Enabled = False
        startButton.Enabled = True
        exitButton.Enabled = True
        Dim currentScore As Integer = Integer.Parse(scoreBox.Text)
        If (currentScore > highScore) Then
            highScoreLabel.Text = currentScore.ToString
            highScore = currentScore
        End If
    End If

    countDownTimer.Text = timeValue.ToString
End Sub
```

Figure 3-29 | Adding Variable highScore

The code is broken down here line by line:

Code (C): Dim currentScore As Integer = Integer.Parse(scoreBox.Text)
Description (D): Get the current text in the scoreBox and convert its value to an integer. Store that value in the local variable called currentScore of type integer.

```
C:   If (currentScore > highScore) Then
         highScoreLabel.Text = currentScore.ToString
         highScore = currentScore
     End If
```
D: If the currentScore is greater than the highScore, then update the highScoreLabel.Text with the new value; also update the global variable highScore with the new value.

Now test what you have. Click the *Save All* button. Click either *Start Debugging* or (*F5*). Click on the *Start* button and test the game. Play multiple games to ensure the High Score is working properly, as can be seen in Figure 3-29 and Figure 3-30.

Figure 3-29 | High Score Of 1

Figure 3-30 | High Score Of 34

Summary

When upgrading or adding code to any Bot application make sure to maintain at least a basic level of version control. The bots created in the following chapters will make use of Labels, Buttons, TextBox, Timers, basic coding, and more. Come back to these chapters to review, if you are having any difficulty with any of the concepts described previously.

Chapter 4:
Basic Mouse Bot

The Basic Mouse Bot enables a programmer to simulate a user by clicking the mouse in a repetitive manner. This is extremely helpful when a game or application requires nonstop clicking.

Implementation Overview

There will be three buttons: Left Start, Right Start, and Stop. There will be two timers: a Left Timer and a Right Timer. The final layout will look like Figure 4-1.

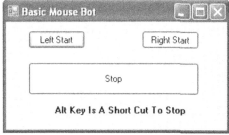

Figure 4-1 | Design View of Basic Mouse Bot

When designing a mouse Bot, the first thing to consider is that there are two very important times. The first is the time between mouse button being pushed down and the button being released up to the default position. Try this experiment to gain a better understanding of what is meant by time between 'mouse down' and 'mouse up'. Click *the left mouse button* and hold *any icon* on the desktop. Now drag it to a new position. Release the *Left button* after counting to three, as shown in Figure 4-2, Figure 4-3, and Figure 4-4.

Figure 4-2 | Left Click Down   Figure 4-3 | The Time Between   Figure 4-4 | Left Click Up

The time between the down-click to the release up is very important in many games and applications. Some games and applications require the click to be within a certain timing range for it to be recognized as a click. Other games with Bot detection software will look at this time and consider if it is humanly possible to click that at that speed. It is best to talk to the developer when testing or creating automations to see if there are any timing restrictions.

The second is the time between clicks. More specifically, the time between the last up click to the next down click. This delay can also be a determining factor as to whether this action is humanly possible. In the Clicker Game, it may take a total of 50 milliseconds to complete the cycle of pushing down on the left mouse when hovered above the Click Me button, and then releasing it to return to the up position. The time between clicks will be the sum total of: reaction time, time to move the mouse to the next Click Me button, and the time it takes to click the mouse. Depending on the distance between buttons and your reaction time, it may take between 700 milliseconds and 2000 milliseconds. After reading this book, you will be able to create a Bot that could reduce 700 milliseconds down to 1 or 2 milliseconds and have it repeat the clicks 24 hours a day, 7 days a week. This is an example of how a person can realize time and money savings by creating automated Bots. Rapid clicks can also be used as a type of load testing.

The combination of the time involved with click down, releasing up, the time between, and clicking down, is known as the double-click speed.

The default double-click speed in Windows is 500ms, or exactly 1/2 of a second. To get a feel for 500ms, or a ½ second, open up Windows Control Panel and double-click on the *Mouse icon*, as shown in Figure 4-5.

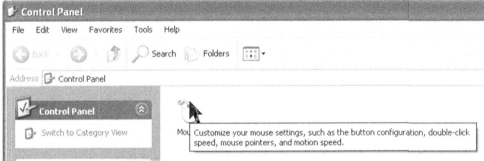

Figure 4-5 | Mouse Properties

Now double-click the *folder icon* multiple times at different speeds to get a sense of the default timing of the double-click, as shown in Figure 4-6.

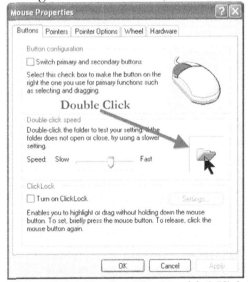

Figure 4-6 | Testing The Double0Click Timing

Setting Up The Project

Start a new project and select *Windows Form Application*. Name it: **basicMouseBot**, as shown in the example below in Figure 4-7.

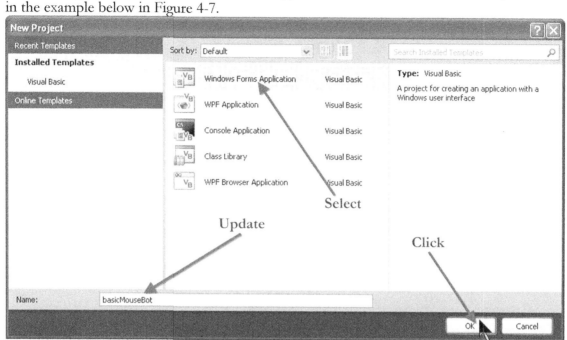

Figure 4-7 | Creating New basicMouseBot Application

Click the *Save All* button, as in Figure 4-8, below.

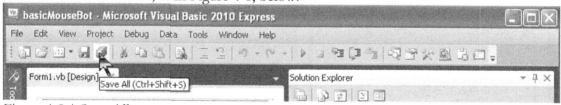

Figure 4-8 | Save All

Click *Save* to create a directory structure for **basicMouseBot** project, as in Figure 4-9.

Figure 4-9 | Saving And Creating Directory For Project

58

Layout Out The Form

The final layout should look like Figure 4-10, shown below.

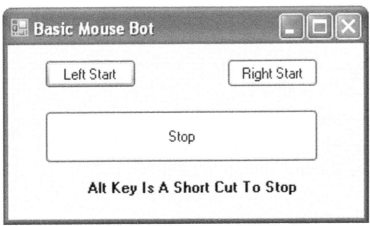

Figure 4-10 | Final Layout Of Basic Mouse Bot

Rename the Form1 title to **Basic Mouse Bot**. Select the *Form1*, as in Figure 4-11, below.

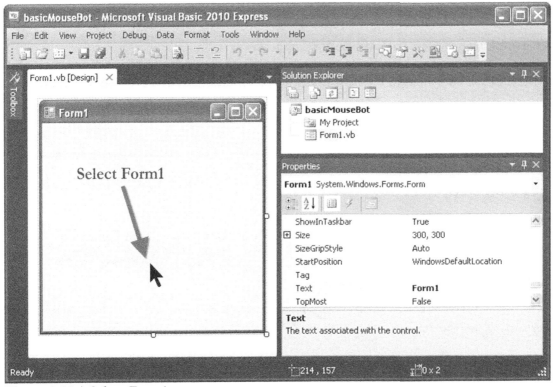

Figure 4-11 | Select Form1

Highlight the *Text* property and update it to **Basic Mouse Bot**, as in Figure 4-12. The Form title change will change to Basic Mouse Bot.

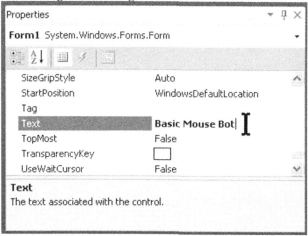

Figure 4-12 | Rename Form1 Text Property To Basic Mouse Bot

Select *Button* from the ToolBox and drag it on to the Form, as in Figure 4-13.

Figure 4-13 | Select Button From ToolBox And Drag On To Form

Repeat the process until three buttons are added to the form, as shown below in Figure 4-14.

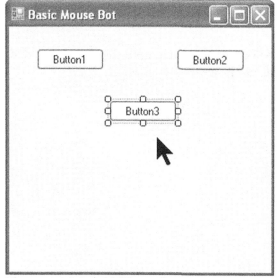

Figure 4-14 | Add Three Buttons

Select *Label* from the ToolBox, and then drag it onto the form, as in Figure 4-15.

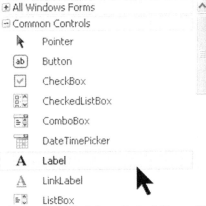

Figure 4-15 | Select Label From ToolBox And Drag Onto Form

Drag the *label* to the center of the form below Button 3, as shown here in Figure 4-16.

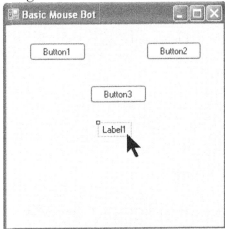

Figure 4-16 | Form With Three Buttons And One Label

To tidy up the form, resize it by moving the mouse to the bottom edge until the double-headed arrow appears. Then click and hold the *form* to resize, as shown below in Figure 4-17.

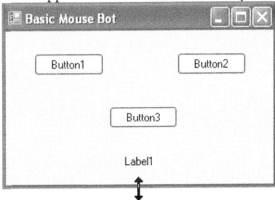

Figure 4-17 | Resize Form

Select *Button1* in order to change the Text and the (Name) Properties, as in Figure 4-18.

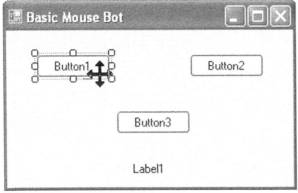

Figure 4-18 | Select Button 1

Highlight and change the *Button1* Text property to **Left Start,** as in Figure 4-19. Change the (Name) property to **leftButton**, as in Figure 4-20.

Figure 4-19 | Change Text   Figure 4-20 | Change (Name)

Repeat the same action to *Button2* by selecting that button, as seen here in Figure 4-21.

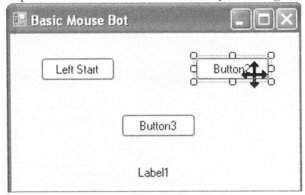

Figure 4-21 | Select Button 2

Highlight and change the *Button2* Text property to **Right Start**, as in Figure 4-22. Change the (Name) property to **rightButton**, as in Figure 4-23.

Figure 4-22 | Change Text   Figure 4-23 | Change (Name)

Select *Button3* in order to change the Text and the (Name) properties, as in Figure 4-24.

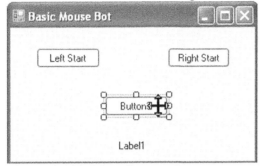

Figure 4-24| Select Button 3

Update *Button3* Text to **Stop,** and (Name) to **stopButton**, as in Figures 4-25 and 4-26.

Figure 4-25 | Change Text   Figure 4-26 | Change (Name) Property

Resize the *Stop* button by moving the mouse to the left and right edges of the image.   Click and drag each edge until the width matches the left of the Left button, and the right of the Right button, as in Figure 4-27.

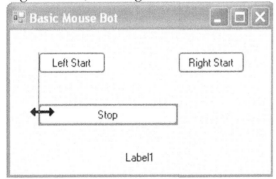

Figure 4-27 | Resize Stop Button

Resize the *Stop* button's height until it looks like Figure 4-28.

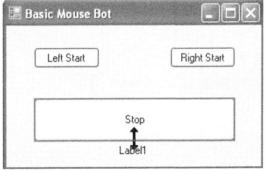

Figure 4-28 | Complete Resizing of Stop Button

Select *Label1*, as shown in Figure 4-29.

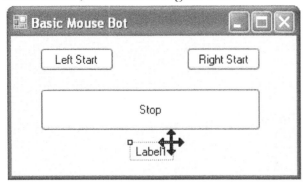

Figure 4-29 | Select Label1

With *Label1* selected, click on the Text property *down arrow* in order to open the edit box, as shown below in the example in Figure 4-30.

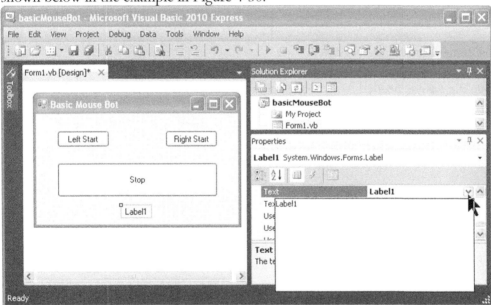

Figure 4-30 | Change The Text Property And Click On Down Arrow To Edit

Update the *Text* property for Label1 to **Alt Key Is A Short Cut To Stop**, as in Figure 4-31.

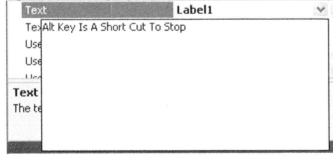

Figure 4-31 | Change Text To Alt Key Is A Short Cut To Stop

Select the *three dots* for the Font property to edit the appearance, as in Figure 4-32.

Figure 4-32 | Update The Font Click On Three Dots

Change the Font style to **Bold** and then click *Ok*, as in Figure 4-33.

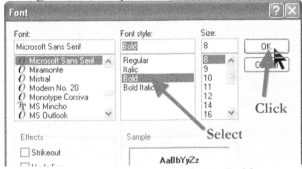

Figure 4-33 | Change Font Style To Bold

Select and move the *label* as needed to look like Figure 4-34.

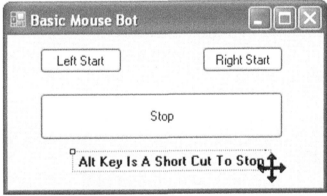

Figure 4-34 | Move Label To Center Bottom Of Form

Now test what you have. Click the *Save All* button, as in Figure 4-35. Click either *Start Debugging*, or (*F5*), as in Figure 4-36. Now you have the form the way you want. The next step is to start coding the project.

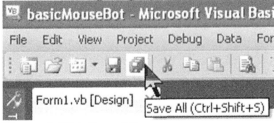

Figure 4-35 | Save All

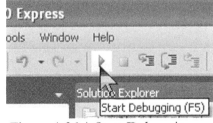

Figure 4-36 | Start Debugging

Coding The Project

To enter the code view, move the mouse over the Solution Explorer until it opens. Now click on *View Code*, as shown in Figure 4-37.

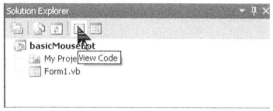

Figure 4-37 | Enter Code View

It is necessary to include the mouse_event library in the global name space, as in Figure 4-38. Libraries save programmers a lot of time because it allows them to use proven code. You don't want to have to reinvent the wheel, so take advantage of these libraries and check to see if one already exists. The mouse_event gives access to functions that simulate mouse clicks.

Reminder, to help with code visibility, I will use multiple lines to display a single line of code. To separate a single line of code into multiple displayed lines, it is necessary to place an underscore _ at the end of the line.

```
Public Class Form1
    Private Declare Sub mouse_event Lib "user32" (ByVal dwFlags As Integer, _
        ByVal dx As Integer, ByVal dy As Integer, ByVal cButtons As Integer, _
        ByVal dwExtraInfo As Integer)
End Class
```

Figure 4-38 | Adding mouse_event Library

Add four constant variables. They will be used to send the down and up clicks for both the right and left mouse buttons, as shown in Figure 4-39.

```
Public Class Form1
    Private Declare Sub mouse_event Lib "user32" (ByVal dwFlags As Integer, _
        ByVal dx As Integer, ByVal dy As Integer, ByVal cButtons As Integer, _
        ByVal dwExtraInfo As Integer)

    Private Const MOUSEEVENTF_LEFTDOWN = &H2
    Private Const MOUSEEVENTF_LEFTUP = &H4
    Private Const MOUSEEVENTF_RIGHTDOWN = &H8
    Private Const MOUSEEVENTF_RIGHTUP = &H10
End Class
```

Figure 4-39 | Adding Const Variables For Mouse Clicks

66

To fire the mouse clicks on a repetitive basis, timers will be used. Two timers are needed, one for the left click and one for the right click. Open the *ToolBox*, page down to *Timer* and drag it onto the form, as in Figure 4-40.

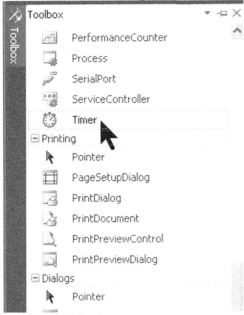

Figure 4-40 | Timer

After dragging the *two timers* onto the form, it should appear like Figure 4-41.

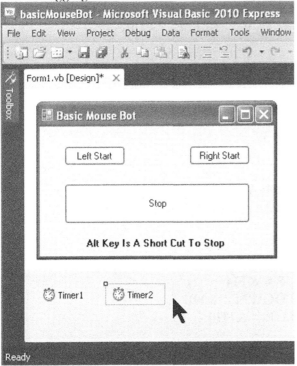

Figure 4-41 | Timer1 And Timer2 Added

Before using any of the timers, begin by renaming them. This will clearly identify which timer is being used at the moment. Highlight *Timer1*, as in Figure 4-42. Then change the (Name) property to **leftTimer**, as in Figure 4-43.

Figure 4-42 | Highlight Timer1

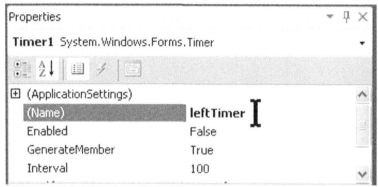

Figure 4-43 | Update (Name) Property To leftTimer

Highlight *Timer2*, as in Figure 4-44. Then change the (Name) property to **rightTimer**, as in Figure 4-45.

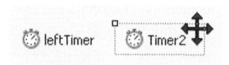

Figure 4-44 | Highlight Timer2

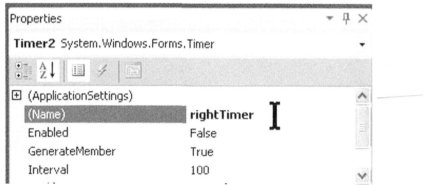

Figure 4-45 | Update (Name) Property To rightTimer

Both timers start with the default property Interval of 100. This is 100 milliseconds or 1/10 of a second. The initial timer value can be changed here, or change it in the code. Setting it in the code allows for updating the timer dynamically.

The Left Start button will be responsible for starting the Basic Mouse Bot, which will simulate the left mouse clicks. To enter the Left Start subroutine, double-click on the *Left Start* button, as in Figure 4-46.

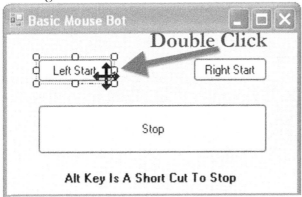

Figure 4-46 | Enter Left Start Subroutine

A timer fires repeatedly at an interval that can either be specified in the Interval property or overridden in the code. Adding a timer to the form does not mean the timer will initially fire. The timer must be started before it will begin to fire. When the timer fires, the code located in the timer subroutine will be executed.

Add the code inside the leftButton subroutine to set the leftTimer interval to a half second and then start the leftTimer, as in Figure 4-47.

```
Private Sub leftButton_Click(ByVal sender As System.Object, _
    ByVal e As System.EventArgs) Handles leftButton.Click
    leftTimer.Interval = 500
    leftTimer.Start()
End Sub
```

Figure 4-47 | Set leftTimer Interval And Start Timer

The code is broken down here line by line:

Code (C): leftTimer.Interval = 500
Description (D): Overwrite the leftTimer Interval time to 500 milliseconds or ½ second.

C: leftTimer.Start()
D: Start the leftTimer and it will begin to fire once every 500 milliseconds after completing leftTimer code block.

Update the leftTimer code block to perform the left mouse click. Double-click on the *leftTimer* to enter the code block, as in Figure 4-48.

Figure 4-48 | Enter leftTimer Subroutine

The left mouse click needs to be performed inside the leftTimer subroutine. A single mouse click involves four separate actions:

- Left mouse click down
- Time delay between down and up click
- Left mouse release to up position
- Time delay between next mouse click (If additional clicks)

Add the left mouse down, delay, and left mouse up inside the leftTimer subroutine, as in Figure 4-49.

```
Private Sub leftTimer_Tick(ByVal sender As System.Object, _
    ByVal e As System.EventArgs) Handles leftTimer.Tick

    mouse_event(MOUSEEVENTF_LEFTDOWN, 0, 0, 0, 0)
    System.Threading.Thread.Sleep(500)
    mouse_event(MOUSEEVENTF_LEFTUP, 0, 0, 0, 0)

End Sub
```

Figure 4-49 | Left Mouse Click Code

The code is broken down here line by line:

C: mouse_event(MOUSEEVENTF_LEFTDOWN, 0, 0, 0, 0)
D: Performs a left down mouse click. The 0,0,0,0 tells it not to change the position on the mouse pointer. So it will perform a click where ever your mouse pointer current is.

C: System.Threading.Thread.Sleep(500)
D: Performs a timed delay for 500 milliseconds or ½ second.

C: mouse_event(MOUSEEVENTF_LEFTUP, 0, 0, 0, 0)
D: Perform a left mouse up release. The 0,0,0,0 tells it not to change the position on the mouse pointer. So it will perform a click where ever your mouse pointer current is.

70

The Right Start button will be responsible for initializing the rightTimer Interval delay and starting the rightTimer. Double-click the *Right Start* button to enter the subroutine, as in Figure 4-50.

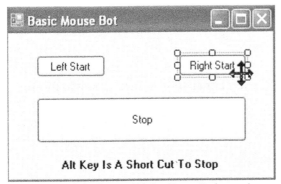

Figure 4-50 | Enter Right Start Subroutine

Set the rightTimer Interval to 2 seconds by setting it to **2000** milliseconds and start the rightTimer, as shown in Figure 4-51.

```
Private Sub rightButton_Click(ByVal sender As System.Object, _
    ByVal e As System.EventArgs) Handles rightButton.Click
    rightTimer.Interval = 2000
    rightTimer.Start()
End Sub
```

Figure 4-51 | Set rightTimer Interval And Start Timer

Double-click *rightTimer* to edit subroutine, as in Figure 4-52.

Figure 4-52 | Enter rightTimer Subroutine

Add the right mouse down, delay, and right mouse up inside the rightTimer subroutine, as in Figure 4-53.

```
Private Sub rightTimer_Tick(ByVal sender As System.Object, _
    ByVal e As System.EventArgs) Handles rightTimer.Tick

    mouse_event(MOUSEEVENTF_RIGHTDOWN, 0, 0, 0, 0)
    System.Threading.Thread.Sleep(1000)
    mouse_event(MOUSEEVENTF_RIGHTUP, 0, 0, 0, 0)

End Sub
```

Figure 4-53 | Right Mouse Click Code

Now there needs to be a means to stop the mouse clicking after it has started. To do this, simply stop the timers. Double-click on the *Stop* button to enter the subroutine, as shown below in Figure 4-54.

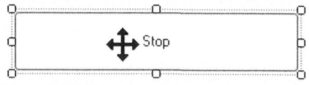

Figure 4-54 | Enter Stop Subroutine

Stop both timers by adding the code included in the box in Figure 4-55.

```
Private Sub stopButton_Click(ByVal sender As System.Object, _
    ByVal e As System.EventArgs) Handles stopButton.Click
    leftTimer.Stop()
    rightTimer.Stop()
End Sub
```

Figure 4-55 | Stop Button Code

The Stop button works great when there are time intervals such as used in the previous code, which range from from a ½ second to 2 seconds. Issues appear when there are very small intervals. For example, 5 milliseconds would make it nearly impossible to click stop between clicks in order to stop the Bot.

This is why there will be an alternative method to shut down the timers. The Bot will use holding down the **Alt Key** as the anternate way to stop the timer.

Stop the left timer by placing the following code inside leftTimer_Tick subroutine, as shown in the box in Figure 4-56.

```
Private Sub leftTimer_Tick(ByVal sender As System.Object, _
    ByVal e As System.EventArgs) Handles leftTimer.Tick

    If (My.Computer.Keyboard.AltKeyDown) Then
        leftTimer.Stop()
    End If

    mouse_event(MOUSEEVENTF_LEFTDOWN, 0, 0, 0, 0)
    System.Threading.Thread.Sleep(500)
    mouse_event(MOUSEEVENTF_LEFTUP, 0, 0, 0, 0)

End Sub
```

Figure 4-56 | Stop leftTimer With Alt Key

The code is broken down here line by line:

C: If (My.Computer.Keyboard.AltKeyDown) Then
D: Check if the Alt Key is currently held down.

C: leftTimer.Stop()
D: Stop the leftTimer.

C: End If
D: Terminate if statement.

To stop the right timer place similar code as above into rightTimer_Tick subroutine, as in Figure 4-57.

```
Private Sub rightTimer_Tick(ByVal sender As System.Object, _
    ByVal e As System.EventArgs) Handles rightTimer.Tick

    If (My.Computer.Keyboard.AltKeyDown) Then
        rightTimer.Stop()
    End If

    mouse_event(MOUSEEVENTF_RIGHTDOWN, 0, 0, 0, 0)
    System.Threading.Thread.Sleep(1000)
    mouse_event(MOUSEEVENTF_RIGHTUP, 0, 0, 0, 0)

End Sub
```

Figure 4-57 | Right Mouse Click Code

Now test what you have. Click the *Save All* button, as in Figure 4-58. Click either *Start Debugging*, or (*F5*), as in Figure 4-59.

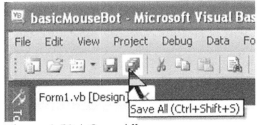

Figure 4-58 | Save All

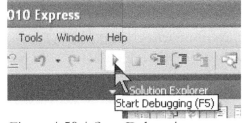

Figure 4-59 | Start Debugging

The Basic Mouse Bot application should appear as shown in Figure 4-60.

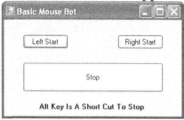

Figure 4-60 | Basic Mouse Bot Application

Now test the Left Start button on the Windows Calculator. Click *Start -> All Programs ->
Accessories -> Calculator*, as in Figure 4-61.

Figure 4-61 | Start Windows Calculator

Place the Basic Mouse Bot next to the Windows Calculator, as in Figure 4-62.

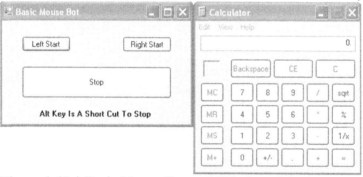

Figure 4-62 | Basic Mouse Bot and Window Calculator

Click the *Left Start* button. Now move the *mouse pointer* to above the number seven on the
Windows Calculator. A new number seven should appear once a second, as in Figure 4-63.
Press and hold the **Alt Key** to stop the Basic Mouse Bot.

Figure 4-63 | Testing Basic Mouse Bot

74

Now test the Right Start Button. Click the *Right Start* button and begin moving the mouse across the screen. The right mouse click will be fired once every three seconds, giving the Windows right mouse menu which will look similar to Figure 4-64. Press and hold the **Alt Key** to stop the Basic Mouse Bot.

Figure 4-64 | Right Mouse Click

Summary

The Basic Mouse Bot shows the steps to automate the clicking of a stopped or moving mouse for either left or right mouse clicks, which is performed with a specific timing pattern.

Testers using software with repetitive clicks can easily put in over a million clicks in a single year. That volume of clicking can lead to carpal tunnel syndrome or other physical issues. Creating a custom basic mouse Bot can reduce such injuries and increase performance.

Chapter 5:
Dynamic Mouse Bot

The Dynamic Mouse Bot will be an upgrade to the Basic Mouse Bot. All of the code will be reused, but with additional updates.

Different games and applications may require different mouse click times. You won't want to recompile the Basic Mouse Bot each time mouse click timing needs to be updated. The Dynamic Mouse Bot will allow for changing the timing setting right on the form.

Creating Dynamic Mouse Bot

When creating the Dynamic Mouse Bot, start with a copy of the Basic Mouse Bot. First, add four TextBoxes to capture times and two Labels. Later, enhance the project a little more with one more TextBox to capture a delay time and another Label.

Setting Up The Project

Follow the same procedure used in upgrading the clicker game as demonstrated in Chapter 3. Create a copy of the Basic Mouse Bot directory and rename it as Dynamic Mouse Bot. Simply follow the steps layed out in Figures 5-1, 5-2, 5-3, 5-4, 5-5, and 5-6.

Click *File* then *Open Project*, as in Figure 5-1.

Figure 5-1 | File -> Open Project

Select the *basicMouseBot* Directory and select *Copy*, as in Figure 5-2.

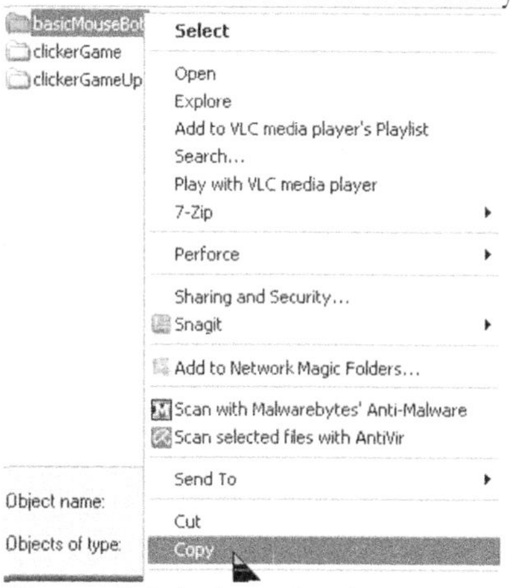

Figure 5-2 | Copy basicMouseBot Directory

Right mouse click and select *Paste*, as shown below in Figure 5-3.

Figure 5-3 | Paste Copy Of Directory

Highlight the directory named *Copy of basicMouseBot*, right mouse click, and then rename it to **dynamicMouseBot**, as in Figure 5-4. Select the folder named *dynamicMouseBot* and click *Open*, also shown in the example in Figure 5-4.

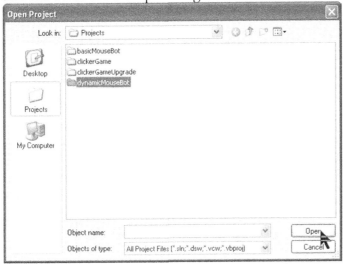

Figure 5-4 | Rename To dynamicMouseBot Then Open Up Directory

Now select the *basicMouseBot.sln* solution file and click *Open*, as in Figure 5-5.

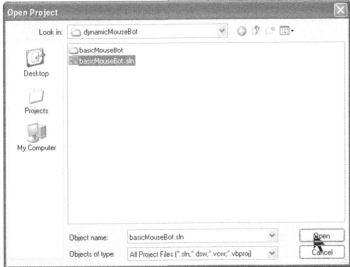

Figure 5-5 | Select And Open Solution File

Select the *Solution Explorer* and double-click on *Form1.vb* to begin upgrading the copy of Basic Mouse Bot to the Dynamic Mouse Bot, as in Figure 5-6.

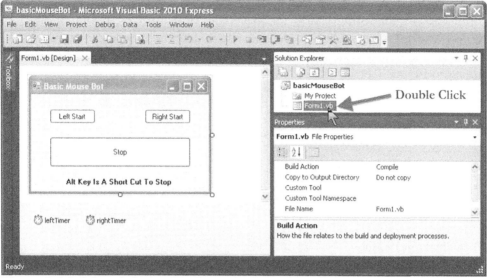

Figure 5-6 | Select Solution Explorer And Double Click On Form1.vb

Select the *form* so the title can be updated, as in Figure 5-7. Update the title by selecting the *Properties* tab, and update the Text property from **Basic Mouse Bot** to **Dynamic Mouse Bot**, as in Figure 5-8. The form then should look like Figure 5-9.

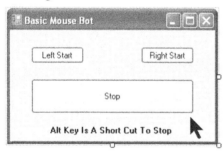

Figure 5-7 | Select Form

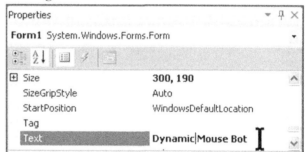

Figure 5-8 | Update Text

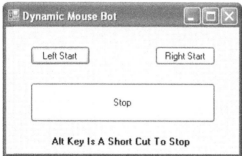

Figure 5-9 | Updated Title

78

Laying Out The Form

Resize and move the items on the form to allow the placement of text boxes, as shown in Figure 5-10. Four new text boxes are needed to dynamically update the mouse click timings. Select *Toolbox*, then click and drag a *TextBox* on to the form. Repeat this three more times until the form looks similar to Figure 5-11.

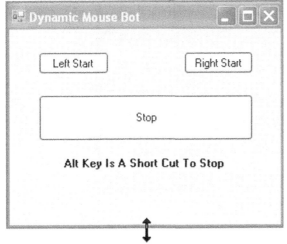

Figure 5-10 | Resized Form

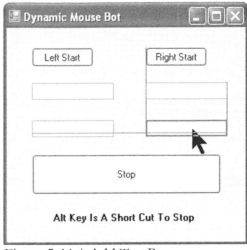

Figure 5-11 | Add TextBoxes

Select the *upper left TextBox*, as in Figure 5-12.

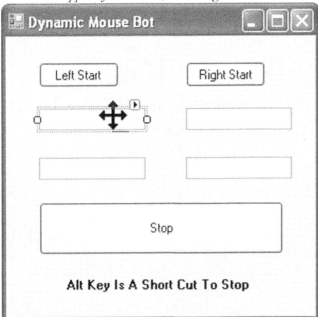

Figure 5-12 | Select Upper Left TextBox

Update the Properties (Name) to **leftDownUpTime** and the Text Property to **500**, as in Figure 5-13 and Figure 5-14.

Figure 5-13 | (Name) = leftDownUpTime   Figure 5-14 | Text = 500

Now select the *upper right TextBox*, as can be seen in Figure 5-15.

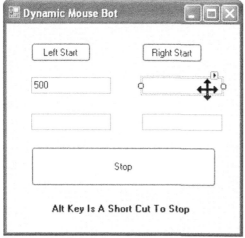

Figure 5-15 | Select Upper Right TextBox

Update the Properties (Name) to **rightDownUpTimer** and Text Property to **500**, as in Figure 5-16 and Figure 5-17.

Figure 5-16 | (Name) = rightDownUpTime   Figure 5-17 | Text = 500

Select the *lower left TextBox*, as in Figure 5-18.

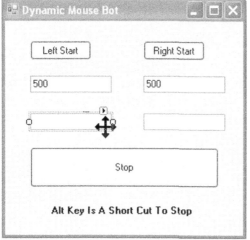

Figure 5-18 | Select Lower Left TextBox

Update the Properties (Name) to **leftBetweenClicksTime** and Text Property to **500**, as in Figure 5-19 and Figure 5-20.

| (Name) | leftBetweenClicksTime | Text | 500 |

Figure 5-19 | (Name) = leftBetweenClicksTime   Figure 5-20 | Text = 500

Select the *lower right TextBox*, as in Figure 5-21.

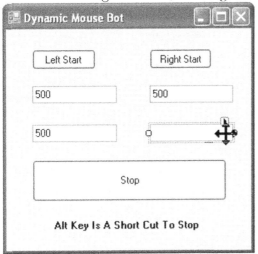

Figure 5-21 | Select Lower Right TextBox

Update the Properties (Name) to **rightBetweenClicksTime** and Text Property to **500**, as in Figure 5-22 and Figure 5-23.

| (Name) | rightBetweenClicksTime | Text | 500 |

Figure 5-22 | (Name) = rightBetweenClicksTime   Figure 5-23 | Text = 500

Resize the *TextBoxes* as shown in Figure 5-24

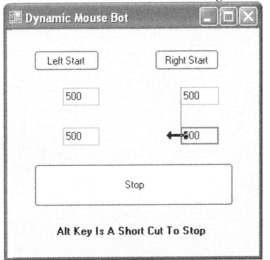

Figure 5-24 | Resize TextBoxes

Select *ToolBox* and click on *Label*, as in Figure 5-2. Drag *two labels* onto the Form, so it appears like Figure 5-26.

Figure 5-25 | Select Label And Drag On To Form

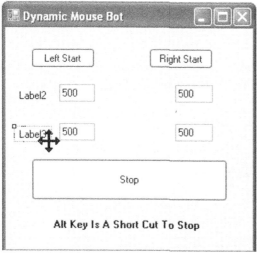

Figure 5-26 | Two Labels Added To Form

Update the top label Text property to **Down/Up**, as in Figure 5-27 and the bottom label Text Property to **Between,** as in Figure 5-28.

Text	Down/Up|	Text	Between|

Figure 5-27 | Text = Down/Up   Figure 5-28 | Text = Between

The Dynamic Mouse Bot's final appearance should look like Figure 5-29.

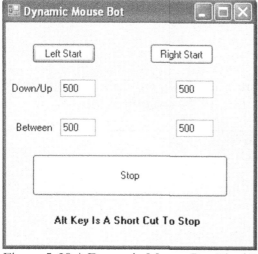

Figure 5-29 | Dynamic Mouse Bot Final Layout

Coding The Project

Start with the existing code from the Basic Mouse Bot. In the Basic Mouse Bot the times for up/down and between were hard coded. Now, read the value from the TextBoxes and update the appropriate times accordingly. Double-click on the *Left Start* button, as in Figure 5-30.

Figure 5-30 | Double-click Left Start

Now update the leftButton_Click subroutine, as in Figure 5-31. The update will dynamically assign the leftTimer.Interval to the value entered into the leftBetweenClicksTime TextBox, when the *Left Start* button is clicked.

```
Private Sub leftButton_Click(ByVal sender As System.Object, _
    ByVal e As System.EventArgs) Handles leftButton.Click

    leftTimer.Interval = Decimal.Parse(leftBetweenClicksTime.Text)
    leftTimer.Start()

End Sub
```

Figure 5-31 | Dynamically Assign The leftTimer.Interval From leftBetweenClicksTime.Text

The code is broken down here line by line:

C: leftTimer.Interval = Decimal.Parse(leftBetweenClicksTime.Text)
D: leftBetweenClicksTime.Text retrieves the value from the TextBox then Decimal.Parse converts the text to a Decimal. Finally, the converted value is stored into leftTimer.Interval.

Now double-click on the *Right Start* button, as in Figure 5-32.

Figure 5-32 | Double-click Right Start

Now update rightButton_Click subroutine, as in Figure 5-33. When the Right Start button is clicked, the value in the rightBetweenClicksTime TextBox will be assigned to the rightTimer.Interval value.

```
Private Sub rightButton_Click(ByVal sender As System.Object, _
    ByVal e As System.EventArgs) Handles rightButton.Click

    rightTimer.Interval = Decimal.Parse(rightBetweenClicksTime.Text)
    rightTimer.Start()

End Sub
```

Figure 5-33 | Dynamically Assign The rightTimer.Interval From rightBetweenClicksTime.Text

Double-click on the *leftTimer* Timer, as in Figure 5-34.

Figure 5-34 | Double-Click leftTimer

Update the leftTimer_Tick subroutine, as in Figure 5-35. The update will dynamically assign the sleep period between down and up state of the left mouse click to the value entered into leftUpDownTime TextBox when the Left Start button is clicked.

```
Private Sub leftTimer_Tick(ByVal sender As System.Object, _
    ByVal e As System.EventArgs) Handles leftTimer.Tick

  If (My.Computer.Keyboard.AltKeyDown) Then
    leftTimer.Stop()
  End If

  mouse_event(MOUSEEVENTF_LEFTDOWN, 0, 0, 0, 0)
  System.Threading.Thread.Sleep(Decimal.Parse(leftDownUpTime.Text))
  mouse_event(MOUSEEVENTF_LEFTUP, 0, 0, 0, 0)

End Sub
```

Figure 5-35| Dynamically Assign Sleep Time From leftDownUpTime.Text

Double click on the *rightTimer*, as in Figure 5-36.

Figure 5-36 | Double-Click rightTimer

Update the rightTimer_Tick subroutine, as in Figure 5-37.

```
Private Sub rightTimer_Tick(ByVal sender As System.Object, _
    ByVal e As System.EventArgs) Handles rightTimer.Tick

  If (My.Computer.Keyboard.AltKeyDown) Then
    rightTimer.Stop()
  End If

  mouse_event(MOUSEEVENTF_RIGHTDOWN, 0, 0, 0, 0)
  System.Threading.Thread.Sleep(Decimal.Parse(rightDownUpTime.Text))
  mouse_event(MOUSEEVENTF_RIGHTUP, 0, 0, 0, 0)

End Sub
```

Figure 5-37| Dynamically Assign Sleep Time From rightDownUpTime.Text

Now test what you have. Click the *Save All* button. Click either *Start Debugging,* or (*F5*). Start the Windows calculator for testing. Place it next to the Dynamic Mouse Bot, as in Figure 5-38.

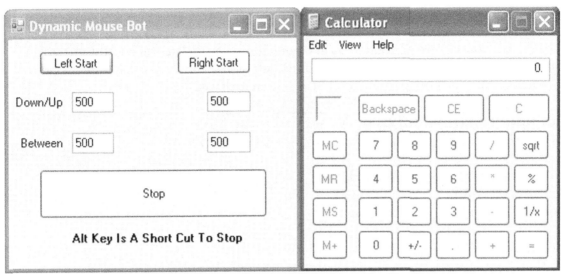

Figure 5-38 | Prepare Dynamic Mouse Bot And Calculator For Testing

Click on the *Left Start* Button and move the mouse to the number 5 on the Calculator. After a little bit of time, press and hold down the **Alt key**. Your results should look like Figure 5-39.

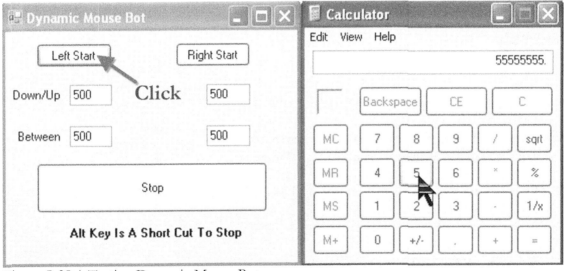

Figure 5-39 | Testing Dynamic Mouse Bot

Now change the Left Down/Up to **50** and Between to **50**. Clear the Calculator and try it again, as in Figure 5-40. As this example shows, a total delay of 100 milliseconds is very quick and it is almost impossible to get to the 5 without clicking something else. A delay before the first click is very helpful, especially when the delay between clicks is extremely small. A solution to this dilemma of the Dynamic Mouse Bot will be added in the next section by adding a delay before first click.

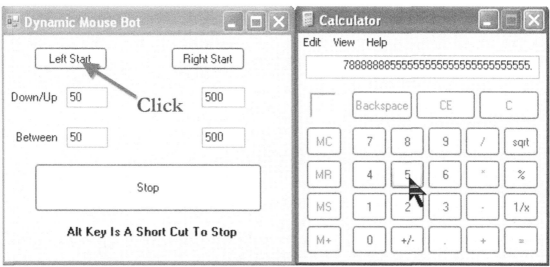

Figure 5-40 | Testing Left Start With Total Of 100 Millisecond Delay

Now test the Right Start button with the default times. Move the mouse around. Once every second the right menu will pop up, as in Figure 5-41.

Figure 5-41 | Right Start Test Results

Close the Dynamic Mouse Bot before starting the next section.

86

Adding A Delay Before First Click

Select *ToolBox* and drag a *Label* on to the form and rename its Text property to **Delay,** as shown in the example in Figure 5-42.

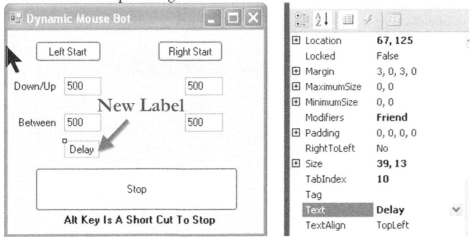

Figure 5-42 | Add Label And Rename Text To Delay

Select *ToolBox* and then click and drag a *TextBox* onto the form. Resize it to appear like Figure 5-43.

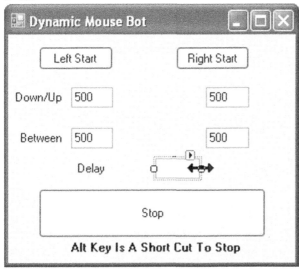

Figure 5-43 | Add A Text Box And Resize

Make sure new *TextBox* is selected. Then update the Properties (Name) to **delayTime** and Text Property to **2000**, as in Figures 5-44, 5-45. Remember, 2000 will give a delay of two seconds.

Figure 5-44 | (Name) = delayTime

Figure 5-45 | Text = 2000

The updated Dynamic Mouse Bot with a delay should look like Figure 5-46.

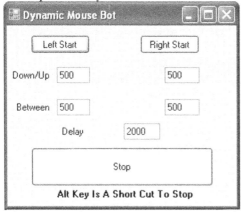

Figure 5-46 | Dynamic Mouse Bot With Delay

Update the code in the leftButton_Click and rightButton_Click subroutines. Double-click on the *Left Start* button to enter leftButton_Click code, as in Figure 5-47.

Figure 5-47 | Double click Left Start

Update the leftButton_Click subroutine, as in Figure 5-48.

```
Private Sub leftButton_Click(ByVal sender As System.Object, _
    ByVal e As System.EventArgs) Handles leftButton.Click
    leftTimer.Interval = Decimal.Parse(leftBetweenClicksTime.Text)

    System.Threading.Thread.Sleep(Decimal.Parse(delayTime.Text))
    leftTimer.Start()
End Sub
```

Figure 5-48 | Dynamically Assign Delay Before Left Mouse Clicking

Next, double-click on the *Right Start* button, as in Figure 5-49.

Figure 5-49| Double-click Right Start

Update the rightButton_Click subroutine, as in Figure 5-50.

```
Private Sub rightButton_Click(ByVal sender As System.Object, _
    ByVal e As System.EventArgs) Handles rightButton.Click
    rightTimer.Interval = Decimal.Parse(rightBetweenClicksTime.Text)

    System.Threading.Thread.Sleep(Decimal.Parse(delayTime.Text))
    rightTimer.Start()
End Sub
```

Figure 5-50| Dynamically Assign Delay Before Right Mouse Clicking

Now test what you have. Click the *Save All* button. Click either *Start Debugging*, or (*F5*). Open up the Windows Calculator for testing and place it next to the Dynamic Mouse Bot. Enter **50** into Left Start Down/Up and Between times. Click the *Left Start* and move the mouse above the number five on the Calculator, as in Figure 5-51.

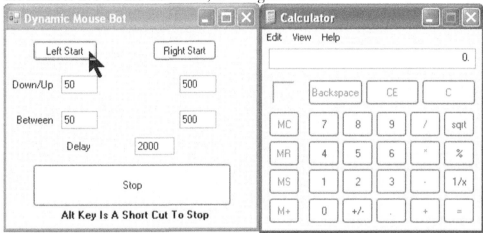

Figure 5-51 | Testing Delay Before Clicking

As the example shows in Figure 5-52, the results are much cleaner now that there is ample time to move the mouse to the desired destination before commencing with the automated clicks.

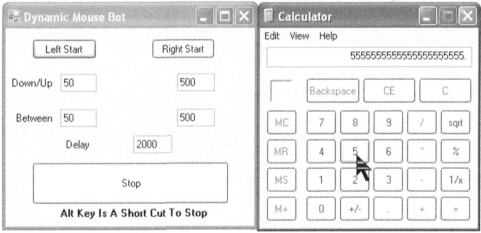

Figure 5-52 | Test Results Of Delay Before Clicking.

Summary

The Dynamic Mouse Bot is a very helpful tool in various mouse clicking automations. Now is the time to practice using Dynamic Mouse Bot to help assist in your automation projects.

Chapter 6:
Application Specific Mouse Bot With Timing Control

The nice thing about most applications is the menu and buttons are always located in the same location. Another way to say that is: they do not randomly appear in different locations around the screen. The times that random placement behavior is utilized is typically in secure logins that attempt to curb Botters.

The fact that the menu and the buttons are typically in the same location will be used to your benefit when creating the Application Specific Mouse Bot.

Everything the Bot does will be relative to the upper left hand corner of the application. This is very helpful in the event that someone moves the application, because by identifying the upper left hand corner as the origin, the Bot will still click in the proper relative location on the application.

Creating the Application Specific Mouse Bot

Four different buttons will be created to demonstrate selecting an application and position specific mouse clicks.

Install Automation Tool Helper

To greatly assist in the botting and automation, I have created a tool call the Automation Tool Helper. The Automation Tool Helper assists by in taking a window screen shot of an application of your choosing, and saving a bitmap image of it for later processing. It also provides a specific pixel color picker.

To download the Automation Tool Helper software for free please visit the website:

http://www.lulu.com/commerce/index.php?fBuyContent=9074577

Download the zip file and extract it to the desktop, as in Figure 6-1. It is important to install it on the desktop because it stores the screen shots where it is installed. This will help keep things simple.

Figure 6-1 | Automation Tool Helper Installed On Desktop

Understanding Automation Tool Helper

To better understand the Automation Tool Helper you are going to use the Windows Calculator again. Please open the Calculator and double-click on the *Automation Tool Helper* icon, as in Figure 6-2.

Figure 6-2 | Start The Automation Tool Helper

The Automation Tool Helper has two main screens: the Screen Capture and the Pixel Color. The Screen Capture allows for creating a screen capture of the whole window of a specific application. The Pixel Color will enable you to specify a bitmap image and retrieve a specific coordinate and get the red green blue (RGB) color. The Automation Tool Helper has been set up in such a way that the newest screen capture is automatically entered into the Pixel Color BMP Image textbox to speed up the most common use of the tool-pixel recognition. The Screen Capture section requires knowing the process name of the application that is being captured. Make sure Windows Calculator is currently open.

The next steps will be used over and over in this book, so make sure you are familiar with them. These steps will show how to retrieve the process name, which needs to be entered into the textbox Process Name in the Screen Capture area in the Automation Tool Helper Application.

Start the Windows Task Manager by clicking all three keys *Ctrl+Alt+Del*. Make sure the *Applications* tab is highlight then select the *Calculator* applications, as in Figure 6-3.

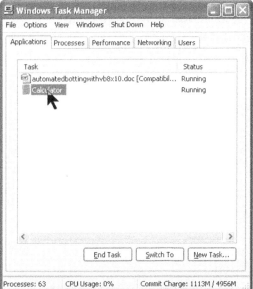

Figure 6-3 | Windows Task Manager Accessed By Ctrl+Alt+Del Keys

Now right mouse click and choose the menu item **Go To Process**, as in Figure 6-4. This will switch to the Process tab, as in Figure 6-5, with the name of the Calculator process.

Figure 6-4 | Select Application Right Mouse Click Go To Process

The Image name for Windows Calculator is **calc.exe**. To get the process name simply remove the dot and anything after it. So calc.exe with provide the process name of **calc**.

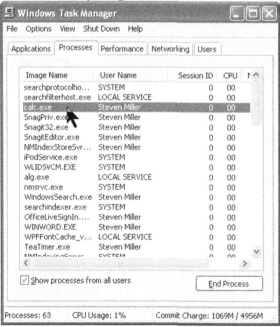

Figure 6-5 | Process Image Name

Application Processing Using Automation Tool Helper

Now place the process name **calc** into the Process Name TextBox, as shown in Figure 6-6.

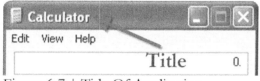

Figure 6-6 | Find calc Process

After clicking on the *Read Applications* button, any applications with the process name containing 'calc' will appear below. The information displayed is: the ID-which is typically the name on the title bar of the application; App Name-which is the applications numerical id; xPos and yPos-are the upper left hand corner grid coordinates of the application on the desktop; Height and Width-are the current size in pixels of the application. In Figure 6-6, above, notice the ids Calculator and CalcMsgPumpWind. The question is: how do you determine which one is the one you are looking for? The first step is simple to look at the title of the application, as shown in Figure 6-7, and then find the ID name that matches.

Figure 6-7 | Title Of Application   Figure 6-8 | Application Screen Capture

After finding a match, confirm that the application is correct, and then click on the *ID* name, as in Figure 6-9. Part of, or the entire image of, the upper left hand corner of the application will appear in the preview area on the bottom of the Automation Tool Helper. At the same time, a whole bitmap screen capture will be saved into the same directory as the Automation Tool Helper as shown, in Figure 6-8 above. In addition to saving a copy of the entire window, it places the name of the bitmap into the BMP Image TextBox as a time saving measure. Notice that every time the ID is clicked, a new bitmap is generated and the name of the bitmap in the BMP Image TextBox is also updated. Remember to delete the old bitmaps to prevent clutter and to free up memory.

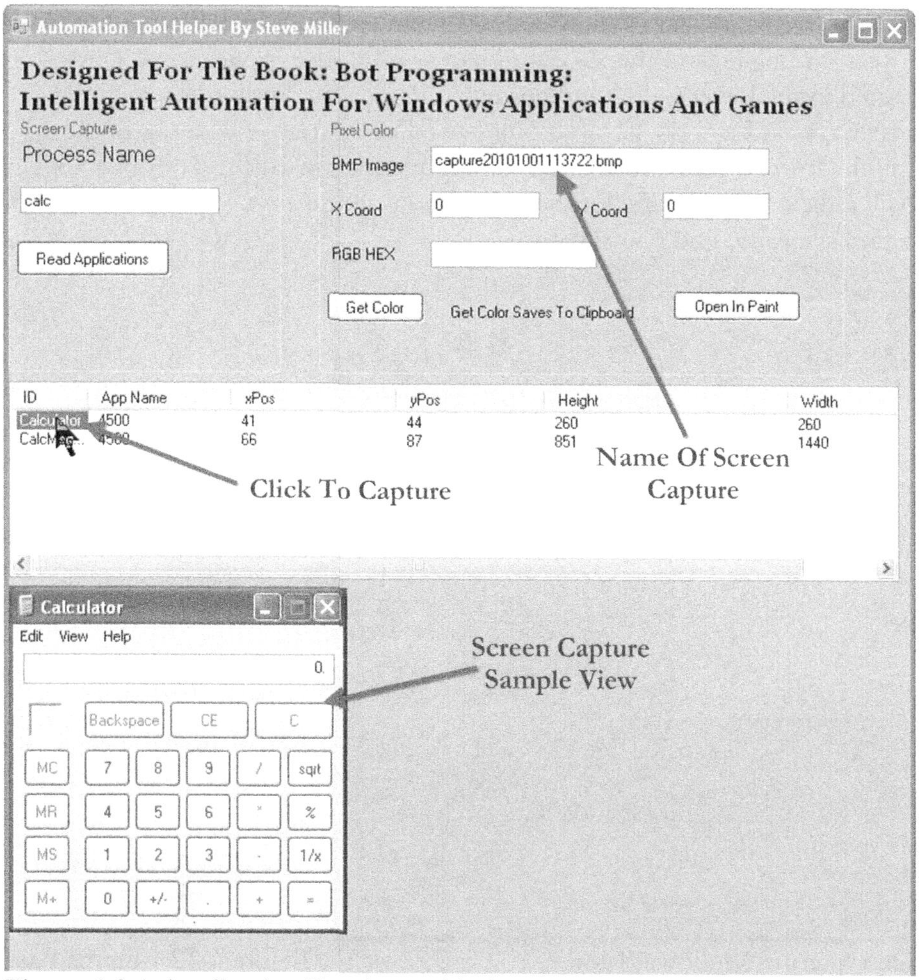

Figure 6-9 | Application Preview With Automation Tool Helper

Now switch the focus from the Screen Capture portion to the Pixel Color portion. You should have the name of the last bitmap that was generated in the BMP Image TextBox. If you want to use a different bitmap simply replace the BMP Image TextBox with the image name including the extension bmp. The next step is to open the bitmap image with Windows Paint application. Making sure the correct BMP Image name entered and click on the *Open In Paint* button, as in Figure 6-10.

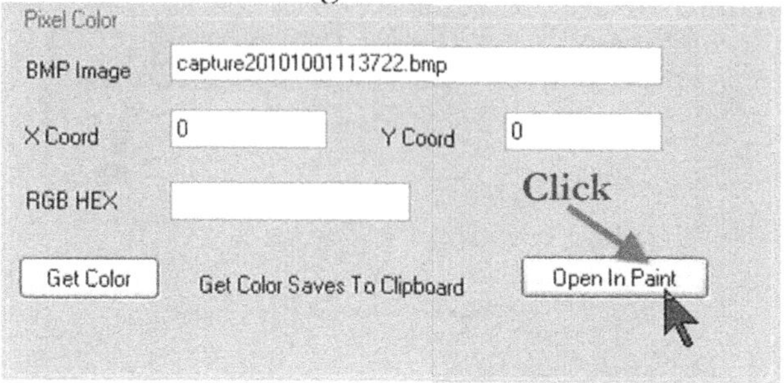

Figure 6-10 | Click Open In Paint Button

The chosen bitmap image should appear in the Windows Paint application, as in Figure 6-11. Use Paint mainly to assist in finging specific x,y coordinates within the applications. The x-y grid coordinate is located in the lower right hand corner of Paint. If you do not see it, make sure Status Bar is checked, as in Figure 6-12. Paint may need to be resized wider until the x,y coordinates appear in the lower right hand corner. When moving any of the Tool Box tools, the x,y coordinates will indicate the specific location within the application. I prefer the Pencil or the Pick Color to find a specific grid coordinate.

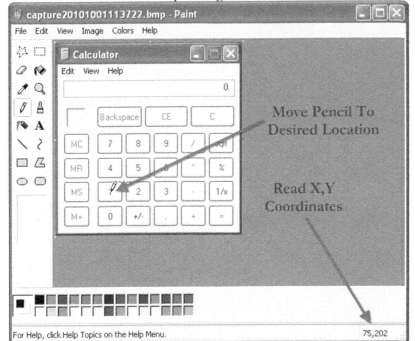

Figure 6-11 | Bitmap Open In Windows Paint   Figure 6-12 | Status Bar

Mapping The Windows Calculator

The x,y Coordinates of all the buttons need to be mapped on the Windows Calculator. Click on the Windows Paint *View* menu, choose *Zoom,* and then select *Custom,* as shown in Figure 6-13. Choose the *200%* option and click the *OK* button, as in Figure 6-14. The example below was done on a Windows XP operating system and Windows Calculator. You will need to perform the calculations on your specific system to ensure correctness.

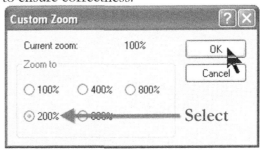

Figure 6-13 | Click View -> Zoom -> Custom   Figure 6-14 | Select Zoom Preference

It is best to create a table of the x,y coordinate range for the Calculator buttons. The simplest way is to choose a single x,y coordinate for the button. However, the best way is to create a range of possible values.

This brings up the following question:
When should a single point be used, as compared to using a range of points?

A single point is fine for most applications. The main reason to use a range would be if creating a Bot for an application with Bot detection. In that instance, avoid clicking in the same place multiple times since it is impossible for a human to actually click on the same pixel over and over and over.

To map the plus (+) button use the simple method, which is simply to find an x,y coordinate near the middle of the plus (+) button, as in Figure 6-15. The middle of the plus (+) is located at 192x and 235y. This means the middle of the plus (+) is 192 pixels to the right and 235 pixels down from the top left hand corner of the application.

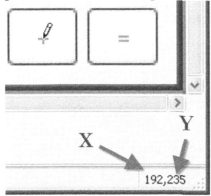

Figure 6-15 | Middle Of Plus 192x and 235y In Windows XP Calculator

To put this in perspective, move the Pencil to the upper left hand corner. Notice that the x equals zero, and y equals zero, as in Figure 6-16.

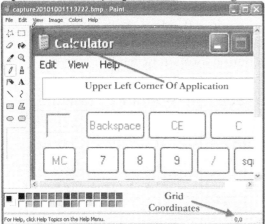

Figure 6-16 | Upper Left Corner Of Application Is Base Of Zero x and Zero y

96

To determine the complete range of possible clicks which will activate a button, four points are needed. Capture the x-Left, x-Right, y-Top, and y-Bottom coordinates, as demonstrated in Figures 6-17 , 6-18, 6-19, and 6-20 respectively.

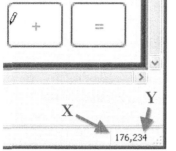

Figure 6-17 | X-Left Coordinate 176

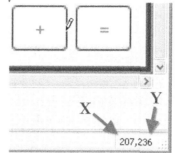

Figure 6-18 | X-Right Coordinate 205

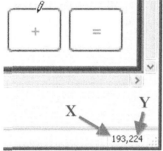

Figure 6-19 | Y-Top Coordinate 224

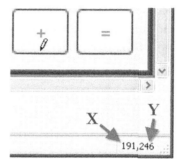

Figure 6-20 | Y-Bottom Coordinate 246

This provides a valid x range for the *Plus* button of 176 to 207; and a valid y range of 224 to 246.

Note: The middle does not have to be the exact middle, since any x or y within the range will work.

I suggest that before starting to bot any application in which you need to automate mouse clicks, create a table with a complete capture of the coordinates of all the buttons or areas that will be used, as in Figure 6-21. It is a helpful short cut to notice that buttons in the same row will have the same y coordinates, and buttons in the same column will have the same x coordinates. If there is any uncertainty, then do each button location by hand.

Button	X –Left	X–Right	X- Middle	Y-Top	Y-Bottom	Y-Middle
0	59	90	75	224	246	235
1	59	90	75	189	213	200
2	98	129	114	189	213	200
3	137	168	154	189	213	200
4	59	90	75	157	181	168
5	98	129	114	157	181	168

6	137	168	154	157	181	168
7	59	90	75	124	148	135
8	98	129	114	124	148	135
9	137	168	154	124	148	135
/	176	207	192	124	148	135
*	176	207	192	157	181	168
-	176	207	192	189	213	200
+	176	207	192	224	246	235
=	215	245	230	224	246	235
C	190	246	218	88	112	90

Figure 6-21 | Window Calculator Button Coordinates In XP Operating System

Setting Up The Project

To practice creating a mouse Bot that is application specific, create four buttons that will perform different automations.

1. Will perform mouse clicks on the desktop.
2. Will set focus on Windows Calculator then perform the calculations.
3. Will set focus on Windows Calculator, perform the calculation, and then use the View Menu.
4. Will set focus on Windows Calculator, perform the calculation, and then use the right mouse -lick.

Start a new project and choose *Windows Form Application* and name it: **calculatorMouseBot**, as in Figure 6-22.

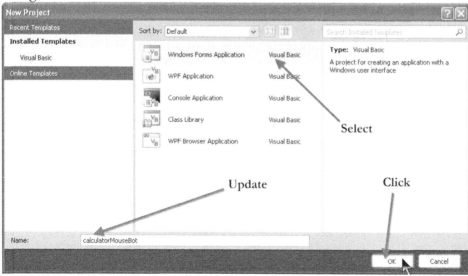

Figure 6-22 | Creating New calculatorMouseBot Application

Now click the *Save All* button, as in Figure 6-23.

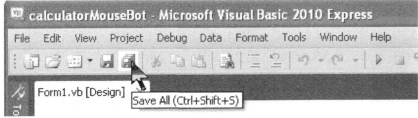

Figure 6-23 | Save All

Click the *Save* button to create directory structure for **calculatorMouseBot** project, as in the example below, Figure 6-24.

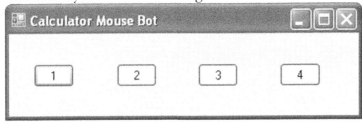

Figure 6-24| Saving And Creating Directory For Project

Layout Out The Form

The form will need four buttons, with each button displaying its text as the number of the calculation.

The final layout will look like Figure 6-25.

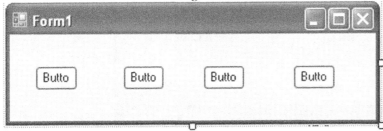

Figure 6-25 | Final Layout

Add four buttons to the form by clicking on *Toolbox* and dragging the *Button* onto the form. Resize the *Form*, as shown in Figure 6-26.

Figure 6-26 | Add Four Buttons And Resize

Begin with the left button, and then move to the right button. For each button, update the Text Properties and the (Name) Property. Press the left most button, select the *Properties* tab, and update the Text to **1** and the (Name) to **one**, as in Figure 6-27 and Figure 6-28.

Figure 6-27 | Left Button Text Property   Figure 6-28 | Left Button (Name) Property

Repeat the process moving from left to right updating so the Text is **2, 3, 4** and the (Name) is **two, three, four** accordingly as in Figures 6-29, 6-30, 6-31, 6-32, 6-33, and 6-34

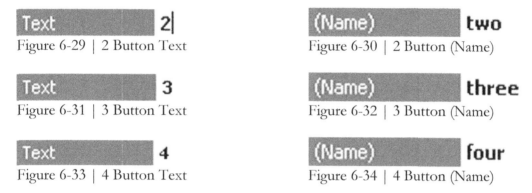

Figure 6-29 | 2 Button Text   Figure 6-30 | 2 Button (Name)

Figure 6-31 | 3 Button Text   Figure 6-32 | 3 Button (Name)

Figure 6-33 | 4 Button Text   Figure 6-34 | 4 Button (Name)

Update the form title to **Calculator Mouse Bot** by clicking on the *Form* anyplace there is no button. Then select the *Properties* tab and update the Text property to Calculator Mouse Bot, as shown in the example in Figure 6-35.

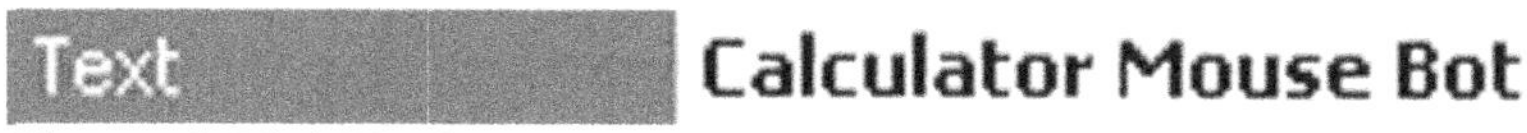

Text   Calculator Mouse Bot

Figure 6-35 | Update Form Text Property

Coding The Project

To enter the code view, move the mouse over the *Solution Explorer* until it opens. Select *Form1.vb* then click on *View Code*, as in Figure 6-36.

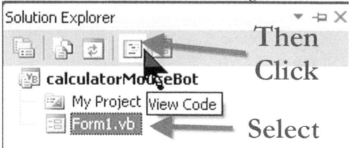

Figure 6-36 | Enter Code View

Including the mouse_event library in the global name space, is necessary, as shown in Figure 6-37. The mouse_event provides access to simulate mouse clicks.

```
Public Class Form1
    Private Declare Sub mouse_event Lib "user32" (ByVal dwFlags As Integer, _
        ByVal dx As Integer, ByVal dy As Integer, ByVal cButtons As Integer, _
        ByVal dwExtraInfo As Integer)
End Class
```

Figure 6-37 | Adding mouse_event Library

Next add four constant variables to send left and right mouse clicks, as shown in Figure 6-38. Each mouse click is separated into a down, and up, action.

```
Public Class Form1

    Private Declare Sub mouse_event Lib "user32" (ByVal dwFlags As Integer, _
        ByVal dx As Integer, ByVal dy As Integer, ByVal cButtons As Integer, _
        ByVal dwExtraInfo As Integer)

    Private Const MOUSEEVENTF_LEFTDOWN = &H2
    Private Const MOUSEEVENTF_LEFTUP = &H4
    Private Const MOUSEEVENTF_RIGHTDOWN = &H8
    Private Const MOUSEEVENTF_RIGHTUP = &H10

End Class
```

Figure 6-38 | Adding Const Variables For Mouse Clicks

Add the SetForegroundWindow library in the global name space, as shown in Figure 6-39.

```
Public Class Form1

    Private Declare Sub mouse_event Lib "user32" (ByVal dwFlags As Integer, _
        ByVal dx As Integer, ByVal dy As Integer, ByVal cButtons As Integer, _
        ByVal dwExtraInfo As Integer)

    Private Const MOUSEEVENTF_LEFTDOWN = &H2
    Private Const MOUSEEVENTF_LEFTUP = &H4
    Private Const MOUSEEVENTF_RIGHTDOWN = &H8
    Private Const MOUSEEVENTF_RIGHTUP = &H10

    Private Declare Function SetForegroundWindow Lib "user32" _
        (ByVal handle As IntPtr) As Integer
End Class
```

Figure 6-39 | Adding SetForegroundWindow Library

SetForegroundWindow allows for setting the active focus on a remote application. Try this on Microsoft Visual Basic 2010 Express by first clicking on any *other application* and then looking at the title bar, as can be seen in Figure 6-40.

VB calculatorMouseBot - Microsoft Visual Basic 2010 Express

Figure 6-40 | VB Express Without Focus

Click anywhere on the *VB Express application* and look at the title bar again, as in Figure 6-41. When an application is not active the title bar appears lighter compared to when the application is selected, or in focus.

VB calculatorMouseBot - Microsoft Visual Basic 2010 Express

Figure 6-41 | VB Express In Focus

It is important to place the application in focus before sending any mouse clicks. If an application is out of focu, the first mouse click may not be received properly.

Finally, add the data structure RECT and the GetWindowRect library into the global name space, as demonstrated in Figure 6-42.

The RECT data structure provides a variable that stores four pieces of information. The four pieces are: Left coordinate, Top coordinate, Right coordinate, and Bottom coordinate.

The GetWindowRect library provides the ability to determine where an application position is relative to the desktop. The upper left hand corner on the desktop is position zero x and zero y. It is similar when finding the position within a specific application.

```
Private Const MOUSEEVENTF_LEFTDOWN = &H2
Private Const MOUSEEVENTF_LEFTUP = &H4
Private Const MOUSEEVENTF_RIGHTDOWN = &H8
Private Const MOUSEEVENTF_RIGHTUP = &H10


Private Declare Function SetForegroundWindow Lib "user32" _
    (ByVal handle As IntPtr) As Integer

Private Structure RECT
    Public Left As Int32
    Public Top As Int32
    Public Right As Int32
    Public Bottom As Int32
End Structure


Private Declare Function GetWindowRect Lib "user32" Alias _
    "GetWindowRect" (ByVal hwnd As IntPtr, ByRef lpRect As RECT) As Integer
```

Figure 6-42 | Adding Rect Datastructure And GetWindowRec Library

Now add a custom subroutine to handle all of the left mouse clicks. Insert it below GetWindowRec Lib, as in Figure 6-43.

```
Private Declare Function GetWindowRect Lib "user32" Alias _
    "GetWindowRect" (ByVal hwnd As IntPtr, ByRef lpRect As RECT) As Integer

Private Sub LeftMouseClick(ByVal x As Integer, ByVal y As Integer, _
    ByVal sleepDelay As Integer, ByVal x2 As Nullable(Of Integer),  _
    ByVal y2 As Nullable(Of Integer), ByVal sleepDelay2 As Nullable(Of Integer))

    If (x2.HasValue) Then
        Dim differenceX As Integer = (x2 - x) + 1
        x = x + (Int(Rnd() * differenceX))
    End If

    If (y2.HasValue) Then
        Dim differenceY As Integer = (y2 - y) + 1
        y = y + (Int(Rnd() * differenceY))
    End If

    If (sleepDelay2.HasValue) Then
        Dim differenceSleepDelay As Integer = (sleepDelay2 - sleepDelay) + 1
        sleepDelay = sleepDelay + (Int(Rnd() * differenceSleepDelay))
    End If

    Cursor.Position = New Point(x, y)
    mouse_event(MOUSEEVENTF_LEFTDOWN, x, y, 0, 0)
    System.Threading.Thread.Sleep(sleepDelay)
    mouse_event(MOUSEEVENTF_LEFTUP, x, y, 0, 0)
    End Sub
End Class
```

Figure 6-43 | Adding LeftMouseClick Subroutine

The code is broken down here line by line:

C: Private Sub LeftMouseClick(ByVal x As Integer, ByVal y As Integer, _
    ByVal sleepDelay As Integer, ByVal x2 As Nullable(Of Integer), _
    ByVal y2 As Nullable(Of Integer), ByVal sleepDelay2 As Nullable(Of Integer))
D: Create a subroutine named LeftMouseClick that accepts six parameters x, y, sleepDelay, x2, y2, and sleepDelay2. All the parameters will accept a value of type integer. The parameters x2, y2, and sleepDelay2 also have the ability to accept no value or also known as Null or Nothing. This ability allows the subroutine to accept a different number of values which then enables you to be more dynamic within the subroutine. The ability to accept multiple values will enable you to accept a range in which it is acceptable to click the mouse.

C: If (x2.HasValue) Then
      Dim differenceX As Integer = (x2 - x) + 1
     x = x + (Int(Rnd() * differenceX))
    End If

D: You check to see if x2 actually has a value. If it does then you take the difference between x2 coordinate and x coordinate and add one to it. This is important because if x equals one and x2 equals three then the valid range is one to three. Three minus one gives the value of two. The range one to three has three values one, two, and three. So you add one after subtracting, so you can calculate the complete range. Int(Rnd() * difference) will give you a random number from zero to the difference minus one. Then you add the random number to x which then gives you a value between and including x to x2. You then take that random x number within the acceptable range of x's and save it into the value of x. If someone only sends you an x value and no x2 value you skip this step completely.

C: If (y2.HasValue) Then
      Dim differenceY As Integer = (y2 - y) + 1
     y = y + (Int(Rnd() * differenceY))
    End If

D: This does the same as above but for the y coordinate value.

C: If (sleepDelay2.HasValue) Then
      Dim differenceSleepDelay As Integer = (sleepDelay2 - sleepDelay) + 1
     sleepDelay = sleepDelay + (Int(Rnd() * differenceSleepDelay))
    End If

D: This does the same for sleepDelay as the above code did for x coordindate and y coordinate.

C: Cursor.Position = New Point(x, y)

D: The x and y coordinates are read in and the mouse in moved to the new location. The new location is calculated from the upper left hand corner of the desktop and not the upper left hand corner of the application.

C: mouse_event(MOUSEEVENTF_LEFTDOWN, x, y, 0, 0)

D: Send a down left mouse click

C: System.Threading.Thread.Sleep(sleepDelay)

D: Create a delay in milliseconds that will determine the amount of time between when the mouse is clicked and when it is released to the default up position.

C: mouse_event(MOUSEEVENTF_LEFTUP, x, y, 0, 0)

D: Send a Release/Up mouse command.

104

Notice that there are three 'if statements' that check for x2, y2, sleepDelay2 independently. This enables the programmer to have the ability of sending no values with a range; just one or two; or all of them. You may want to click in a specific x,y coordinate, but have a range in milliseconds of when it occurs. You might want to have a range for x, and specific value for y and sleepDelay. Or, maybe send a specific x coordinate and a range for both y and SleepDelay. Head spinning? The point is that it is very flexible depending on your automation needs.

Now add a similar subroutine called RightMouseClick, but this is specific to the right mouse-click, as in Figure 6-43. Insert the RightMouseClick subroutine below the LeftMouseClick subroutine, but before the End Class.

```
      Cursor.Position = New Point(x, y)
      mouse_event(MOUSEEVENTF_LEFTDOWN, x, y, 0, 0)
      System.Threading.Thread.Sleep(sleepDelay)
      mouse_event(MOUSEEVENTF_LEFTUP, x, y, 0, 0)
   End Sub

Private Sub RightMouseClick(ByVal x As Integer, ByVal y As Integer, _
   ByVal sleepDelay As Integer, ByVal x2 As Nullable(Of Integer),  _
   ByVal y2 As Nullable(Of Integer), ByVal sleepDelay2 As Nullable(Of Integer))

      If (x2.HasValue) Then
         Dim differenceX As Integer = (x2 - x) + 1
         x = x + (Int(Rnd() * differenceX))
      End If


      If (y2.HasValue) Then
         Dim differenceY As Integer = (y2 - y) + 1
         y = y + (Int(Rnd() * differenceY))
      End If

      If (sleepDelay2.HasValue) Then
         Dim differenceSleepDelay As Integer = (sleepDelay2 - sleepDelay) + 1
         sleepDelay = sleepDelay + (Int(Rnd() * differenceSleepDelay))
      End If

      Cursor.Position = New Point(x, y)
      mouse_event(MOUSEEVENTF_RIGHTDOWN, x, y, 0, 0)
      System.Threading.Thread.Sleep(sleepDelay)
      mouse_event(MOUSEEVENTF_RIGHTUP, x, y, 0, 0)
   End Sub
End Class
```

Figure 6-43 | Adding RightMouseClick Subroutine

The only difference between LeftMouseClick and RightMouseClick is the name of the subroutine and the mouse_event is updated to use MOUSEEVENTF_RIGHTDOWN and MOUSEEVENTF_RIGHTUP.

Button 1 will not use the calculator. Button 1 will lay the ground work of how mous-clicks work in reference to the desktop and the application.
- Button 1 will left click at grid coordinate 100x and 130y, with a ½ to 1 second pause.
- It will left click at 200x and 100y with a second pause.
- It will right click at 0x and 0y with a one to second pause
- It will left click 300x and 0 to 300y range with a 1 ½ second pause.
- It will click in a range of 100 to 200x and 200 to 300yy with a ½ - 1 second pause.

To assist in clearly demonstrating the mouse moves I created a grid background that is 300 pixels by 300 pixels and 10 pixel increment between lines, as shown in Figure 6-44.

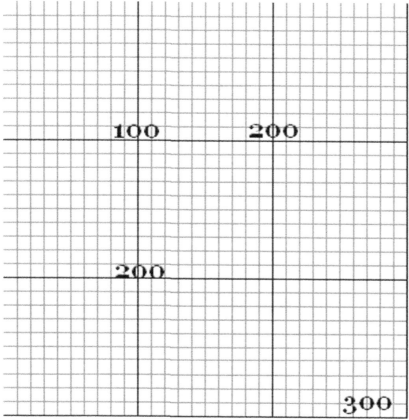

Figure 6-44| Pixel Grid Background

A desktop wallpaper with the above 300 by 300 grid and the size 1024x768 can be downloaded for free at:

http://www.lulu.com/commerce/index.php?fBuyContent=9427825

Double-click on *button 1* to create the one_Click subroutine, as in Figure 6-45.

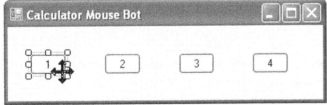

Figure 6-45 | Create And Enter one_Click Subroutine

The result will place you inside the one_Click subroutine as in Figure 6-46.

```
Private Sub one_Click(ByVal sender As System.Object, _
  ByVal e As System.EventArgs) Handles one.Click


End Sub
```

Figure 6-46 | one_Click Subroutine

The subroutine LeftMouseClick and RightMouseClick will do all the work for you. You just need to call it and give it the proper information. LeftMouseClick or RightMouseClick requires the information is sent like: LeftMouseClick(x, y, sleepDelay , x2, y2, sleepDelay2) or RightMouseClick(x, y, sleepDelay , x2, y2, sleepDelay2). Remember x2, y2, and sleepDelay2 are only used if you want a random number generated in the range of those two numbers. If only sending a specific value and not a range then you need to fill x2, y2, and/or sleepDelay2 with the word Nothing. Nothing is equivalent to null or NULL in many other languages.

The first action is to perform a left click at grid coordinate 100x and 130y with a range of 500 milliseconds to 1000 milliseconds. One nice thing about VB.net is when begin to type LeftMouseClick, it reminds you of the order and type of all the parameters you need to send it, as in Figure 6-47.

```
Private Sub one_Click(ByVal sender As System.Object, ByVal e As System.EventArgs) Handles one.Click
    LeftMouseClick(
End   LeftMouseClick(x As Integer, y As Integer, sleepDelay As Integer, x2 As Integer?, y2 As Integer?, sleepDelay2 As Integer?)
```

Figure 6-47 | Begin To Type LeftMouseClick in one_Click

The finished code for the first click for Button 1 is shown below in Figure 6-48.

```
Private Sub one_Click(ByVal sender As System.Object, _
ByVal e As System.EventArgs) Handles one.Click

    LeftMouseClick(100, 130, 500, Nothing, Nothing, 1000)

End Sub
```

Figure 6-48 | one_Click Add LeftMouseClick

Now test what you have. Click the *Save All* button. Click either *Start Debugging*, or (*F5*).

Again, I set my background to have a 300 by 300 pixel grid to clearly show the placement of the clicks, as in Figure 6-49. The upper left hand corner or the grid is the upper left hand corner of your monitor and is position zero x and zero y.

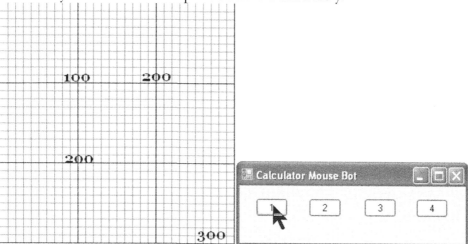

Figure 6-49 | Test Grid With Calculator Mouse Bot

Test Button 1 by clicking on *Button 1* and your result should position the mouse, as shown below in Figure 6-50. Notice the point of the mouse is 100 pixels to the right or the x position and 130 pixels down or the y position, from the upper left corner of your screen. The delay range between the down click and the up click will become apparent after adding the second click command.

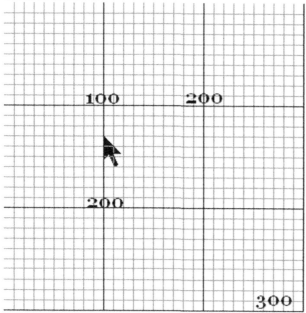

Figure 6-50 | Button 1 Test

108

After testing make sure to close the Calculator Mouse Bot and add the next mouse click.

Now add a LeftMouseClick at 200x and 100y with a second delay, as in Figure 6-51.

```
Private Sub one_Click(ByVal sender As System.Object, ByVal e As System.EventArgs) _
    Handles one.Click

    LeftMouseClick(100, 130, 500, Nothing, Nothing, 1000)
    LeftMouseClick(200, 100, 1000, Nothing, Nothing, Nothing)

End Sub
```
Figure 6-51 | one_Click Add LeftMouseClick

Now test what you have. Click the *Save All* button. Click either *Start Debugging*, or (*F5*). Test it multiple times to observe the range in sleepDelay for the first click. The result should look like Figure 6-52 and 6-53. After testing make sure to close the Calculator Mouse Bot and add the next mouse click.

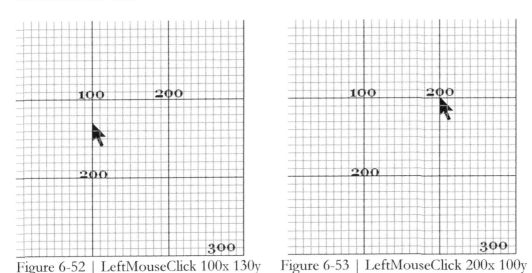

Figure 6-52 | LeftMouseClick 100x 130y   Figure 6-53 | LeftMouseClick 200x 100y

Now add RightMouseClick at 0x and 0y with a second delay, as in Figure 6-54.

```
Private Sub one_Click(ByVal sender As System.Object, ByVal e As System.EventArgs) _
    Handles one.Click

    LeftMouseClick(100, 130, 500, Nothing, Nothing, 1000)
    LeftMouseClick(200, 100, 1000, Nothing, Nothing, Nothing)
    RightMouseClick(0, 0, 1000, Nothing, Nothing, Nothing)

End Sub
```
Figure 6-54 | one_Click Add RightMouseClick

Now test what you have. Click the *Save All* button. Click either *Start Debugging*, or (*F5*).   The result should look like Figures 5-55, 5-56, and 5-57.

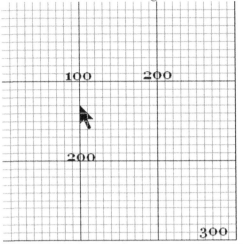

Figure 6-55 | LeftMouseClick 100x 130y

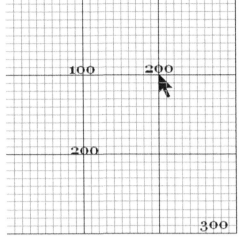

Figure 6-56 | LeftMouseClick 200x 100y

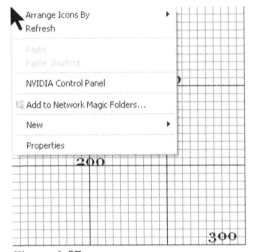

Figure 6-57

Add a LeftMouseClick with the parameters of 300x, y with a range of 0 to 300, and 1500 millisecond delay, as in Figure 6-58.

```
Private Sub one_Click(ByVal sender As System.Object, ByVal e As System.EventArgs) _
    Handles one.Click
        LeftMouseClick(100, 130, 500, Nothing, Nothing, 1000)
        LeftMouseClick(200, 100, 1000, Nothing, Nothing, Nothing)
        RightMouseClick(0, 0, 1000, Nothing, Nothing, Nothing)
        LeftMouseClick(300, 0, 1500, Nothing, 300, Nothing)

    End Sub
```

Figure 6-58 | one_Click Add LeftMouseClick

110

Now test what you have. Click the *Save All* button. Click either *Start Debugging*, or (*F5*). Rerun multiple times to see the random results for the range of y from 0 to 300 along the 300x axis. Examples of the last click are shown below, in Figures 6-59 and 6-60.

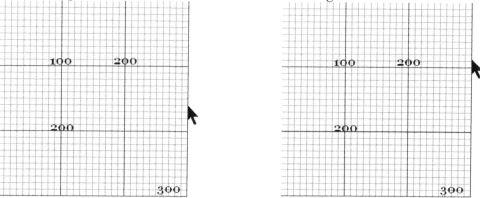

Figure 6-59 | LeftMouseClick 0 to 300y   Figure 6-60 | LeftMouseClick 0 to 300y

Close the Calculator Mouse Bot and add LeftMouseClick with 100 to 200x range, 200 to 300y range, and 500 to 1000 millisecond time delay, as in Figure 6-61.

```
Private Sub one_Click(ByVal sender As System.Object, ByVal e As System.EventArgs) _
    Handles one.Click

    LeftMouseClick(100, 130, 500, Nothing, Nothing, 1000)
    LeftMouseClick(200, 100, 1000, Nothing, Nothing, Nothing)
    RightMouseClick(0, 0, 1000, Nothing, Nothing, Nothing)
    LeftMouseClick(300, 0, 1500, Nothing, 300, Nothing)
    LeftMouseClick(100, 200, 500, 200, 300, 1000)

End Sub
```

Figure 6-61 | one_Click Add LeftMouseClick

Now test what you have. Click the *Save All* button. Click either *Start Debugging*, or (*F5*). Rerun multiple times to see the random results for the ranges, as in Figure 6-62 and 6-63.

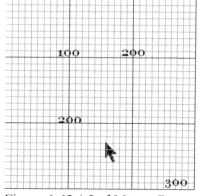

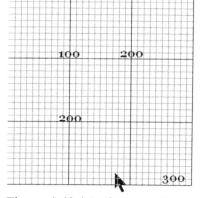

Figure 6-62 | LeftMouse Range   Figure 6-63 | LeftMouse Range

To add a time delay between the down and up mouse click, add the desired delay using System.Threading.Thread.Sleep, as shown in Figure 6-64.

```
Private Sub one_Click(ByVal sender As System.Object, ByVal e As System.EventArgs) _
    Handles one.Click

    LeftMouseClick(100, 130, 500, Nothing, Nothing, 1000)
    System.Threading.Thread.Sleep(500)
    LeftMouseClick(200, 100, 1000, Nothing, Nothing, Nothing)
    System.Threading.Thread.Sleep(1000)
    RightMouseClick(0, 0, 1000, Nothing, Nothing, Nothing)
    System.Threading.Thread.Sleep(250)
    LeftMouseClick(300, 0, 1500, Nothing, 300, Nothing)
    System.Threading.Thread.Sleep(500)
    LeftMouseClick(100, 200, 500, 200, 300, 1000)

End Sub
```

Figure 6-64 | one_Click Add Delays Between Clicks

Remember that all of the mouse clicks' grid coordinates are determined by using the desktop with the upper left hand corner being 0x and 0y. This gets a little challenging when using multiple monitors, but you will see in the next section that when working with applications you have an easy way to code it, no matter its location.

Make sure the Calculator Mouse Bot is closed. Double click on *Button 2* to create two_Click subroutine, as in Figure 6-65, and then begin to edit the code, as in Figure 6-66.

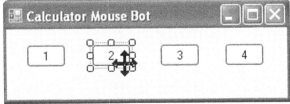

Figure 6-65 | Create Button 2 Subroutine

```
Private Sub two_Click(ByVal sender As System.Object, ByVal e As System.EventArgs) _
    Handles two.Click

    End Sub
```

Figure 6-66 | two_Click Subroutine

Button 2 is application specific and will set the focus on Windows Calculator, which you determined earlier to be the process name of calc. You also need to get the grid coordinate of the upper left hand corner of the application that you are working with in relation to its

112

position on the desktop. Remember, you can use the Automation Tool Helper to determine the current position of the upper left hand corner of an application, as in Figure 6-67.

ID	App Name	xPos	yPos	Height	Width
Calculator	5868	100	100	260	260

Figure 6-67 | Automation Tool Helper Determine Location Of Windows Calculator

As you can see from the result in Figure 6-67, I have the location of the Windows Calculator at 100x and 100y. Page back and review Figure 6-21, which is the table of the Windows Calculator buttons mapped out. The number 5 button's middle was: 129x, 168y. This means to get to the number 5 button with the Windows Calculator at 100x, 100y, you must click at an absolute position on the desktop of 229x and 268y, as shown in Figure 6-68. The absolute position will be the distance to the upper left hand corner of the application plus the relative position within the application to its location.

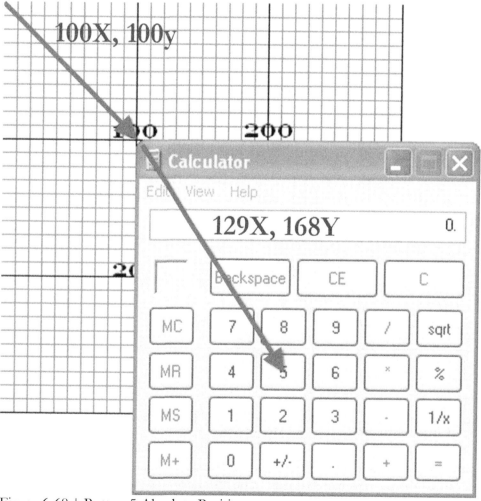

Figure 6-68 | Button 5 Absolute Position

Now you need to add code to the two_Click subroutine that will set the focus on Window Calculator and get the grid coordinates of its current location on the desktop, as in Figure 6-69.

```
Private Sub two_Click(ByVal sender As System.Object, ByVal e As System.EventArgs) _
    Handles two.Click

        Dim ps() As Process = Process.GetProcessesByName("calc")
        If ps.Length > 0 Then
            'Set Focus
            Dim p As Process = ps(0)
            Dim hWnd As IntPtr = p.MainWindowHandle
            SetForegroundWindow(hWnd)
            'get Window Position
            Dim Prop As New RECT()
            GetWindowRect(p.MainWindowHandle.ToInt32, Prop)
            Dim xAppPos As Integer
            Dim yAppPos As Integer
            Dim appHeight As Integer
            Dim appWidth As Integer
            xAppPos = Prop.Left
            yAppPos = Prop.Top
            appHeight = Prop.Bottom - Prop.Top
            appWidth = Prop.Right - Prop.Left
        End If

End Sub
```

Figure 6-69 | Adding Focus And Position Determining Code To two_Click Subroutine

The code is broken down here line by line:
C: Dim ps() As Process = Process.GetProcessesByName("calc")
D: This gives you the process object for the application Calculator.

C: If ps.Length > 0 Then
D: Determines is the application you want to find information on is open.

C: Dim p As Process = ps(0)
    Dim hWnd As IntPtr = p.MainWindowHandle
D: This gives you the handle to the application you want

C: SetForegroundWindow(hWnd)
D: Takes the handle of the application and sets the focus on the application

C: Dim Prop As New RECT()
D: Create a new datastructure of type RECT to store coordinates and height and width.

C: GetWindowRect(p.MainWindowHandle.ToInt32, Prop)

D: Calls the process to GetWindowRect and assigns the applications coordinates, height, and width into the datastructure variable Prop.

C: Dim xAppPos As Integer
      Dim yAppPos As Integer
      Dim appHeight As Integer
      Dim appWidth As Integer

D: Declare four local variables to store application coordinates, height, and width.

C: xAppPos = Prop.Left
    yAppPos = Prop.Top
    appHeight = Prop.Bottom - Prop.Top
    appWidth = Prop.Right - Prop.Left

D: Assign the applications coordinates, height, and width into the local variables. xAppPos and yAppPos give you the upper left hand corner of the application. appHeight and appWidth give you just that the height and width of the application, which can be helpful.

Now that you have laid the ground work for setting focus on the Windows Calculator, it is time to perform the clicks on the Windows Calculator.   You will be coding the clicking on Windows Calculator to do:

- Left mouse click on number 5 in the middle 129x, 168y and time delay of 200 milliseconds.
- 1 second delay between clicks.
- Left mouse on the + using the 176 to 207 x range, 224 to 246 y range and time delay of 100 milliseconds.
- 1 second delay between clicks.
- Left mouse click on number 7 in the middle 75x, 135y and time delay range 75 to 150 milliseconds.
- 1 second delay between clicks.
- Left mouse click on the = in the middle 230x, 235y and time delay of 50 milliseconds.

I would suggest making a copy of the Windows Calculator table coordinates from Figure 6-21 to use as a reference. You need to add the mouse clicks between the **If ps.Length > 0 Then** and the **End If**. This ensures you have a valid application to work with. You will begin by adding the click on Number 5.

To correctly calculate the absolute 'x' coordinate for the number 5, you need to add 129 plus xAppPos. To calculate the absolute 'y' coordinate, you need to add 168 plus yAppPos.

You can add the value simply by adding them in the call to LeftMouseClick, as in Figure 6-70.

```
appWidth = Prop.Right - Prop.Left

LeftMouseClick(129 + xAppPos, 168 + yAppPos, 200, Nothing, _
    Nothing, Nothing)

End If
```

Figure 6-70 | LeftMouseClick On Windows Calculator

Now test what you have. Click the *Save All* button. Click either *Start Debugging*, or (*F5*).

Make sure the Windows Calculator is open and its result is cleared to zero. Click on the Calculator Mouse Bot number *2 button* and you should see the mouse move to the number 5 on Windows Calculator and click, as in Figure 6-71.

Figure 6-71 | Test Number 5 Mouse Click

If you want to do additional tests, move the Windows Calculator to multiple positions on the desktop and determine if the code dynamic reads the position on the Windows Calculator each time.

Add a one second delay. Then add a left mouse click on the plus (+) sign with a 176 to 207x range and 224 to 246y range, and also including a time delay of 100 milliseconds, as shown in Figure 6-72.

```
LeftMouseClick(129 + xAppPos, 168 + yAppPos, 200, Nothing, _
    Nothing, Nothing)
System.Threading.Thread.Sleep(1000)
LeftMouseClick(176 + xAppPos, 224 + yAppPos, 100, 207 + xAppPos, _
    246 + yAppPos, Nothing)

End If
```

Figure 6-72 | Time Delay And LeftMouseClick +

Add a one second delay before the number 7. Then add a left mouse click on the number 7 by clicking at 75x and 135y, and also with a time delay ranage of 75 to 150 milliseconds.

Add a one second delay between clicks. Then add a left mouse click on the equal (=) sign by clicking at 230x and 235y with a time delay of 50 milliseconds, as in Figure 6-73.

```
   LeftMouseClick(129 + xAppPos, 168 + yAppPos, 200, Nothing, _
      Nothing, Nothing)
   System.Threading.Thread.Sleep(1000)
   LeftMouseClick(176 + xAppPos, 224 + yAppPos, 100, 207 + xAppPos, _
      246 + yAppPos, Nothing)
   System.Threading.Thread.Sleep(1000)
   LeftMouseClick(75 + xAppPos, 135 + yAppPos, 75, Nothing, _
         Nothing, 125)
   System.Threading.Thread.Sleep(1000)
   LeftMouseClick(230 + xAppPos, 235 + yAppPos, 50, Nothing, _
         Nothing, Nothing)
End If
```

Figure 6-73 | Time Delay And LeftMouseClick number 7

Now test what you have. Click the *Save All* button. Click either *Start Debugging*, or (*F5*). The result is shown in Figure 6-74.

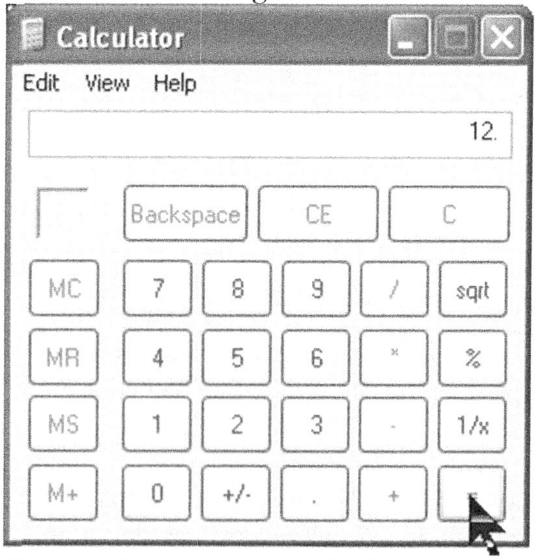

Figure 6-74 | Summation Of Button 2

When finished testing, make sure the Calculator Mouse Bot is closed.

Now create a random time delay subroutine with a range for the time between the clicks. To make it reusable you will create a subroutine to handle this for you, as in Figure 6-77.

```
Private Declare Function GetWindowRect Lib "user32" Alias _
    "GetWindowRect" (ByVal hwnd As IntPtr, ByRef lpRect As RECT) As Integer

Private Sub RandomTimeDelay(ByVal milliseconds As Integer, _
    ByVal milliseconds2 As Integer)

    Dim difference As Integer = (milliseconds2 - milliseconds) + 1
    Dim result As Integer = milliseconds + (Int(Rnd() * difference))
    System.Threading.Thread.Sleep(result)

End Sub
```

Figure 6-77 | RandomTimeDelay Function

The code is broken down here line by line:
C: Private Sub RandomTimeDelay(ByVal milliseconds As Integer, _
    ByVal milliseconds2 As Integer)
D: Declare a subroutine RandomTimeDelay that accepts two parameters of type Integer.

C: Dim difference As Integer = (milliseconds2 - milliseconds) + 1
D: Calculate the range total between the two times.

C: Dim result As Integer = milliseconds + (Int(Rnd() * difference))
D: Generate a random number within the total range and add it to the smaller number.

C: System.Threading.Thread.Sleep(result)
D: Sleep with the randomly generated time within the predetermined range.

Double click on *Button 3* to create three_Click subroutine, as in Figure 6-75, and begin to edit the code as in Figure 6-76.

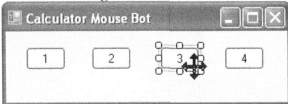

Figure 6-75 | Create Button 3 Subroutine

```
Private Sub three_Click(ByVal sender As System.Object, ByVal e As System.EventArgs) _
    Handles three.Click

End Sub
```

Figure 6-76 | three_Click Subroutine

You will be coding the clicking onWindows Calculator to do:

- Click on View pull down menu with 200 millisecond delay.
- Wait 500 to 1000 milliseconds.
- Select Scientific option with 100 to 200 millisecond delay.
- Wait between 4 to 8 seconds.
- Click on View pull down menu with 50 millisecond delay.
- Wait 1500 to 3000 milliseconds.
- Select Standard option with 100 to 200 millisecond delay.

Map out the grid coordinates for the View menu, Scientific option, and Standard option on the Calculator. Below are my results:

- View pull down menu 45x and 40y
- Scientific option 75x and 75y
- Standard option 75x and 55y

Add the code that sets the focus on Windows Calculator and gives you the application's coordinates on the desktop, as in Figure 6-78. The below code layout is used many times and it essentially becomes a copy and paste every time you make an application specific Bot.

```
Private Sub three_Click(ByVal sender As System.Object, ByVal e As System.EventArgs) _
    Handles three.Click
    Dim ps() As Process = Process.GetProcessesByName("calc")

    If ps.Length > 0 Then
        'Set Focus
        Dim p As Process = ps(0)
        Dim hWnd As IntPtr = p.MainWindowHandle
        SetForegroundWindow(hWnd)

        'get Window Position
        Dim Prop As New RECT()
        GetWindowRect(p.MainWindowHandle.ToInt32, Prop)
        Dim xAppPos As Integer
        Dim yAppPos As Integer
        Dim appHeight As Integer
        Dim appWidth As Integer
        xAppPos = Prop.Left
        yAppPos = Prop.Top
        appHeight = Prop.Bottom - Prop.Top
        appWidth = Prop.Right - Prop.Left

    End If
End Sub
```

Figure 6-78 | Application Focus And Coordinates

Now add the View menu click by placing a left click at 45x and 40y, as in Figure 6-79.

```
        Dim appWidth As Integer
        xAppPos = Prop.Left
        yAppPos = Prop.Top
        appHeight = Prop.Bottom - Prop.Top
        appWidth = Prop.Right - Prop.Left


        LeftMouseClick(45 + xAppPos, 40 + yAppPos, 200, Nothing, _
            Nothing, Nothing)


    End If
End Sub
```

Figure 6-79 | Windows Calculator View Menu Click

Now test what you have. Click the *Save All* button. Click either *Start Debugging*, or (*F5*). Click on Calculator Mouse Bot *Button 3* and the test results should look like Figure 6-80.

Figure 6-80 | Button 3 Test

Next, use the subroutine RandomTimeDelay you created earlier to generate a random time delay between 500 to 1000 milliseconds, as in Figure 6-81.

```
    LeftMouseClick(45 + xAppPos, 40 + yAppPos, 200, Nothing, _
        Nothing, Nothing)
    RandomTimeDelay(500, 1000)


End If
```

Figure 6-80 | Call RandomTimeDelay Subroutine

120

Add the Select Scientific option at coordinate 75x and 75y with 100 to 200 millisecond delay, as in Figure 6-81.

```
    RandomTimeDelay(500, 1000)
    LeftMouseClick(75 + xAppPos, 75 + yAppPos, 100, Nothing, _
        Nothing, 200)

End If
```

Figure 6-81 | Click Scientific Option

Now complete the rest of the code. Insert a 4 to 8 second delay. Click on View pull down menu at 45x and 40y with 50 millisecond delay, then wait 1500 to 3000 milliseconds. Finally, select Standard option at 75x and 55y with 100 to 200 millisecond delay, as in Figure 6-82.

```
LeftMouseClick(75 + xAppPos, 75 + yAppPos, 100, Nothing, _
        Nothing, 200)
    RandomTimeDelay(4000, 8000)
    LeftMouseClick(45 + xAppPos, 40 + yAppPos, 50, Nothing, _
        Nothing, Nothing)
    RandomTimeDelay(1500, 8000)
    LeftMouseClick(75 + xAppPos, 55 + yAppPos, 100, Nothing, _
        Nothing, 200)
End If
```

Figure 6-82 | Button 3 Complete Code

Now test what you have. Click the *Save All* button. Click either *Start Debugging*, or (*F5*). Run the test multiple times to see the variance in time delays.

Calculator Mouse Bot Button 4 will add the requirement that it must repeat the process once every ten seconds. You must add a timer to the form to create the repetitive process. Make sure to click on the *Form Designer* tab, as in Figure 6-83. Click on the *Toolbox* and drag a *Timer* onto the form. It should then appear below, as in Figure 6-84.

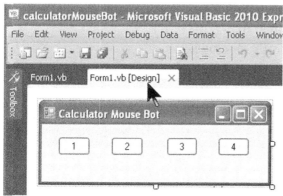

Figure 6-83 | Select Form Designer

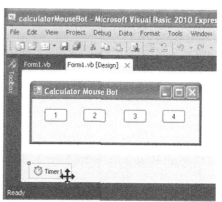

Figure 6-84 | Timer Placed On Form

You will use the default name of the timer which is Timer1. Double click on *Button 4* to create four_Click subroutine, as in Figure 6-85. Button 4 will simply turn on Timer1. You will use the Alt Key to turn off Timer1.

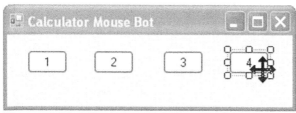

Figure 6-85 | Double Click Button 4

Add the below code to turn on Timer1 within Button 4, as in Figure 6-86.

```
Private Sub four_Click(ByVal sender As System.Object, ByVal e As System.EventArgs) _
    Handles four.Click

    Timer1.Start()

End Sub
```

Figure 6-86 | Click Scientific Option

Double click on *Timer1* so you can create the Timer1_Click subroutine to begin coding, as Figure 6-87.

Figure 6-87 | Edit Timer1 Code

First, add code to Timer1 to allow the Alt Key (while being held down) to disable the Timer, as in Figure 6-88.

```
Private Sub Timer1_Tick(ByVal sender As System.Object, ByVal e As System.EventArgs) _
    Handles Timer1.Tick

    If (My.Computer.Keyboard.AltKeyDown) Then
        Timer1.Stop()
    Else
        Timer1.Stop()

        Timer1.Start()
    End If

End Sub
```

Figure 6-88 | Click Scientific Option

The code is broken down here line by line:

C: If (My.Computer.Keyboard.AltKeyDown) Then
      Timer1.Stop()
D: If the Alt Key is pressed then stop Timer1 and exit the subroutine

C: Else
    Timer1.Stop()
    Timer1.Start()
  End If
D: Timers can behave oddly if its property interval is set to one second, but the code in the Timer subroutine happens to take more than one second. So, I suggest placing the code in the Else statement to stop the timer when you begin, and to restart it when you exit, as in Figure 6-88.

You will be coding the clicking on Windows Calculator to do:
- Right mouse click the number 7 with a 100 millisecond delay.
  - Number 7 at 90x and 148y
- Wait 1 to 2 seconds.
- Add 5x and 5y to number 7 coordinates and left mouse click with a 100 millisecond delay.
  - Click on number 7 pop up at 95x and 153y
- Wait 2 to 3 seconds
- Right mouse click the equal (=) sign with a 100 millisecond delay
  - Equal sign at 245x and 246y
- Wait 1 to 2 seconds.
- Add 5x and 5y to equal sign coordinate and left mouse click with a 100 millisecond delay
  - Click on equal sign pop up at 250x and 251y
- Wait 2 to 3 seconds

Note the default Timer interval is 100 milliseconds. You want the timer to fire once every ten seconds. Ten seconds would be equivalent to 10000 milliseconds. Make sure *Timer1* is selected, as in Figure 6-89.

Figure 6-89 | Select Timer1

Click on the *Properties* tab and update the Interval to **10000**, as in Figure 6-90.

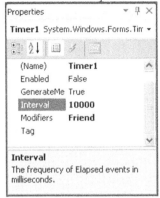

Figure 6-90 | Timer1 Set 10 Second Delay

Now add the section of code that detects the application, sets it to the foreground, and also gets the location, and size, into the subroutine Timer1_Tick, as in Figure 6-91.

```
If (My.Computer.Keyboard.AltKeyDown) Then
        Timer1.Stop()
    Else
        Timer1.Stop()
        Dim ps() As Process = Process.GetProcessesByName("calc")

        If ps.Length > 0 Then
          'Set Focus
          Dim p As Process = ps(0)
          Dim hWnd As IntPtr = p.MainWindowHandle
          SetForegroundWindow(hWnd)

          'get Window Position
          Dim Prop As New RECT()
          GetWindowRect(p.MainWindowHandle.ToInt32, Prop)
          Dim xAppPos As Integer
          Dim yAppPos As Integer
          Dim appHeight As Integer
          Dim appWidth As Integer
          xAppPos = Prop.Left
          yAppPos = Prop.Top
          appHeight = Prop.Bottom - Prop.Top
          appWidth = Prop.Right - Prop.Left
        End If
        Timer1.Start()
    End If
```

Figure 6-91 | Application Detection

Now add the code for performing the right and left mouse clicks, as in Figure 6-92.

```
appWidth = Prop.Right - Prop.Left
RightMouseClick(90 + xAppPos, 148 + yAppPos, 100, Nothing, Nothing,Nothing)
RandomTimeDelay(1000, 2000)
LeftMouseClick(95 + xAppPos, 153 + yAppPos, 100, Nothing, Nothing, Nothing)
RandomTimeDelay(2000, 3000)
RightMouseClick(245 + xAppPos,246 + yAppPos,100,Nothing,Nothing,Nothing)
RandomTimeDelay(1000, 2000)
LeftMouseClick(250 + xAppPos, 251 + yAppPos, 100, Nothing, Nothing, Nothing)
RandomTimeDelay(2000, 3000)
End If
Timer1.Start()
End If
```

Figure 6-92 | Right And Left Mouse Clicks In A Timer

Now test what you have. Click the *Save All* button. Click either *Start Debugging*, or (*F5*). The test should contain clicks as displayed in Figure 6-93 and 6-94, below. With the timer set to 10 seconds, you will experience a 10 second delay before the first click. Note: If you have multiple monitors there may be a bug in which the right mouse click only appears on the primary monitor.

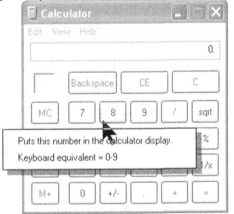

Figure 6-93 | Number 7 Left Mouse Click

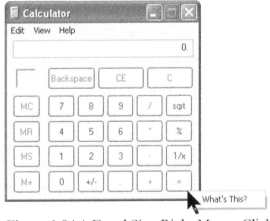

Figure 6-94 | Equal Sign Right Mouse Click

Summary

The code in the Calculator Mouse Bot gives you the ability to automate left and right mouse clicks with high definition to an applications location and time with a specific coordinate or to a range of coordinates and specific time delay or a range for a time delay.

Important things to remember: The desktop grid coordinates start at 0x,0y in the upper left hand corner of your desktop. If you want to generate a click on an application you must first find the location on the application, and then find the relative location of the click within that application. If you need to repeat a series of clicks over and over at a specific time interval, then place your code inside a timer.

Chapter 7: Individual Keys Botting With Timing Control

Sending individual key strokes with timing control is extremely powerful. Just like the mouse click, there is a press down and a release of the keys. Games are typically the pickiest of applications when it comes to timing. This type of key botting allows you to specify the time between the down and up key stroke. Compare that with menu driven application that have little, to no, timing restrictions. This enables you to take a process that might take up to three minutes to complete by hand on a menu driven application, and condense it down to seconds.

Creating Individual Keyboard Bot

You will create three different buttons to demonstrate selecting an application and sending key strokes.

- Normal Timing – Will perform a calculation on the Windows Calculator.
- Faster Timer – Will perform a calculation on the Windows Calculator as fast as possible.
- Notepad – Sending letters to Windows Notepad in lower case and upper case.

Setting Up The Project

Start a new project and choose **Windows Form Application** and name it: **calculatorKeyBot**, as in Figure 7-1.

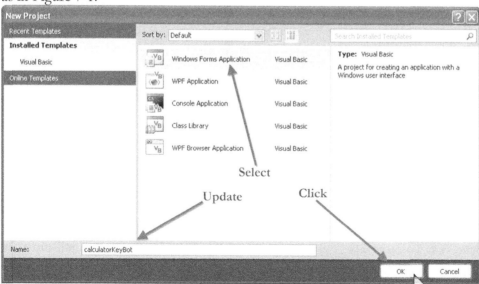

Figure 7-1 | Creating New calculatorKeyBot Application

Now click the *Save All* button, as shown below in Figure 7-2.

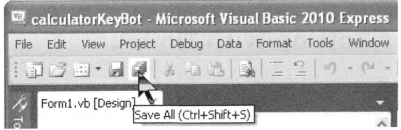

Figure 7-2 | Save All

Click *Save* to create directory structure for **calculatorKeyBot** project, as in Figure 7-3.

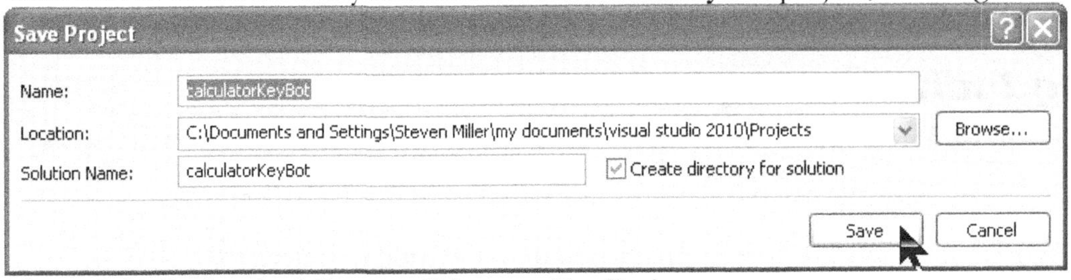

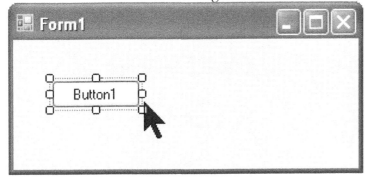

Figure 7-3| Saving And Creating Directory For Project

Laying Out The Form

Click on *Toolbox* and click and drag a *Button* onto the form, as in Figure 7-4.

Figure 7-4 | Add Normal Button

Make sure *Button1* is selected then change the property Text to **Normal,** and (Name) to **normalButton**, as in Figure 7-5 and 7-6.

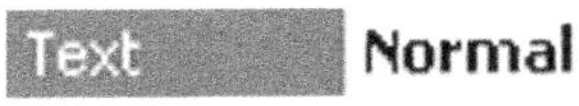

Figure 7-5 | Update Text To Normal

Figure 7-6 | Update (Name) To normalButton

Again, click on the *Toolbox* and drag another *Button* on to the form, as in Figure 7-7.

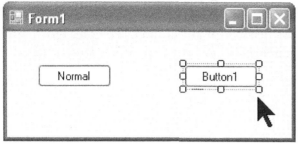

Figure 7-7 | Add Fast Button

Update the text property to **Fast** and the (Name) property to **fastButton**, as in Figure 7-8 and 7-9.

Figure 7-8| Update Text To Fast

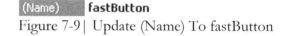

Figure 7-9| Update (Name) To fastButton

Update the form title to Calculator Key Bot by clicking on the *form* anyplace there is not a button. Select the *Properties* tab and update the Text property to **Calculator Key Bot**, as in Figure 7-10.

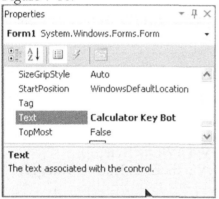

Figure 7-10 | Update Form Text Title

You will add the third button later. For now, the form should look like Figure 7-11 below.

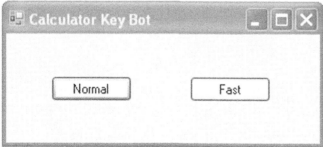

Figure 7-11 | Form Layout

128

Coding The Project

The first thing you need to do is insert the libraries needed for key botting. To enter the coding area, choose the Solution Explorer and double click on *View Code*, as in Figure 7-12.

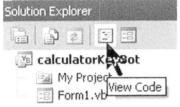

Figure 7-12 | Double Click View Code

You then get the basic form code outline, as in Figure 7-13.

```
Public Class Form1

End Class
```

Figure 7-13 | Basic Form Outline

Now insert the two libraries needed to perform sending of individual keys and setting focus on the specific application, as in Figure 7-14. It is important to realize that just sending keys will only send keys to whichever application is currently in focus.

```
Public Class Form1

    Private Declare Function SetForegroundWindow Lib "user32" _
        (ByVal handle As IntPtr) As Integer

    Private Declare Sub keybd_event Lib "user32.dll" (ByVal bVk As Byte, _
        ByVal bScan As Byte, ByVal dwFlags As Integer, ByVal dwExtraInfo As Integer)

    Private Declare Function MapVirtualKey Lib "user32" Alias "MapVirtualKeyA" _
        (ByVal wCode As Integer, ByVal wMapType As Integer) As Integer

End Class
```

Figure 7-14 | Add Libraries

The code is broken down here line by line:

C: Private Declare Function SetForegroundWindow Lib "user32" _
    (ByVal handle As IntPtr) As Integer
D: Allows you to set the active focus on an application on your choice by passing the applications handle.

C: Private Declare Sub keybd_event Lib "user32.dll" (ByVal bVk As Byte, _
ByVal bScan As Byte, ByVal dwFlags As Integer, ByVal dwExtraInfo As Integer)
D: Simulates a key stoke in either the down or up direction for a specific key.

C: Private Declare Function MapVirtualKey Lib "user32" Alias "MapVirtualKeyA" _
(ByVal wCode As Integer, ByVal wMapType As Integer) As Integer
D: Translates a virtual-key code into a character value. For a complete list of virtual key codes do a search on Virtual-Key Codes.

It will be helpful to create random time delays within a time range. To do this you will simply reuse the subroutine from the previous chapter called RandomTimeDelay, as in Figure 7-15.

```
Private Declare Function SetForegroundWindow Lib "user32" _
    (ByVal handle As IntPtr) As Integer

Private Sub RandomTimeDelay(ByVal milliseconds As Integer, _
  ByVal milliseconds2 As Integer)

    Dim difference As Integer = (milliseconds2 - milliseconds) + 1
    Dim result As Integer = milliseconds + (Int(Rnd() * difference))
    System.Threading.Thread.Sleep(result)

End Sub
```

Figure 7-15| Add RandomTimeDelay Subroutine

At the end of this book is the Bot Automation Tool Box Directory, which will allow you to easily copy and paste useful code sections such as the RandomTimeDelay.

Next, create a subroutine called pressKeys that will enable you to send a specific key, with a specific or random time range, as in Figure 7-16.

```
Private Sub RandomTimeDelay(ByVal milliseconds As Integer, _
   ByVal milliseconds2 As Integer)
    Dim difference As Integer = (milliseconds2 - milliseconds) + 1
    Dim result As Integer = milliseconds + (Int(Rnd() * difference))
    System.Threading.Thread.Sleep(result)
  End Sub
 Private Sub pressKeys(ByVal key As Integer, ByVal milliseconds As Integer, _
   ByVal key2 As Nullable(Of Integer), _
   ByVal milliseconds2 As Nullable(Of Integer))

    If (milliseconds2.HasValue) Then
       Dim differenceTime As Integer = (milliseconds2 - milliseconds) + 1
       milliseconds = milliseconds + (Int(Rnd() * differenceTime))
    End If
```

```
      keybd_event(key, MapVirtualKey(key, 0), 0, 0)
      If (key2.HasValue) Then
         keybd_event(key2, MapVirtualKey(key2, 0), 0, 0)
      End If
      System.Threading.Thread.Sleep(milliseconds)
      If (key2.HasValue) Then
         keybd_event(key2, MapVirtualKey(key2, 0), 2, 0)
      End If
      keybd_event(key, MapVirtualKey(key, 0), 2, 0)
   End Sub
```

Figure 7-16 | Add RandomTimeDelay Subroutine

The code is broken down here line by line:

C: Private Sub pressKeys(ByVal key As Integer, ByVal milliseconds As Integer, _
      ByVal key2 As Nullable(Of Integer), _
      ByVal milliseconds2 As Nullable(Of Integer))
D: The subroutine pressKeys allows you to send one or two keys to be pressed at the same time with a specific or random time range.

C: If (milliseconds2.HasValue) Then
      Dim differenceTime As Integer = (milliseconds2 - milliseconds) + 1
      milliseconds = milliseconds + (Int(Rnd() * differenceTime))
   End If
D: If two times were sent to the subroutine it then calculates a random time within the range of times submitted.

C: keybd_event(key, MapVirtualKey(key, 0), 0, 0)
D: Press down the first key

C: If (key2.HasValue) Then
      keybd_event(key2, MapVirtualKey(key2, 0), 0, 0)
   End If
D: If a second key was sent then press down the key. Notice that there is no time delay between the second key and the first key. Without a time delay, this will be the same as pressing one key, then holding both keys down at the same time.

C: System.Threading.Thread.Sleep(milliseconds)
D: Create a time delay between the press down and the release up of the key or keys.

C: If (key2.HasValue) Then
      keybd_event(key2, MapVirtualKey(key2, 0), 2, 0)
   End If
D: If a second key was sent then release the second key.

C: keybd_event(key, MapVirtualKey(key, 0), 2, 0)
D: Release the first key

C: End Sub
D: End subroutine and return to caller.

Now return to the View Designer and double click on the *Normal* button to enter the normalButton_Click subroutine, as in Figure 7-17.

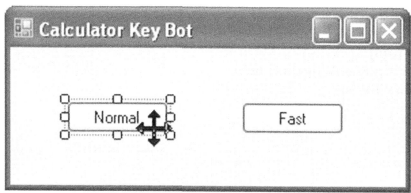

Figure 7-17 | Edit Normal Button Code

The normal button code will perform the following function:
- Set focus on Windows Calculator.
- Press the 7 key with a 350 millisecond delay.
- Wait one to two seconds.
- Press the Ctrl and C key at the same time with a 300 to 400 millisecond delay.
- Wait one to two seconds.
- Press the Delete Key with a 350 millisecond delay.
- Wait one to two seconds.
- Press the Ctrl and V key at the same time with a 350 millisecond delay.
- Wait one to two seconds.
- Press the plus key with a 350 millisecond delay.
- Wait one to two seconds.
- Press the 5 key with a 350 millisecond delay.
- Wait one to two seconds.
- Press the enter key with a 350 millisecond delay.

The first part is to set focus on the Windows Calculator application. You will use a portion of the same code you used in chapter 6 to set focus, as in Figure 7-18. You will leave out the portion that determines the position of the application. You will not need the location since you will be sending keystrokes to the application, and not to specific mouse clicks position.

```
Private Sub normalButton_Click(ByVal sender As System.Object, _
    ByVal e As System.EventArgs) Handles normalButton.Click
    Dim ps() As Process = Process.GetProcessesByName("calc")

    If ps.Length > 0 Then
        'Set Focus
        Dim p As Process = ps(0)
        Dim hWnd As IntPtr = p.MainWindowHandle
        SetForegroundWindow(hWnd)


    End If
    End Sub
```

Figure 7-18| Add Set Focus To normalButton_Click Subroutine

Begin the first keystroke of the number 7 with a 350 millisecond delay, as in Figure 7-19. Start by entering **pressKeys**, then use virtual keys to send the number 7.

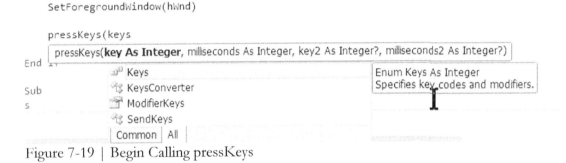

Figure 7-19 | Begin Calling pressKeys

To use the virtual keys to assist in sending the number 7, press the dot, page down, and then select **D7** or NumPad7, as in Figure 7-20.

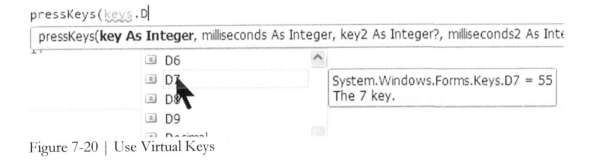

Figure 7-20 | Use Virtual Keys

Notice the pop up message System.Windows.Forms.Keys.D7 = 55 and the 7 key, as in Figure 7-19. You could have just sent the number 55 instead of Keys.D7, but this is very cryptic and can be confusing, so I advise against it.

The complete code for pressing the number 7 is shown below in Figure 7-21.

```
Private Sub normalButton_Click(ByVal sender As System.Object, _
    ByVal e As System.EventArgs) Handles normalButton.Click

    Dim ps() As Process = Process.GetProcessesByName("calc")

    If ps.Length > 0 Then
      'Set Focus
      Dim p As Process = ps(0)
      Dim hWnd As IntPtr = p.MainWindowHandle
      SetForegroundWindow(hWnd)

      pressKeys(Keys.D7, 350, Nothing, Nothing)

    End If

  End Sub
```

Figure 7-21 | Add Keystroke Of Number 7

Now test what you have. Click the *Save All* button. Click either *Start Debugging* or (*F5*). Make sure the Windows Calculator is currently running and clear the value to zero.

Click on the *Normal* button on the calculatorKeyBot, as in Figure 7-22.

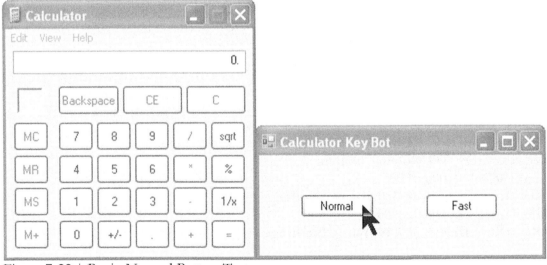

Figure 7-22 | Begin Normal Button Test

The result should be that the focus has switched from the Bot to Windows Calculator. The number 7 being pressed and released can now be viewed, as seen below in Figure 7-23.

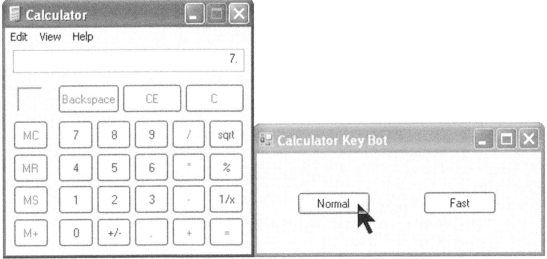

Figure 7-23 | Bot Test Results

Add a one to two second delay. Then, hold down the Ctrl + C keys at the same time to copy the resulting 7 into memory, as Figure 7-24. It is very important the Ctrl key be first and the C key second, otherwise it will not work. Try it on your own keyboard. Ctrl needs to be pressed first, followed by the C key.

```
SetForegroundWindow(hWnd)

pressKeys(Keys.D7, 350, Nothing, Nothing)
RandomTimeDelay(1000, 2000)
pressKeys(Keys.ControlKey, 350, Keys.C, Nothing)
```

Figure 7-24| Add Delay And Copy Windows Calculator Result

Add a one to two second delay. Then, send a Delete key press with 350 millisecond delay between the down and up keystrokes, as in Figure 7-25.

```
SetForegroundWindow(hWnd)

pressKeys(Keys.D7, 350, Nothing, Nothing)
RandomTimeDelay(1000, 2000)
pressKeys(Keys.ControlKey, 350, Keys.C, Nothing)
RandomTimeDelay(1000, 2000)
pressKeys(Keys.Delete, 350, Nothing, Nothing)
```

Figure 7-25| Add Delay And Delete Keystroke

Add a one to two second delay. Then, paste using the Ctrl+ V key with a 350 millisecond delay between down and up keystroke, as in Figure 7-26.

```
pressKeys(Keys.D7, 350, Nothing, Nothing)
RandomTimeDelay(1000, 2000)
pressKeys(Keys.ControlKey, 350, Keys.C, Nothing)
RandomTimeDelay(1000, 2000)
 pressKeys(Keys.Delete, 350, Nothing, Nothing)
RandomTimeDelay(1000, 2000)
pressKeys(Keys.ControlKey, 350, Keys.V, Nothing)
```

Figure 7-26| Add Delay And Combination Ctrl + V Keystroke

Add one to two second delay. Add the plus(+) keystroke with a 350 millisecond delay between the down and up keystrokes, as in Figure 7-27. Notice: there is no Keys.Plus in the pull down menu. However, there is a Keys.Add, which you could use. Sometimes you need to scan the list of keys to find what you are looking for. If you cannot find it, remember you can always send a mouse click.

```
RandomTimeDelay(1000, 2000)
 pressKeys(Keys.ControlKey, 350, Keys.V, Nothing)
RandomTimeDelay(1000, 2000)
pressKeys(Keys.Add, 350, Nothing, Nothing)
```

Figure 7-27| Add Delay And Combination Ctrl And V Keystroke

Add a one to two second delay. Send the number 5 keystroke, as in Figure 7-28. Note: this time I am using NumPad5 instead of D5. Both will work. If you ever find a situation where one does not work, try the other option.

```
RandomTimeDelay(1000, 2000)
 pressKeys(Keys.Add, 350, Nothing, Nothing)
 RandomTimeDelay(1000, 2000)
 pressKeys(Keys.NumPad5, 350, Nothing, Nothing)
```

Figure 7-28| Add Delay And Number 5 Keystroke

Finally, add a one to two second delay. Send the enter key, as in Figure 7-29. Again, notice that I had to use the enter key since there was no equals key.

```
RandomTimeDelay(1000, 2000)
 pressKeys(Keys.NumPad5, 350, Nothing, Nothing)
 RandomTimeDelay(1000, 2000)
 pressKeys(Keys.Enter, 350, Nothing, Nothing)
```

Figure 7-29| Add Delay And Enter Keystroke

Now test what you have. Click the *Save All* button. Click either *Start Debugging*, or (*F5*). Make sure the Windows Calculator is currently running and clear the value to zero. Click on the *Normal* button on the calculatorKeyBot. Your result should look like Figure 7-30, below.

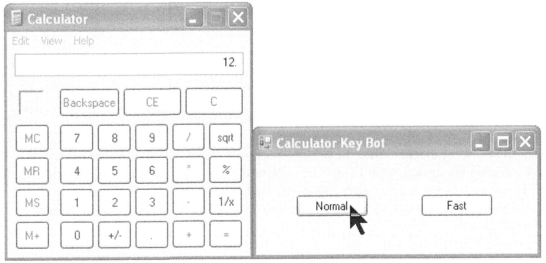

Figure 7-30 | Normal Button Test Results

The range of the total time using the Normal button is between 1150 to 6750 milliseconds. For the Fast button you are going to remove all time delays and see how the Bot responds. In the View Designer, double click on the *Fast* button to edit the code, as in Figure 7-31.

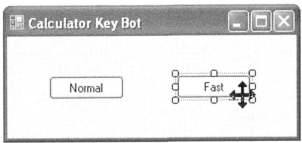

Figure 7-31 | Edit Code For Fast Button

You have now created the fastButton_Click subroutine, as the example inFigure 7-32 shows.

```
Private Sub fastButton_Click(ByVal sender As System.Object, _
    ByVal e As System.EventArgs) Handles fastButton.Click

End Sub
```

Figure 7-32| fastButton Subroutine

The next step is to copy all the code within the numberButton_Click subroutine and paste it into the fastButton_Click subroutine, shown in Figure 7-33. Make sure not to copy subroutine declaration and ending.

```
Private Sub normalButton_Click(ByVal sender As System.Object, _
    ByVal e As System.EventArgs) Handles normalButton.Click

    Dim ps() As Process = Process.GetProcessesByName("calc")

    If ps.Length > 0 Then
        'Set Focus
        Dim p As Process = ps(0)
        Dim hWnd As IntPtr = p.MainWindowHandle
        SetForegroundWindow(hWnd)

        pressKeys(Keys.D7, 350, Nothing, Nothing)
        RandomTimeDelay(1000, 2000)
        pressKeys(Keys.ControlKey, 350, Keys.C, Nothing)
        RandomTimeDelay(1000, 2000)
        pressKeys(Keys.Delete, 350, Nothing, Nothing)
        RandomTimeDelay(1000, 2000)
        pressKeys(Keys.ControlKey, 350, Keys.V, Nothing)
        RandomTimeDelay(1000, 2000)
        pressKeys(Keys.Add, 350, Nothing, Nothing)
        RandomTimeDelay(1000, 2000)
        pressKeys(Keys.NumPad5, 350, Nothing, Nothing)
        RandomTimeDelay(1000, 2000)
        pressKeys(Keys.Enter, 350, Nothing, Nothing)
    End If
End Sub
```

Figure 7-33 | Copy Code Within normalButton_Click Subroutine

Now, paste the contents into the fastButton_Click subroutine, as Figure 7-34 shows. (Note: Figure 7-34 is continued on the next page .)

```
Private Sub fastButton_Click(ByVal sender As System.Object, _
    ByVal e As System.EventArgs) Handles fastButton.Click
    Dim ps() As Process = Process.GetProcessesByName("calc")
    If ps.Length > 0 Then
        'Set Focus
        Dim p As Process = ps(0)
        Dim hWnd As IntPtr = p.MainWindowHandle
        SetForegroundWindow(hWnd)
        pressKeys(Keys.D7, 350, Nothing, Nothing)
        RandomTimeDelay(1000, 2000)
```

```
            pressKeys(Keys.ControlKey, 350, Keys.C, Nothing)
            RandomTimeDelay(1000, 2000)
            pressKeys(Keys.Delete, 350, Nothing, Nothing)
            RandomTimeDelay(1000, 2000)
            pressKeys(Keys.ControlKey, 350, Keys.V, Nothing)
            RandomTimeDelay(1000, 2000)
            pressKeys(Keys.Add, 350, Nothing, Nothing)
            RandomTimeDelay(1000, 2000)
            pressKeys(Keys.NumPad5, 350, Nothing, Nothing)
            RandomTimeDelay(1000, 2000)
            pressKeys(Keys.Enter, 350, Nothing, Nothing)
        End If
    End Sub
```

Figure 7-34 | fastButton Subroutine

Now update the delay to **zero** and remove all the **RandomTimeDelays**, as in Figure 7-35.

```
Private Sub fastButton_Click(ByVal sender As System.Object, _
    ByVal e As System.EventArgs) Handles fastButton.Click
    Dim ps() As Process = Process.GetProcessesByName("calc")

    If ps.Length > 0 Then
        'Set Focus
        Dim p As Process = ps(0)
        Dim hWnd As IntPtr = p.MainWindowHandle
        SetForegroundWindow(hWnd)

        pressKeys(Keys.D7, 0, Nothing, Nothing)
        pressKeys(Keys.ControlKey, 0, Keys.C, Nothing)
        pressKeys(Keys.Delete, 0, Nothing, Nothing)
        pressKeys(Keys.ControlKey, 0, Keys.V, Nothing)
        pressKeys(Keys.Add, 0, Nothing, Nothing)
        pressKeys(Keys.NumPad5, 0, Nothing, Nothing)
        pressKeys(Keys.Enter, 0, Nothing, Nothing)



    End If
End Sub
```

Figure 7-35 | fastButton Subroutine Updated

Now test what you have. Click the *Save All* button. Click either *Start Debugging*, or (*F5*). Make sure the Windows Calculator is currently running and clear the value to zero. Click on the *Fast* button on the calculatorKeyBot.

Your result should look like Figure 7-36 below. Run the Calculator Bot a couple of times and compare the difference in times between the Normal and Fast buttons.

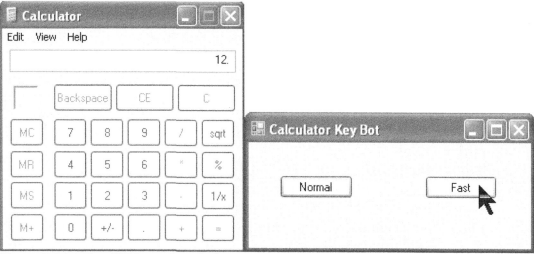

Figure 7-36 | Fast Without Any Delays

You have focused mainly on numbers, but what about letters? To add letters, the process is the same as for numbers. You will simply find the appropriate letters instead, as in Figure 7-37.

Figure 7-37 | Adding Letters

Did you notice that there were no lower case letters? You will add one more button to the form in order to work with letters, and this time you will use Windows Notepad as the application.

Click on the *Toolbox* and drag another *Button* onto the form, as in Figure 7-38, shown below.

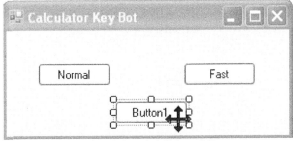

Figure 7-38 | Add An Additional Button

Update the Text property to **Notepad,** and the (Name) property to **notepad**, as shown below in Figure 7-39 and Figure 7-40.

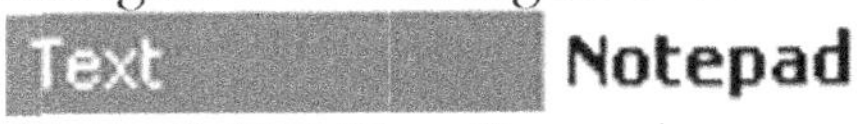

| Text | **Notepad** | (Name) | **notepad** |

Figure 7-39 | Text Properties   Figure 7-40 | (Name) Property

Now double click on *Notepad* button to edit the code, as in Figure 7-41.

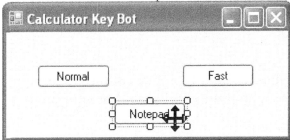

Figure 7-41 | Enter Code Edit For Notepad Button

You have now created the notepad_Click subroutine, as the example in Figure 7-42 shows.

```
Private Sub notepad_Click(ByVal sender As System.Object, _
   ByVal e As System.EventArgs) Handles notepad.Click


End Sub
```

Figure 7-42| notepad Subroutine

Open up the Windows Notepad. Click on the *Start menu -> All Programs -> Accessories -> Notepad*, as in Figure 7-43.

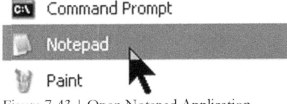

Figure 7-43 | Open Notepad Application

Capture the process name of Windows Notepad. Press Ctrl+Alt+Delete to open up the Windows Task Manager. Then, highlight and right mouse click on *Untitled – Notepad* and select *Go To Process*, as in Figure 7-44.

Figure 7-44 | Notepad Go To Process

The image name is notepad.exe, as in Figure 7-45. Again, you remove the .exe and are left with **notepad** as the process name.

Figure 7-45 | notepad.exe Process

Inside notepad_Click you need to set the focus on notepad, as shown in Figure 7-46.

```
Private Sub notepad_Click(ByVal sender As System.Object, _
    ByVal e As System.EventArgs) Handles notepad.Click


    Dim ps() As Process = Process.GetProcessesByName("notepad")
    If ps.Length > 0 Then
      'Set Focus
      Dim p As Process = ps(0)
      Dim hWnd As IntPtr = p.MainWindowHandle
      SetForegroundWindow(hWnd)
    End If


End Sub
```

Figure 7-46| Set Focus On Notepad

Next type the abc's on notepad, as shown in Figure 7-47 below.

```
Private Sub notepad_Click(ByVal sender As System.Object, _
     ByVal e As System.EventArgs) Handles notepad.Click
      Dim ps() As Process = Process.GetProcessesByName("notepad")
      If ps.Length > 0 Then
         'Set Focus
         Dim p As Process = ps(0)
         Dim hWnd As IntPtr = p.MainWindowHandle
         SetForegroundWindow(hWnd)

         pressKeys(Keys.A, 0, Nothing, Nothing)
         pressKeys(Keys.B, 0, Nothing, Nothing)
         pressKeys(Keys.C, 0, Nothing, Nothing)


      End If
End Sub
```
Figure 7-47 | Send Keystroks abc

Now test what you have. Click the *Save All* button. Click either *Start Debugging*, or (*F5*). Make sure the Windows Notepad is currently running. Click on the *Notepad* button on the calculatorKeyBot. Your result should look the same as Figure 7-48, below.

Figure 7-48 | abc Keystrokes On Notepad

So Keys.A sends an 'a'; Keys.B sends a 'b'; and Keys.C sends a 'c'. What if you want to send a capital letter? You can do it the same way you do on a keyboard, hold down the shift key and then press your letter. You will add an uppercase 'D', lowercase 'e', and uppercase 'F', as shown in Figure 7-49.

```
pressKeys(Keys.A, 0, Nothing, Nothing)
pressKeys(Keys.B, 0, Nothing, Nothing)
pressKeys(Keys.C, 0, Nothing, Nothing)

pressKeys(Keys.ShiftKey, 0, Keys.D, Nothing)
pressKeys(Keys.E, 0, Nothing, Nothing)
pressKeys(Keys.ShiftKey, 0, Keys.F, Nothing)
```
Figure 7-49 | Send Keystroks abcDeF

Now test what you have. Click the *Save All* button. Click either *Start Debugging*, or (*F5*). Make sure the Windows Notepad is currently running and clear any existing text. Click on the *Notepad* button on the calculatorKeyBot. Your result should look like Figure 7-50, below.

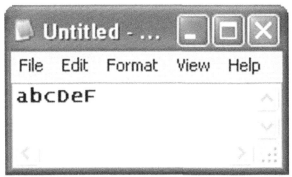

Figure 7-50 | abcDeF Keystrokes On Notepad

Summary

The library keybd_event allows you to send an individual keystroke, control both the down and up keystrokes, and set a time delay between the strokes, if needed. There are many different ways to send keystrokes in VB.net, but I have found keybd_event to be the most reliable of all the methods.

The first step is always to set focus on the application that you want to send the keystrokes to. Next, is to send the keystrokes with their appropriate timing. If a keystroke cannot be found to work with the application, resort to using application specific mouse clicks.

Chapter 8:
Multiple And/Or Individual Keys Without Timing Control

Using keybd_event works great if you need to specify keystroke timing and sending smaller amounts of text. What if you want to send a couple pages of text? This chapter will show you how to use Sendkeys to send multiple or individual keystrokes without timing control. A word of caution: Sendkeys works with most applications but if a specific timing control is needed you will need to use keybd_event. As always, make sure to test your Bot completely to make sure that it works the way you expecte it to.

Creating Sendkeys Keyboard Bot

The Sendkeys Bot will have only one button. You will have another opportunity in the next chapter, Starting Remote Applications, to get another chance to practice using SendKeys.

Setting Up The Project

Start a new project and choose *Windows Form Application* and name it **sendKeysBot**, as shown in the example in Figure 8-1.

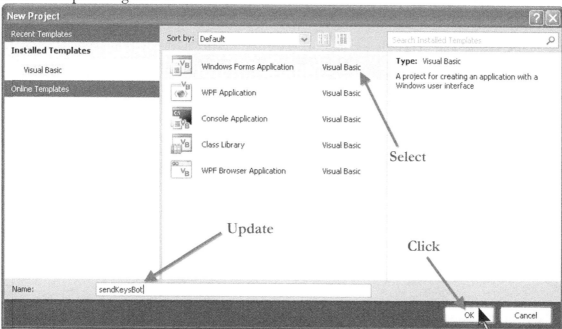

Figure 8-1 | Creating New sendKeysBot Application

Now click the *Save All* button, as in Figure 8-2, below.

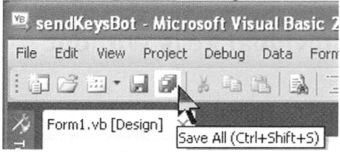

Figure 8-2 | Save All

Click *Save* to create a directory structure for **sendKeysBot** project, as in Figure 8-3.

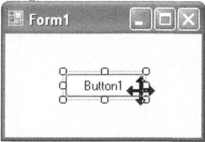

Figure 8-3 | Saving And Creating Directory For Project

Laying Out The Form

Click on the *Toolbox* and drag a *Button* on to the Form and resize as needed, and shown below in Figure 8-4.

Figure 8-4 | Add A Button

Update the Text property to **SendKeys,** and the (Name) property to **sendKeys**, as shown below in Figure 8-5 and Figure 8-6.

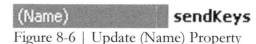

Figure 8-5 | Update Text Property

Figure 8-6 | Update (Name) Property

Update the form title to Send Keys Bot by clicking on the form any place there is no button. Select the *Properties* tab and update the Text property to **Send Keys Bot**, as in Figure 8-7.   The resulting form should look like Figure 8-8.

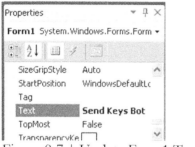

Figure 8-7 | Update Form1 Text

Figure 8-8 | Updated Form Title

Coding The Project

Sendkeys allow you to send one keystroke, or a whole string of keystrokes, in one call. Sendkeys does not require the inclusion on a library to use. However, you still need to include the library SetForegroundWindow to set the focus on the application to which you will be sending the keystrokes.

Click on the *Solution Explorer* and click on *View Code*, as in Figure 8-9.

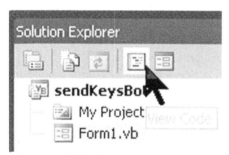

Figure 8-9 | Select View Code In Solution Explorer

Now add the SetForegroundWindow library, as shown in Figure 8-10 below.

```
Public Class Form1

    Private Declare Function SetForegroundWindow Lib "user32" _
        (ByVal handle As IntPtr) As Integer

End Class
```

Figure 8-10| Add SetForegroundWindow Library

The next step is to double click on the *SendKeys* button to add the subroutine and edit the code, as in Figure 8-11. This will create the sendKeys_Click subroutine, as in Figure 8-12.

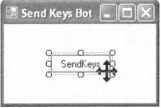

Figure 8-11 | Edit SendKeys Code

```
Public Class Form1
    Private Declare Function SetForegroundWindow Lib "user32" _
        (ByVal handle As IntPtr) As Integer

    Private Sub sendKeys_Click(ByVal sender As System.Object, _
        ByVal e As System.EventArgs) Handles sendKeys.Click

    End Sub
End Class
```

Figure 8-12| sendKeys_Click Subroutine Created

Sendkeys has two main methods to send keystokes. SendKeys.Send will send keystrokes to the active application. SendKeys.SendWait will send keystrokes to the active application and then wait for the messages to be processed. I **strongly suggest** you use SendWait instead of Send to help ensure your keystrokes are properly received. Because Send does not wait for application processing, your application may not be ready to process all the keys and what had been sent to the application may get truncated, or not received.

To send special keys such as Shift, Tab, F1 you need to use the codes shown in Figure 8-13:

Keystroke	Code	Keystroke	Code
ALT	%	RIGHT ARROW	{RIGHT}
BACKSPACE	{BACKSPACE}, {BS}, or {BKSP}	SCROLL LOCK	{SCROLLLOCK}
BREAK	{BREAK}	SHIFT	+
CAPS LOCK	{CAPSLOCK}	TAB	{TAB}
CTRL	^	UP ARROW	{UP}
DEL or DELETE	{DEL} or {DELETE}	F1	{F1}
DOWN ARROW	{DOWN}	F2	{F2}
END	{END}	F3	{F3}
ENTER	{ENTER} or ~	F4	{F4}
ESC	{ESC}	F5	{F5}
HELP	{HELP}	F6	{F6}

HOME	{HOME}	F7	{F7}
INS or INSERT	{INSERT} or {INS}	F8	{F8}
Keypad add	{ADD}	F9	{F9}
Keypad subtract	{SUBTRACT}	F10	{F10}
Keypad multiply	{MULTIPLY}	F11	{F11}
Keypad divide	{DIVIDE}	F12	{F12}
LEFT ARROW	{LEFT}	F13	{F13}
NUM LOCK	{NUMLOCK}	F14	{F14}
PAGE DOWN	{PGDN}	F15	{F15}
PAGE UP	{PGUP}	F16	{F16}
PRINT SCREEN	{PRTSC}		

Figure 8-13 | SendKeys Keystroke To Code Table

To create keystroke combinations with ALT, CTRL, and SHIFT you need to precede the key code with the corresponding code from above.

Examples:
- Ctrl C would be ^C
- Hold down SHIFT with also held down E and C would be +(EC)
- Hold down SHIFT with E pressed followed by C would be +EC

To send repeating keystrokes, use the format {keystroke repeatNumber}.

Examples
- 12 A's would be {A 12}
- 4 Down Arrows would be {Down 4}
- 3 Tabs would be {Tab 3}

The SendKeys button will be working with Windows Notepad. So the next step is to set the focus on the Windows Notepad inside of the subroutine sendKey_Clicks, as in Figure 8-14.

```
Private Sub sendKeys_Click(ByVal sender As System.Object, _
    ByVal e As System.EventArgs) Handles sendKeys.Click

    Dim ps() As Process = Process.GetProcessesByName("notepad")
    If ps.Length > 0 Then
        'Set Focus
        Dim p As Process = ps(0)
        Dim hWnd As IntPtr = p.MainWindowHandle
        SetForegroundWindow(hWnd)
    End If

End Sub
```

Figure 8-14 | Set Focus On Windows Notepad

150

Helpful Hint: If you ever notice that the first couple SendKeys or keybd_event keystrokes work some times, and do not at other times, I suggest placing at least a one second delay after the SetForegroundWindow call in order to give enough time for the focus to be applied. Add a one second delay after SetForegroundWindow, as shown in the example below, Figure 8-15.

Start by sending your name to Windows Notepad. Make sure to update the code in Figure 8-15 to be **your name**, (unless your name is actually Steve Miller, of course).

```
Private Sub sendKeys_Click(ByVal sender As System.Object, _
    ByVal e As System.EventArgs) Handles sendKeys.Click

    Dim ps() As Process = Process.GetProcessesByName("notepad")
    If ps.Length > 0 Then
      'Set Focus
      Dim p As Process = ps(0)
      Dim hWnd As IntPtr = p.MainWindowHandle
      SetForegroundWindow(hWnd)
      System.Threading.Thread.Sleep(1000)

      System.Windows.Forms.SendKeys.SendWait("Steve Miller")

    End If
End Sub
```
Figure 8-15 | Send Your Name With SendKeys

Now test what you have. Click the *Save All* button. Click either *Start Debugging*, or (*F5*). Make sure the Windows Notepad is currently running. Click on the *SendKeys* button on the sendKeysBot. Your result should look like Figure 8-16 below, except it would be your name.

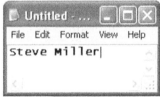

Figure 8-16 | Your Name With SendKeys

Next, you are going to send an **Enter** Keystroke following by the string **Likes Bot Programming**, as in Figure 8-17. Note: you still use quotes around the {Enter} code with SendKeys.

```
System.Windows.Forms.SendKeys.SendWait("Steve Miller")
System.Windows.Forms.SendKeys.SendWait("{Enter}")
System.Windows.Forms.SendKeys.SendWait("Likes Bot Programming")
```
Figure 8-17 | Send Your Name With SendKeys

Now test what you have. Click the *Save All* button. Click either *Start Debugging*, or (*F5*). Make sure the Windows Notepad is currently running and cleared out. Click on the *SendKeys* button on the sendKeysBot. Your result should look like Figure 8-18 below, except it would be your name.

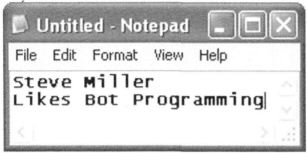

Figure 8-18 | Enter Keystroke And String

Next you are going to change the Font style of all the text to Bold. Under the Edit menu you see the keyboard short cut for select all is Ctrl+A, as seen in Figure 8-19.

Figure 8-19 | Select All Keyboard Short Cut

Now add the code for Ctrl+A which is **^a** within SendKeys, as in Figure 8-20. Note: the code must be ^a with a lowercase a and not ^A with a upper case a.

System.Windows.Forms.SendKeys.SendWait("Steve Miller")
System.Windows.Forms.SendKeys.SendWait("{Enter}")
System.Windows.Forms.SendKeys.SendWait("Likes Bot Programming")
System.Windows.Forms.SendKeys.SendWait("^a")

Figure 8-20| Select All With SendKeys

Now test what you have. Click the *Save All* button. Click either *Start Debugging*, or (*F5*). Make sure the Windows Notepad is currently running and cleared out. Click on the *SendKeys* button on the sendKeysBot. Your result should look like Figure 8-21 below, except it would be your name.

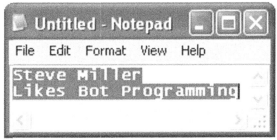

Figure 8-21 | Test Select All

When working with applications it is extremely helpful to know how to identify all the keyboard short cuts for the program. Simply hold down the **ALT key** to identify the short cut codes for Windows Notepad, as in Figure 8-22.

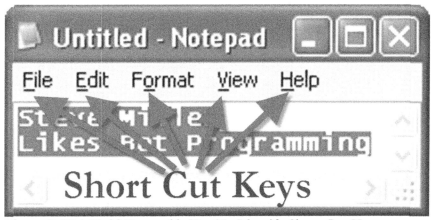

Figure 8-22 | Hold Down Alt Key To Identify Short Cut Keys

Now you are going to select the Format menu using the "**o**" short cut key by sending ALT+o. So **%o** is the code. Insert this into SendKeys, as shown below in Figure 8-23.

```
System.Windows.Forms.SendKeys.SendWait("Steve Miller")
 System.Windows.Forms.SendKeys.SendWait("{Enter}")
 System.Windows.Forms.SendKeys.SendWait("Likes Bot Programming")
System.Windows.Forms.SendKeys.SendWait("^a")
System.Windows.Forms.SendKeys.SendWait("%o")
```

Figure 8-23| Select Format Short Cut Alt 0

Now test what you have. Click the *Save All* button. Click either *Start Debugging*, or (F5).
Make sure the Windows Notepad is currently running and cleared out. Click on the *SendKeys*
button on the sendKeysBot. With the Format pull down menu visible, press the **Alt key** to
show the short cut choices listed on the pull down. Your result should look like Figure 8-24
below, except it would be your name.

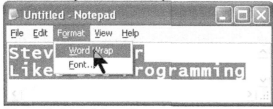

Figure 8-24 | Select Format Menu With Alt o Short Cut Key

To access Word Wrap you would now use "**w**", and to access Font use "**f**". Notice that to
access the pull down menu you do not use the Alt Key again, but simply use the letter shown
on the pull down menu.

The next step is to select Font using Alt 0, as shown in Figure 8-25 below.

```
System.Windows.Forms.SendKeys.SendWait("Steve Miller")
 System.Windows.Forms.SendKeys.SendWait("{Enter}")
 System.Windows.Forms.SendKeys.SendWait("Likes Bot Programming")
System.Windows.Forms.SendKeys.SendWait("^a")
System.Windows.Forms.SendKeys.SendWait("%o")
System.Windows.Forms.SendKeys.SendWait("f")
```

Figure 8-25| Select Font Pull Down Option

Now test what you have. Click the *Save All* button. Click either *Start Debugging*, or (F5).
Make sure the Windows Notepad is currently running. Click on the *SendKeys* button on the
sendKeysBot. Your result should have popped up the Font menu, as in Figure 8-26.

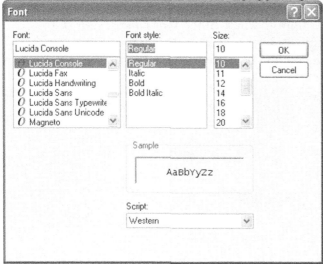

Figure 8-26 | Font Menu

154

Again, you can press the **Alt Key** to show the keyboard short cuts, as shown in Figure 8-27.

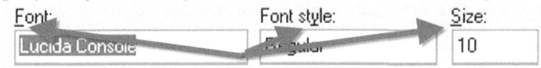

Figure 8-27 | Font Menu With Keyboard Short Cuts Identified.

Now change the Font Style to Bold. Two different paths will accomplish that. Either use the short cut Alt+y to access the Font Style, as in Figure 8-28, or press the Tab key to access the Font Style, as Figure 8-29. I would suggest trying both.

```
System.Windows.Forms.SendKeys.SendWait("^a")
System.Windows.Forms.SendKeys.SendWait("%o")
System.Windows.Forms.SendKeys.SendWait("f")
System.Windows.Forms.SendKeys.SendWait("%y")
```

Figure 8-28| Select Font Style With Short Cut Alt+y

```
System.Windows.Forms.SendKeys.SendWait("^a")
System.Windows.Forms.SendKeys.SendWait("%o")
System.Windows.Forms.SendKeys.SendWait("f")
System.Windows.Forms.SendKeys.SendWait("{TAB}")
```

Figure 8-29| Select Font Style With Sending Tab Key

Both methods work well. My preference would be to use the short cut in case the developer ever decided to change the order of the menus.

Now test what you have. Click the *Save All* button. Click either *Start Debugging*, or (*F5*). Make sure the Windows Notepad is currently running. Click on the *SendKeys* button on the sendKeysBot. Your result should have the with the Font style selected, as in Figure 8-30.

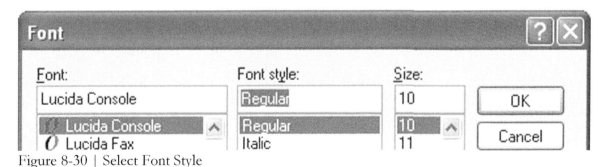

Figure 8-30 | Select Font Style

To choose the Bold Style you can take two different paths. The first would be to send the word Bold, as in Figure 8-31. The second would be to send two down arrows keystrokes, as in Figure 8-32. If you used the Tab for the previous example, your second line of code will be different.

```
System.Windows.Forms.SendKeys.SendWait("f")
System.Windows.Forms.SendKeys.SendWait("%y")
System.Windows.Forms.SendKeys.SendWait("Bold")
```
Figure 8-31 | Select Bold By Typing Bold

```
System.Windows.Forms.SendKeys.SendWait("f")
System.Windows.Forms.SendKeys.SendWait("%y")
System.Windows.Forms.SendKeys.SendWait("{Down 2}")
```
Figure 8-32| Select Bold By Tabbing Down to Bold

A word of caution: Notepad remembers the last Font style update, so running the Bot more than once by using two down arrows might cause a problem. My preference would be to select via typing the Font style.

Now test what you have. Click the *Save All* button. Click either *Start Debugging*, or (F5). Make sure the Windows Notepad is currently running. Click on the *SendKeys* button on the sendKeysBot. Your result should look like Figure 8-33, below, with the Bold Font Style.

Figure 8-33 | Update Bold Font Style

To update the font, you simply need to send an Enter keystroke. The code for Enter is {Enter} or ~. Add an Enter keystroke, as shown below in Figure 8-34.

```
System.Windows.Forms.SendKeys.SendWait("%y")
System.Windows.Forms.SendKeys.SendWait("Bold")
System.Windows.Forms.SendKeys.SendWait("{Enter}")
```
Figure 8-34| Apply Bold Font Style By Sending Enter Key

Now test what you have. Click the *Save All* button. Click either *Start Debugging*, or (F5). Make sure the Windows Notepad is currently running. Click on the *SendKeys* button on the sendKeysBot. Your result should look like Figure 8-35 with Bold Font Style Applied.

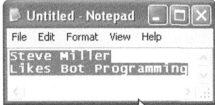

Figure 8-35 | Updated Font With Bold Style

Summary

SendKeys is extremely powerful for sending complete strings, or individual characters, where down and up keystroke timing is not needed. You can combine sending mouse clicks, keybd_event, and Sendkeys to automate applications and games. The Alt key will help highlight the short cuts keys for Windows applications. To increase the reliability, add a one second delay after calling SetForegroundWindow before sending any keys.

I would suggest mapping out the keys you want to use in your automation ahead of time.

Example for this chapter:
- String: Your Name
- Enter key
- String: Likes Bot Programming
- CTRL a
- ALT o
- f Key
- Alt y
- Bold
- Enter Key

Additional Windows program key combinations that might help you in automating are:

- Copy is CTRL+C
- Cut is CTRL+X
- Paste is CTRL+V
- Undo is CTRL+Z
- Bold is CTRL+B
- Underline is CTRL+U
- Italic is CTRL+I

Chapter 9:
Starting Remote Applications

It is helpful to be able to have your Bot start the Windows application that you're going to automate. This enables the application to be open before starting the Bot, and before mouse clicks and keystrokes are sent.

It is typically necessary to be able to start an application when using a Task Scheduler or Cron Job. In Windows, you can use Scheduled Task to run an application at either a given reoccurring time, or a one-time event. This ensures that the application you want to automating at 3:00 am each day is open.

Creating Starting Remote Application

The automation Bot will have four buttons.

- Windows Calculator – Open
- Windows Media Player – Open with Music
- Internet Explorer – Open
- Internet Explorer – Open with Website Address

Setting Up The Project

Start a new project and choose *Windows Form Application* and name it: **startRemoteApplicationsBot**, as shown in the example in Figure 9-1.

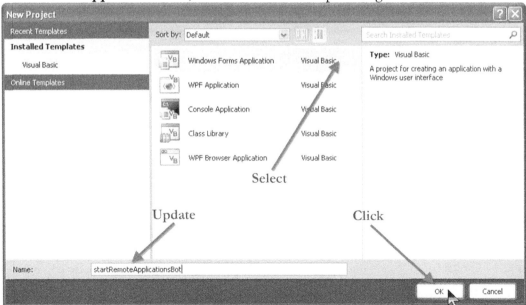

Figure 9-1 | Creating New startRemoteApplicationsBot

158

Now click the *Save All* button, as shown in Figure 9-2.

Figure 9-2 | Save All

Click *Save* to create directory structure for project, as in Figure 9-3.

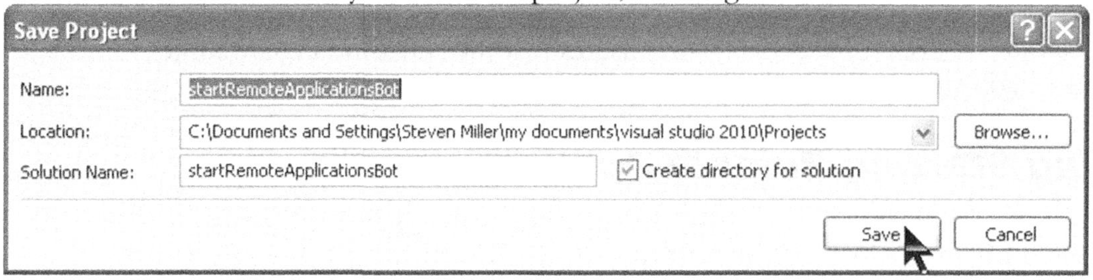

Save Project		? X
Name:	startRemoteApplicationsBot	
Location:	C:\Documents and Settings\Steven Miller\my documents\visual studio 2010\Projects	Browse...
Solution Name:	startRemoteApplicationsBot	☑ Create directory for solution
		Save Cancel

Figure 9-3| Saving And Creating Directory For Project

Laying Out The Form

Add four buttons on the form, as in Figure 9-4 below.

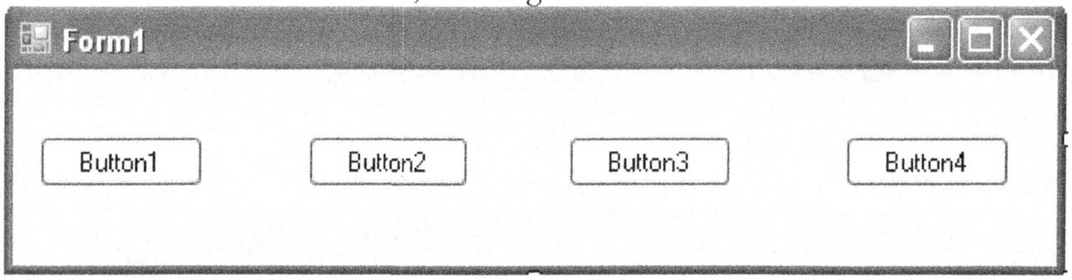

Form1   _ □ X

Button1   Button2   Button3   Button4

Figure 9-4 | Add Four Buttons

Update the form title to Start Remote Applications Bot by clicking on the *form* any place there is no button. Select the *Properties* tab and update the Text property to **Start Remote Applications Bot**, as in Figure 9-5.

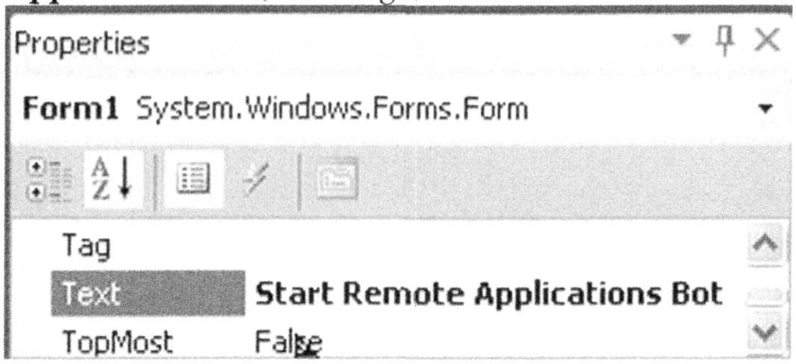

Properties   ▼ ⚲ ×

Form1 System.Windows.Forms.Form   ▼

Tag	
Text	**Start Remote Applications Bot**
TopMost	False

Figure 9-5 | Update Form Text Title To Start Remote Applications Bot

Update the Text property to **Calculator,** and the (Name) property to **calculator** for Button 1. Update the Text property to **WMP,** and the (Name) property to **wmp** for Button 2. Update the Text property to **Explorer,** and the (Name) property to **explorer** for Button 3. Update the Text property to **Explorer Site,** and the (Name) property to **explorerSite** for Button 4. The final result should look like Figure 9-6.

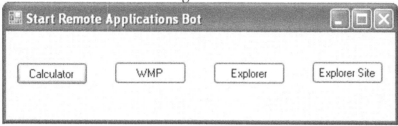

Figure 9-6 | Update Form Buttons

Coding The Project

You will be using both SendKeys and keybd_event to send keystrokes. You will need to include the libraries keybd_event and MapVirtualKey. Select the *Solution Explorer*, and then click on *View Code* to enter code, as shown in Figure 9-7.

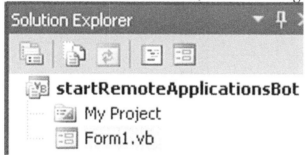

Figure 9-7 | Edit Code

Now add keybd_event and MapVirtualKey libraries, as in Figure 9-8.

```
Public Class Form1

    Private Declare Sub keybd_event Lib "user32.dll" (ByVal bVk As Byte, _
        ByVal bScan As Byte, ByVal dwFlags As Integer, _
        ByVal dwExtraInfo As Integer)

    Private Declare Function MapVirtualKey Lib "user32" Alias "MapVirtualKeyA" _
        (ByVal wCode As Integer, ByVal wMapType As Integer) As Integer

End Class
```

Figure 9-8| Include keybd_event and MapVirtualKey Libraries

160

The next step is to get the absolute path for Windows Calculator. Click on *Start -> All Programs -> Accessories ->* then right click on *Calculator* and select *Properties*, as shown below in Figure 9-9 and Figure 9-10.

Figure 9-9 | Right Mouse Click   Figure 9-10 | Select Properties

This will show the Calculator Properties, as in Figure 9-11.

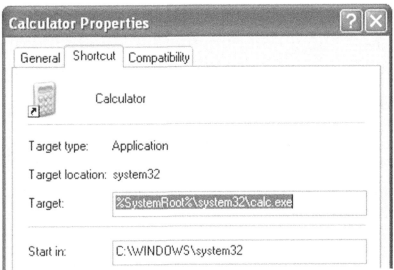

Figure 9-11 | Calculator Properties

"Start in:" shows the location C:\Windows\system32 ; and "Target:" shows the name calc.exe. The complete path is then C:\Windows\system32\calc.exe. Double-check your system to make sure it is the same. You can also perform a search to find locations of files.

Double click on *Calculator* button to edit the code, as in Figure 9-12.

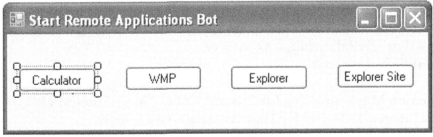

Figure 9-12 | Edit Calculator Button Code

This will create the calculator_Click subroutine, as shown below in Figure 9-13.

```
Public Class Form1

   Private Declare Sub keybd_event Lib "user32.dll" (ByVal bVk As Byte, _
       ByVal bScan As Byte, ByVal dwFlags As Integer, _
       ByVal dwExtraInfo As Integer)

   Private Declare Function MapVirtualKey Lib "user32" Alias "MapVirtualKeyA" _
      (ByVal wCode As Integer, ByVal wMapType As Integer) As Integer

   Private Sub calculator_Click(ByVal sender As System.Object, _
     ByVal e As System.EventArgs) Handles calculator.Click

   End Sub
End Class
```
Figure 9-13 | calculator_Click Subroutine Created.

The next step is to add the code to calculator_Click subroutine that will start the remote application Windows Calculator, as in Figure 9-14.

```
Private Sub calculator_Click(ByVal sender As System.Object, _
    ByVal e As System.EventArgs) Handles calculator.Click

    Dim p As Process
    p = Process.Start("C:\Windows\system32\calc.exe")
    p.WaitForInputIdle()

End Sub
```
Figure 9-14 | Start Windows Calculator

The code is broken down here line by line:
C: Dim p As Process
D: Create a variable named p of type Process to hold the Calculator process

C: p = Process.Start("C:\Windows\system32\calc.exe")
D: Start up Windows Calculator

C: p.WaitForInputIdle()
D: Allow time for the application to open up before processing anymore lines of code.

162

Now test what you have. Click the *Save All* button. Click either *Start Debugging*, or (*F5*). To make it a clean test shut down any Windows Calculators. Click on the Calculator button on the startRemoteApplicationsBot, as in Figure 9-15. Note that each time you click on the Calculator button, another Windows Calculator appears.

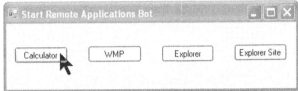

Figure 9-15 | Remote Start Windows Calculator

Your result should look like Figure 9-16.

Calculator

Edit   View   Help

Now Has Focus   0.

	Backspace	CE	C
MC	7	8	9	/	sqrt
MR	4	5	6	*	%
MS	1	2	3	.	1/x
M+	0	+/-	.	+	=

Figure 9-16| Windows Calculator Started

It is very important to notice that when you start an application remotely, as in Figure 9-16, it becomes the Windows application in focus. If you are Botting only one application at a time, the focus will automatically be set on the newly started Windows Calculator. Keystrokes can be sent to it without having to set the focus on it first. If you Bot more than one application concurrently, you will have to set focus on each application before sending keystrokes. Now send keystrokes to the Windows Calculator using the code provided, in Figure 9-17.

```
Private Sub calculator_Click(ByVal sender As System.Object, _
    ByVal e As System.EventArgs) Handles calculator.Click
    Dim p As Process
    p = Process.Start("C:\Windows\system32\calc.exe")
    p.WaitForInputIdle()

    System.Windows.Forms.SendKeys.SendWait("7")
    System.Windows.Forms.SendKeys.SendWait("{ADD}")
    System.Windows.Forms.SendKeys.SendWait("3")
    System.Windows.Forms.SendKeys.SendWait("{Enter}")
End Sub
```

Figure 9-17| Add 7 + 3 = With Windows Calculator

Now test what you have. Click the *Save All* button. Click either *Start Debugging*, or (*F5*). To make it a clean test shut down any Windows Calculators. Click on the *Calculator* button on the startRemoteApplicationsBot. The result will be 7 + 3 = 10, as shown in Figure 9-18.

Figure 9-18 | Remote Start With Keystrokes Test

There are times when you want your Bot to start the application, and then process the automation, and then shut down the application when complete. To do that you will use a Process method called closeMainWindow. Add the below line to close the Windows Calculator after being automated to add 7 + 3 =, as in Figure 9-19, below.

```
Private Sub calculator_Click(ByVal sender As System.Object, _
  ByVal e As System.EventArgs) Handles calculator.Click

  Dim p As Process
  p = Process.Start("C:\Windows\system32\calc.exe")
  p.WaitForInputIdle()

  System.Windows.Forms.SendKeys.SendWait("7")
  System.Windows.Forms.SendKeys.SendWait("{ADD}")
  System.Windows.Forms.SendKeys.SendWait("3")
  System.Windows.Forms.SendKeys.SendWait("{Enter}")
  p.CloseMainWindow()
End Sub
```

Figure 9-19 | Close Windows Calculator

Now test what you have. Click the *Save All* button. Click either *Start Debugging*, or (*F5*). To make it a clean test shut down any Windows Calculators. Click on the *Calculator* button on the startRemoteApplicationsBot. The result will be 7 + 3 = 10 and then the Windows Calculator will be closed immediately after that.

The next application that you will be starting remotely is the Windows Media Player. The goal is to create a Bot that will start the Windows Media Player with specific items to display and play.

The first step is to find the location on the Windows Media Player. Click on the *Start Menu -> All Programs -> Window Media Player* then right mouse click and choose *Properties*, as in Figure 9-20.

Figure 9-20 | Window Media Player In Start Menu

This time the Target contains the full path to WMP, which on my machine is: C:\Program Files\Windows Media Player\wmplayer.exe. The Target is longer than the Target box so be sure to click and drag your mouse all the way from left to right to copy the complete target path, as in Figure 9-21. Double-check the path on your machine.

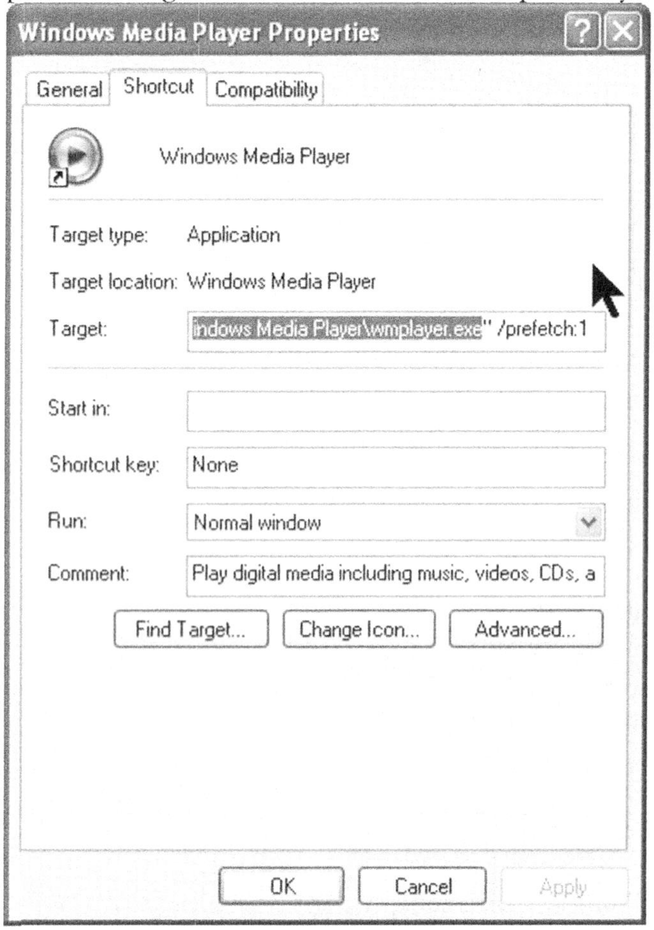

Figure 9-21 | Windows Media Player Properties.

Next, double click on *WMP* button, as in Figure 9-22, to create the wmp_Click subroutine, and also to edit the button's code, as shown in Figure 9-23.

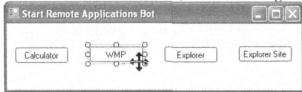

Figure 9-22 | Double Click To Edit WMP Button Subroutine

```
Private Sub wmp_Click(ByVal sender As System.Object, _
    ByVal e As System.EventArgs) Handles wmp.Click
End Sub
```

Figure 9-23 | wmp_Click Subroutine Created

Now add the code to start the Windows Media Player remotely, as in Figure 9-24. This is the simplest example you will use with the Windows Media Player.

```
Private Sub wmp_Click(ByVal sender As System.Object, _
    ByVal e As System.EventArgs) Handles wmp.Click

    Dim p As Process
    p = Process.Start("C:\Program Files\Windows Media Player\wmplayer.exe")
    p.WaitForInputIdle()

End Sub
```

Figure 9-24 | Remote Start Windows Media Player

Now test what you have. Click the *Save All* button. Click either *Start Debugging*, or (*F5*). To make it a clean test shut down any Windows Media Players. Click on the *WMP* button on the startRemoteApplicationsBot. Your result will look similar to Figure 9-25, based on Windows Media Player version and setup. Note: if you click the WMP button it does not spawn a second Windows Media Player like the Windows Calculator did.

Figure 9-25 | Windows Media Player Started

166

The Process Start method has a second optional argument, as shown in Figure 9-26. This allows you to include a starting string with your application.

```
Public Shared Function Start(fileName As String, arguments As String) As System.Diagnostics.Process
Starts a process resource by specifying the name of an application and a set of command-line arguments
```
Figure 9-26 | Process Start Structure

The Windows Media Player will display images, play songs and videos, and much more. To keep it simple you will start with displaying images. Typically, the default backgrounds are located in the Windows directory. I will start by having the Windows Media Player starting up and displaying the Greenstone.bmp image located in the C:\Windows directory. Do a search on your computer to find the image, or find the path and name of a favorite image of yours.

It is very important that you include the argument provided for Start to be wrapped in double quotes.

Below are two examples of how to include the double quotes, as in Figures 9-27 and 9-28. Once again, use the option you prefer. Chr(34) is the same as double quotes and can be used to visually clean up the code. Also, there is a short cut to calling wmplayer.exe. Since it is typically configure in a default path, you do not need to include the full path. Update the Process.Start to one of the examples, below.

```
Dim p As Process
p = Process.Start("wmplayer.exe", """C:\Windows\Greenstone.bmp""")
p.WaitForInputIdle()
```
Figure 9-27 | Using Quotes Wrapped With Double Quotes Or Triple Quotes

```
Dim p As Process
p = Process.Start("wmplayer.exe", _
    Chr(34) & "C:\Windows\Greenstone.bmp" & Chr(34))
p.WaitForInputIdle()
```
Figure 9-28 | Using Chr(34) For Double Quotes

Now test what you have. Click the *Save All* button. Click either *Start Debugging*, or (*F5*). To make it a clean test shut down any Windows Media Players. Click on the *WMP* button on the startRemoteApplicationsBot.

Your result will look similar to Figure 9-29; results will vary based on your Windows Media Player version and setup.

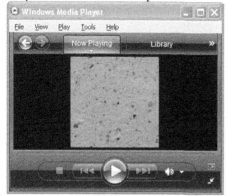

Figure 9-29 | Windows Media Player Displaying Greenstone.bmp

The Windows Media Player also accepts additional command line arguments when starting up. One such useful command line argument is /fullscreen which will display or play in full-screen mode.

Now apply that when you open up the Greenstone.bmp, as in Figure 9-30, below.

```
Dim p As Process
p = Process.Start("wmplayer.exe", _
        Chr(34) & "C:\Windows\Greenstone.bmp" & Chr(34) & " /fullscreen")
p.WaitForInputIdle()
```
Figure 9-30| Opening In Full Screen Mode

Now test what you have. Click the *Save All* button. Click either *Start Debugging*, or (F5). To make it a clean test shut down any Windows Media Players. Click on the *WMP* button on the startRemoteApplicationsBot. Your result should be the Greenstone.bmp taking up the whole screen.

You can create a virtual slide show when starting up the Windows Media Player by sending it a list of items to open. Create the list to include two pictures and one video. Start with the Greenstone.bmp, then Zapotec.bmp, and finally clock.avi . All are located in the Windows directory.

To do this without making a big mess, you will create a String called playlist by concatenating the lines together, as in Figure 9-31.

```
Dim playlist As String
playlist = Chr(34) & "C:\Windows\Greenstone.bmp" & Chr(34)
playlist &= " " & Chr(34) & "C:\Windows\Zapotec.bmp" & Chr(34)
playlist &= " " & Chr(34) & "C:\Windows\clock.avi" & Chr(34)
```
Figure 9-31| Create playList

Now, pull it all together. Start Windows Media Player, display Greenstone.bmp, then Zapotec.bmp, and finally clock.avi, in order and in full-screen mode, as in Figure 9-32.

```
Private Sub wmp_Click(ByVal sender As System.Object, _
    ByVal e As System.EventArgs) Handles wmp.Click

    Dim playlist As String
    playlist = Chr(34) & "C:\Windows\Greenstone.bmp" & Chr(34)
    playlist &= " " & Chr(34) & "C:\Windows\Zapotec.bmp" & Chr(34)
    playlist &= " " & Chr(34) & "C:\Windows\clock.avi" & Chr(34)

    Dim p As Process
    p = Process.Start("wmplayer.exe", playlist & " /fullscreen")
    p.WaitForInputIdle()

End Sub
```

Figure 9-32 | Create playList

Now test what you have. Click the *Save All* button. Click either *Start Debugging*, or (*F5*). To make it a clean test shut down any Windows Media Players. Click on the *WMP* button on the startRemoteApplicationsBot.

Your result should have the Windows Media Player in full screen mode, and then the Greenstone.bmp should appear, followed by Zapotec.bmp, and finally clock.avi. Next, double-click on *Explorer* button, as in Figure 9-33, to create the explorer_Click subroutine, and also to edit the button's code, as shown in Figure 9-34.

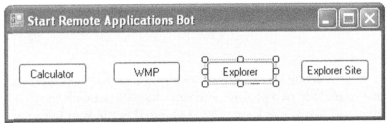

Figure 9-33 | Double Click To Edit Explorer Button Subroutine

```
Private Sub explorer_Click(ByVal sender As System.Object, _
    ByVal e As System.EventArgs) Handles explorer.Click

End Sub
```

Figure 9-34 | explorer_Click Subroutine Created

The first step again is to find the location of Internet Explorer. Click on the *Start Menu -> All Programs -> Internet Explorer* then right mouse click to choose *Properties*, as in Figure 9-35.

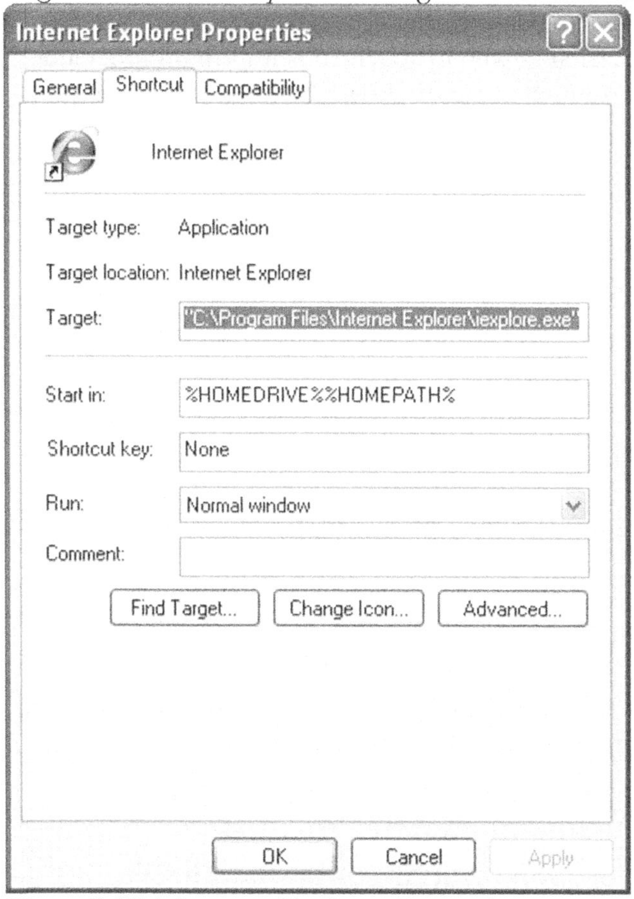

Figure 9-35 | Internet Explorer Properties

The application name is iexplore.exe and the path is C:\Program Files\Internet Explorer\iexplore.exe. Find the name and path on your machine.

Again, with iexplore.exe being set in the default Windows path, you may simply use the name iexplore.exe. Or, you may include the full path if you want.

Now add the code, as the example in Figure 9-36 shows, to start Internet Explorer.

```
Private Sub explorer_Click(ByVal sender As System.Object, _
    ByVal e As System.EventArgs) Handles explorer.Click
    Dim p As Process
    p = Process.Start("iexplore.exe")
    p.WaitForInputIdle()
End Sub
```

Figure 9-36| Remote Start Internet Explorer

Next, you will open up the web site http://www.google.com. Send an **Alt+F** for the File menu, then the letter 'o', to be able to enter a web address using keybd_event. Then send the website address **http://www.google.com** , followed by an **Enter** key using Sendkeys, as in Figure 9-37. When working with applications such as web browsers, it is important to include time delays between keystrokes. I had issues running the code shown below without time delays.

```
Private Sub explorer_Click(ByVal sender As System.Object, _
    ByVal e As System.EventArgs) Handles explorer.Click

    Dim p As Process
    p = Process.Start("iexplore.exe")
    p.WaitForInputIdle()

    System.Threading.Thread.Sleep(1000)

    keybd_event(Keys.LMenu, MapVirtualKey(Keys.LMenu, 0), 0, 0)
    keybd_event(Keys.F, MapVirtualKey(Keys.F, 0), 0, 0)

    System.Threading.Thread.Sleep(1000)

    keybd_event(Keys.F, MapVirtualKey(Keys.F, 0), 2, 0)
    keybd_event(Keys.LMenu, MapVirtualKey(Keys.LMenu, 0), 2, 0)

    System.Threading.Thread.Sleep(1000)

    keybd_event(Keys.O, MapVirtualKey(Keys.O, 0), 0, 0)
    keybd_event(Keys.O, MapVirtualKey(Keys.O, 0), 2, 0)

    System.Threading.Thread.Sleep(1000)

    System.Windows.Forms.SendKeys.SendWait("http://www.google.com")
    System.Windows.Forms.SendKeys.SendWait("{Enter}")

End Sub
```

Figure 9-37 | Remote Start Internet Explorer

When automating web surfing, it is extremely important to consider download times and insert timed delays where appropriate.

Now test what you have. Click the *Save All* button. Click either *Start Debugging*, or (*F5*). To make it a clean test shut down any Internet Explorer. Click on the *Explorer* button on start Internet Explorer with the http://www.google.com website, as Figure 9-38. Notice: if you press the button more than once it spawns multiple Internet Explorers.

Figure 9-38 | Internet Explorer Started With Website Address Typed In

Next, double-click on *Explorer Site* button, as in Figure 9-39, to create the explorerSite_Click subroutine, and also to edit the button's code, as in Figure 9-40.

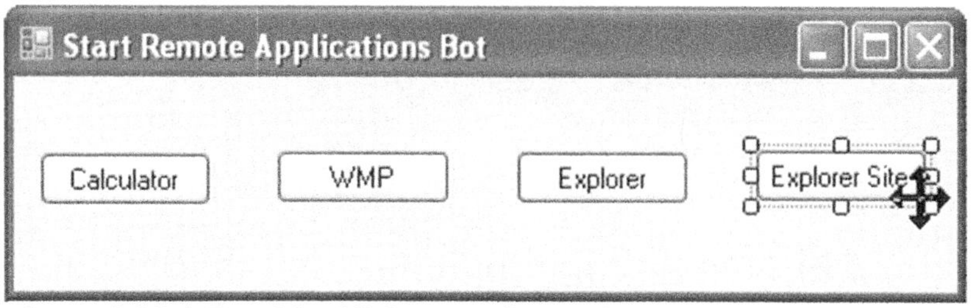

Figure 9-39 | Double Click To Edit Explorer Site Button Subroutine

```
Private Sub explorerSite_Click(ByVal sender As System.Object, _
    ByVal e As System.EventArgs) Handles explorerSite.Click

End Sub
```

Figure 9-40| explorerSite_Click Subroutine Created

This time you will use a second argument from the Start Process to open up the website http://www.google.com, as shown in the code below, in Figure 9-41.

```
Private Sub explorerSite_Click(ByVal sender As System.Object, _
    ByVal e As System.EventArgs) Handles explorerSite.Click

    Dim p As Process
    p = Process.Start("iexplore.exe", """http://www.google.com""")
    p.WaitForInputIdle()
    End Sub

End Sub
```

Figure 9-41 | explorerSite_Click Subroutine Created

Now test what you have. Click the *Save All* button. Click either *Start Debugging*, or (*F5*). To make it a clean test shut down any Internet Explorer. Click on the *Explorer Site* button on the startRemoteApplicationsBot which gives you the results seen below, in Figure 9-42.

Figure 9-42 | Internet Explorer Started With Specific Website

Now open up a new tab after the website has loaded. Again, you need to provide enough time delays for the automation to work properly. To open up a tab you issue an **ALT+F**, followed by the letter 't'. I have include a four second delay after the website has loaded, then one second delays between keystrokes, as shown in Figure 9-43, below.

```
Private Sub explorerSite_Click(ByVal sender As System.Object, _
    ByVal e As System.EventArgs) Handles explorerSite.Click
    Dim p As Process
    p = Process.Start("iexplore.exe", """http://www.google.com""")
    p.WaitForInputIdle()
    System.Threading.Thread.Sleep(4000)
    keybd_event(Keys.LMenu, MapVirtualKey(Keys.LMenu, 0), 0, 0)
    keybd_event(Keys.F, MapVirtualKey(Keys.F, 0), 0, 0)

    System.Threading.Thread.Sleep(1000)
    keybd_event(Keys.F, MapVirtualKey(Keys.F, 0), 2, 0)
    keybd_event(Keys.LMenu, MapVirtualKey(Keys.LMenu, 0), 2, 0)

    System.Threading.Thread.Sleep(1000)
    keybd_event(Keys.T, MapVirtualKey(Keys.T, 0), 0, 0)
    System.Threading.Thread.Sleep(1000)
    keybd_event(Keys.T, MapVirtualKey(Keys.T, 0), 2, 0)
End Sub
```

Figure 9-43 | Open Tab After Website Loads

Now test what you have. Click the *Save All* button. Click either *Start Debugging*, or (*F5*). To make it a clean test shut down any Internet Explorer. Click on the *Explorer Site* button on the startRemoteApplicationsBot. You should see Internet Explorer started up followed by a pause, then ALT+F and the Letter 't' then the new tab will appear, as in Figure 9-44.

Figure 9-44 | Internet Explorer With Second Tab

Summary

The ability to start a remote application ensures an application will be open when testing begins, and allows you to control the order and timing involved in starting up an application.

It is crucial to pay attention to the time it takes an application to settle down before it can properly accept keystrokes and mouse clicks. This makes it doubly important to test your automated Bot and to make time adjustments as needed.

The examples in this chapter were the starting of a single application, then sending keystrokes. If your automation includes more than one application, you will need to set focus when switching back and forth between applications.

Chapter 10:
Resize Remote Applications

The size of any application can determine the position and visibility of buttons and text within an application. The ability to resize a specific application can ensure that your Bot works consistently each time. Just resize a web browser on any of your favorite websites and watch areas be resized or disappear completely out of view. Resize applications does not work on all applications, but works best when the application can be resized by clicking and dragging the lower right hand corner of the application, as in Figure 10-1.

Figure 10-1 | Resizing Application

Creating Resize Remote Application

The resize automation Bot will have two buttons.

- Internet Explorer– 600 pixels wide by 800 pixels high
- Internet Explorer – Dynamic pixels wide by dynamic pixels high

Setting Up The Project

Start a new project and choose *Windows Form Application* and name it: **resizeRemoteApplicationsBot**, as in Figure 10-2.

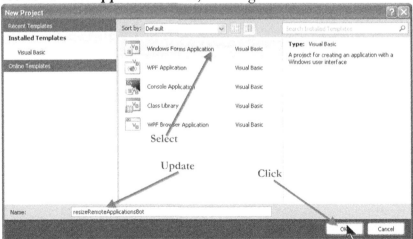

Figure 10-2 | Creating New resizeRemoteApplicationsBot

Now click the *Save All* button, as in the below Figure 10-3.

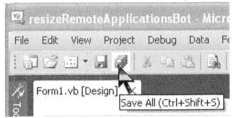

Figure 10-3 | Save All

Click *Save* to create directory structure for the project, as in Figure 10-4.

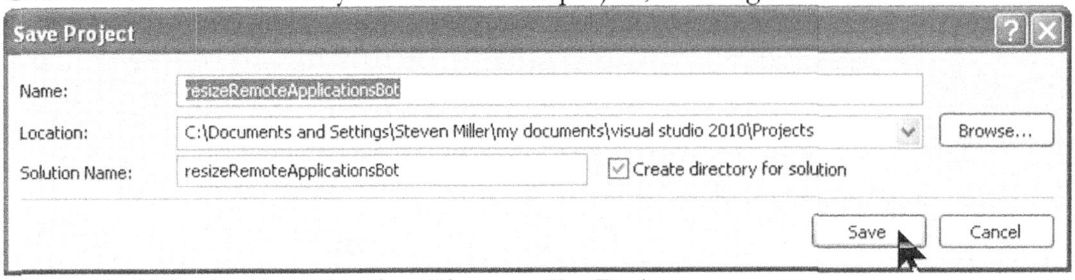

Figure 10-4| Saving And Creating Directory For Project

Laying Out The Form

Add two buttons to the form by clicking on the *Toolbox* and dragging the *Button* onto the form, as in Figure 10-5.

Figure 10-5 | Add Two Buttons

Click on *Toolbox*. Select *TextBox* and drag two of them onto the form, as shown in Figure 10-6.

Figure 10-6 | Add Two TextBoxes

Click on *ToolBox*. Select *Label* and drag two of them onto the form, as in Figure 10-7 below.

Figure 10-7 | Add Two Labels

Select *Button1*, as in Figure 10-8, and update the Text property to equal **800 X 600** and the (Name) property to equal **width800Height600**, as in Figures 10-9 and 10-10, below.

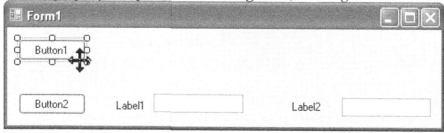
Figure 10-8 | Select Button1

Figure 10-9 | Button1 Text Property   Figure 10-10 | Button1 (Name) Property

Select *Button2*, as in Figure 10-11, and update the Text property to equal **Resize** and the (Name) property to equal **resize**, as in Figure 10-12 and Figure 10-13.

Figure 10-11 | Select Button2

Figure 10-12 | Button2 Text Property   Figure 10-13 | Button2 (Name) Property

Select *Label1*, as in Figure 10-14, and update the Text property to **Width**, as in Figure 10-15. Since you are not updating the label you can just leave the (Name) property as is.

Figure 10-14 | Select Label1   Figure 10-15 | Label1 Text Property

178

Select *Label2*, as in Figure 10-16, and update the Text property to **Height**, as in Figure 10-17.

Figure 10-16 | Select Label 2   Figure 10-17 | Label2 Text Property

Now select *TextBox1*, as in Figure 10-18, and update the Text property to a default value of **800** and the (Name) property to **widthValue**, as in Figures 10-19 and 10-20.

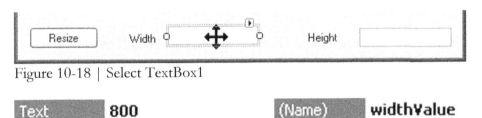

Figure 10-18 | Select TextBox1

Figure 10-19 | TextBox1Text Property   Figure 10-20 | TextBox1 (Name) Property

Now select *TextBox2*, as in Figure 10-21, and update the Text property to a default value of **600** and the (Name) property to **heightValue**, as in Figures 10-22 and 10-23.

Figure 10-21 | Select TextBox2

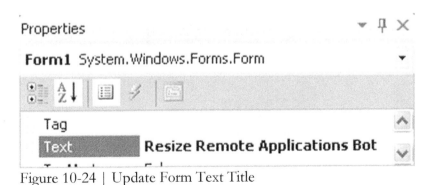

Figure 10-22 | TextBox2 Text Property   Figure 10-23 | TextBox2 (Name) Property

Update the form title to Resize Remote Applications Bot by clicking on the *form* any place there is no button. Select the *Properties* tab, as in Figure 10-24, and update the Text property to **Resize Remote Applications Bot**.

Figure 10-24 | Update Form Text Title

Coding The Project

You will be using two libraries; SetForegroundWindow and SetWindowPos. To add the libraries, click on the *Solution Explorer*, then *Form1.vb*, and finally *View Code*, as in then example shown below in Figure 10-25.

Figure 10-25 | Select View Code In Solution Explorer

First, add the SetForegoundWindow library code, as in Figure 10-26 below.

```
Public Class Form1
    Private Declare Function SetForegroundWindow Lib "user32" _
        (ByVal handle As IntPtr) As Integer
End Class
```

Figure 10-26| Add SetForegroundWindow Library

Next, add the SetWindowPos library code, as in Figure 10-27.

```
Public Class Form1
    Private Declare Function SetForegroundWindow Lib "user32" _
        (ByVal handle As IntPtr) As Integer
    Public Declare Function SetWindowPos Lib "user32" Alias _
        "SetWindowPos" (ByVal hwnd As IntPtr, _
        ByVal hWndInsertAfter As IntPtr, ByVal x As Integer, _
        ByVal y As Integer, ByVal cx As Integer, _
        ByVal cy As Integer, ByVal wFlags As Integer) As Integer
End Class
```

Figure 10-27| Add SetWindowPos Library

You will also need to add a constant to set the value of wFlags in SetWindowPos, as in Figure 10-28. SWP_NOMOVE will force the application to remain in the same location in reference to the upper left hand corner after you resize it. If you do not do this, the application is typically moved to the position 0x, 0y when you resize it.

```
Public Declare Function SetWindowPos Lib "user32" Alias _
    "SetWindowPos" (ByVal hwnd As IntPtr, _
    ByVal hWndInsertAfter As IntPtr, ByVal x As Integer, _
    ByVal y As Integer, ByVal cx As Integer, _
    ByVal cy As Integer, ByVal wFlags As Integer) As Integer
Public Const SWP_NOMOVE = &H2
```

Figure 10-28| Add SWP_NOMOVE Constant

180

Return to the View Designer by clicking on the *Form1.vb[Design]* tab, as in Figure 10-29.

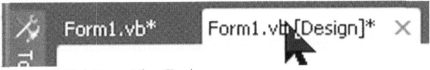

Figure 10-29 | Enter View Designer

Double-click on the *800X600* button, as in Figure 10-30, to create the width800Height600_Click subroutine, and also to edit the botton's code, as in Figure 10-31.

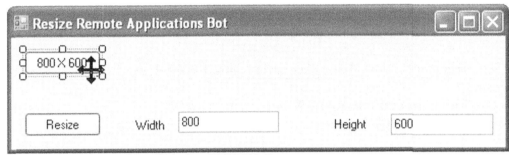

Figure 10-30 | Double Click On 800X600 Button

```
Private Sub width800Height600_Click(ByVal sender As System.Object, _
    ByVal e As System.EventArgs) Handles width800Height600.Click

    End Sub
```

Figure 10-31 | width800Height600 Subroutine Created

In this example you will remotely start Internet Explorer, wait four seconds, and then resize it to 800 pixels wide X 600 pixels high by adding the code included in Figure 10-32.

```
Private Sub width800Height600_Click(ByVal sender As System.Object, _
    ByVal e As System.EventArgs) Handles width800Height600.Click

    Dim p As Process
    p = Process.Start("iexplore.exe")
    p.WaitForInputIdle()

    System.Threading.Thread.Sleep(4000)

    SetWindowPos(p.MainWindowHandle, IntPtr.Zero, 0, 0, 800, 600, SWP_NOMOVE)

End Sub
```

Figure 10-32 | Open Internet Explorer And Resize It

The code is broken down here line by line:

C: Dim p As Process
    p = Process.Start("iexplore.exe")
    p.WaitForInputIdle()
D: Remotely Start Internet Explorer

C: System.Threading.Thread.Sleep(4000)
D: Wait for four seconds before proceeding

C: SetWindowPos(p.MainWindowHandle, IntPtr.Zero, 0, 0, 800, 600, SWP_NOMOVE)
D: Resize Internet Explorer to 800 X 600, the parameters you sent broken down in order
- p.MainWindowHandle – Application handle
- IntPtr.Zero, - Set value to zero
- 0 – X coordinate used in moving Application, SWP_NOMOVE overrides this
- 0 – y coordinate used in moving Application, SWP_NOMOVE overrides this
- 800 – Resize width of application in pixels
- 600 - Resize height of application in pixels
- SWP_NOMOVE – Inactivates the moving on the application.

Now test what you have. Click the *Save All* button. Click either *Start Debugging*, or (*F5*). To make it a clean test shut down any Internet Explorers. Click on the *800X600* button on the resizeRemoteApplicationsBot. A new Internet Explorer with be started, then pause of four seconds, and finally Internet Explorer will be resized to 800x600.

When capturing the applications handle after starting it and using p.MainWindowHandle you run into one issue, and that is: it crashes when you attempt to open a second application with one currently open.

Click on the *800X600* button again and you will get an error, as in Figure 10-33. This same error can occur if you have an existing version on Internet Explorer open.

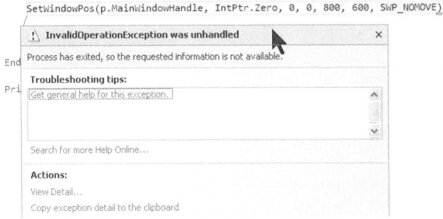

Figure 10-33 | SetWindowPos Error When Called Twice

182

Use SetForegroundWindow to capture the handle when you need start multiple versions of the same application when botting.   To do that you need to modify the width800Height600 subroutine, as in Figure 10-34.

```
Private Sub width800Height600_Click(ByVal sender As System.Object, _
    ByVal e As System.EventArgs) Handles width800Height600.Click

    Dim p As Process
    p = Process.Start("iexplore.exe")
    p.WaitForInputIdle()
    System.Threading.Thread.Sleep(4000)

    Dim IE() As Process
    Dim n As Integer
    IE = Process.GetProcessesByName("iexplore")
    If IE.Length > 0 Then
      For n = 0 To IE.Length - 1
        SetWindowPos(IE(n).MainWindowHandle, IntPtr.Zero, _
              0, 0, 800, 600, SWP_NOMOVE)
      Next
    End If

End Sub
```

Figure 10-34| Open Internet Explorer And Resize It

The new code broken down line by line:
C: Dim IE() As Process
D: Create a new variable called IE of type Process

C: Dim n As Integer
D: Create a new variable called n of type Integer

C: IE = Process.GetProcessesByName("iexplore")
D: Store the process of Internet Explorer into variable IE

C: If IE.Length > 0 Then
D: Check if the process exist

C: For n = 0 To IE.Length - 1
        SetWindowPos(IE(n).MainWindowHandle, IntPtr.Zero, _
              0, 0, 800, 600, SWP_NOMOVE)
    Next
D: Loop through process and resize the most recent application

Now test what you have. Click the *Save All* button. Click either *Start Debugging*, or (*F5*).   To make it a clean test shut down any Internet Explorers. Click on the *800X600* button on the resizeRemoteApplicationsBot.   Then updated code allows for multiple calls to the width800Height600_Click subroutine.

Now, double click on the Resize button, as shown below in Figure 10-35, to creae the resize_Click Subroutine, and also to edit the btton's code, as in Figure 10-36.

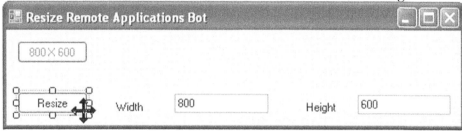

Figure 10-35 | Double Click On Resize Button

```
Private Sub resize_Click(ByVal sender As System.Object, _
    ByVal e As System.EventArgs) Handles resize.Click


End Sub
```

Figure 10-36| resize_Click Subroutine Created

You will resize an existing Internet Explorer when you click the *Resize* button. Each time you click Resize it will read the Width and Height textboxes value. Add the code to the resize_Click subroutine, as in Figure 10-37.

```
Private Sub resize_Click(ByVal sender As System.Object, _
    ByVal e As System.EventArgs) Handles resize.Click

    Dim ps() As Process = Process.GetProcessesByName("iexplore")

    If ps.Length > 0 Then
       Dim p As Process = ps(0)
       Dim hWnd As IntPtr = p.MainWindowHandle
       SetForegroundWindow(hWnd)
       Dim applicationWidth As Integer = Integer.Parse(widthValue.Text)
       Dim applicationHeight As Integer = Integer.Parse(heightValue.Text)

       SetWindowPos(hWnd, IntPtr.Zero, 0, 0, _
          applicationWidth, applicationHeight, SWP_NOMOVE)
    End If
End Sub
```

Figure 10-37| Resize Internet Explorer

184

Now test what you have. Click the *Save All* button. Click either *Start Debugging*, or (*F5*). Have at least one Internet Explorer open and click on the *Resize* button, as in Figure 10-38. You will see the results as shown in the example in Figure 10-39.

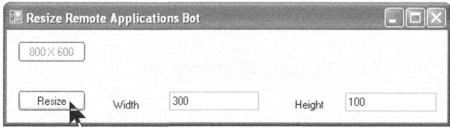

Figure 10-38 | Resize Internet Explorer To 300 By 100

Figure 10-39 | Resized IE 300 Wide By 100 High

Summary

Resizing is very important for botting applications that can be resized. Remember, when creating an automation that bots one open application simply call SetWindowPos directly. If you are working with multiple open versions of a specific application, make sure you approach it in the same manner as the code in Figure 10-34.

Chapter 11:
Move Remote Applications

The position of your application is important when sending mouse clicks. You want to ensure complete visibility of the application on the desktop that you are botting. It is also important when you are using multiple applications and you want ensure they do not overlap. Setting focus can overcome this issue of overlap. If you are watching your Bot during automation, it is very helpful not to allow the applications to visually overlap.

Creating Move Remote Application

The Move Remote Applications Bot will have three buttons
- Start new Internet Explorer and move it to zero x and zero y position on the screen
- Start new Internet Explorer and move it to zero x and zero y and start new Notepad and move it to 200x and 100y
- Start new Notepad resize it to 200 Wide by 300 High and move it to zero x and zero y

Setting Up The Project

Start a new project and choose *Windows Form Application* and name it: **moveRemoteApplicationsBot**, as in Figure 11-1.

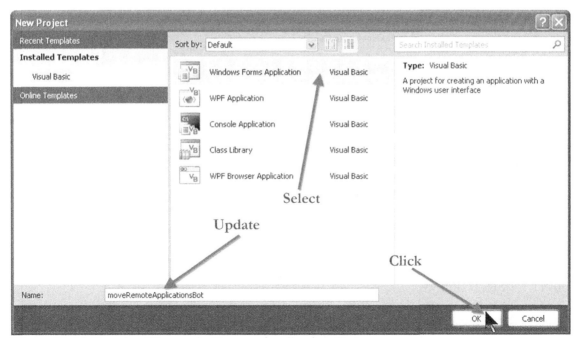

Figure 11-1 | Creating New resizeRemoteApplicationsBot

Now click the *Save All* button, as in the below Figure 11-2.

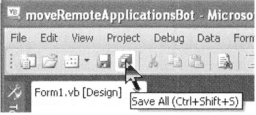

Figure 11-2 | Save All

Click *Save* to create directory structure for project, as in Figure 11-3.

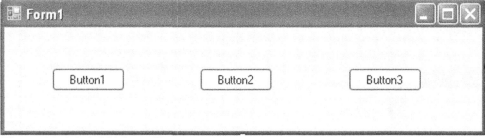

Figure 11-3 | Saving And Creating Directory For Project

Laying Out The Form

Add three buttons to the form by clicking on the *Toolbox* and dragging the *buttons* on the form, with the final result looking like Figure 11-4.

Figure 11-4 | Add Three Buttons To Form

Select *Button1*, as in Figure 11-5 below. Then update Button1 Text Properties to **Move** and the (Name) property to **move**, as in Figure 11-6 and Figure 11-7.

Figure 11-5 | Select Button1

Figure 11-6 | Text Property   Figure 11-7 | (Name) Property

Select *Button2*, as in Figure 11-8. Update Button2 Text Properties to **Move2** , and the (Name) property to **move2**, as in Figure 11-9 and Figure 11-10.

Figure 11-8 | Select Button 2

Figure 11-9 | Text Property   Figure 11-10 | (Name) Property

Select *Button3*, as in Figure 11-11. Update Button3 Text Properties to **Resize Move,** and the (Name) property to **resizeMove**, as in Figure 11-12 and Figure 11-13. Note: you may need to resize Button3 for the whole text Resize Move to appear.

Figure 11-11 | Select Button 3

Figure 11-12 | Text Property   Figure 11-13 | (Name) Property

Update the form title to Move Remote Applications Bot by clicking on the *form* any place there is no button. Select the *Properties* tab and update the Text property to **Move Remote Applications Bot**, as in Figure 11-14.

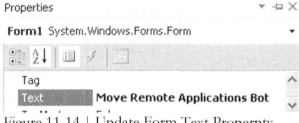

Figure 11-14 | Update Form Text Properpty

Coding The Project

You will be using the SetWindowPos library. To add the libraries click on the *Solution Explorer*, then *Form1.vb*, and finally *View Code*, as in Figure 11-15.

Figure 11-15 | Select View Code In Solution Explorer

Add the SetWindowPos library code, as in Figure 11-16.

```
Public Class Form1

    Public Declare Function SetWindowPos Lib "user32" Alias _
        "SetWindowPos" (ByVal hwnd As IntPtr, _
        ByVal hWndInsertAfter As IntPtr, ByVal x As Integer, _
        ByVal y As Integer, ByVal cx As Integer, _
        ByVal cy As Integer, ByVal wFlags As Integer) As Integer

End Class
```

Figure 11-16 | Add SetWindowPos Library

You also need to add two constants to set the value of wFlags in SetWindowPos, as in Figure 11-17. SWP_NOMOVE will force the application to remain in the same location in reference to the upper left hand corner after you resize it. SWP_NOSIZE will force the application to remain the same size.

```
Public Class Form1

    Public Declare Function SetWindowPos Lib "user32" Alias _
        "SetWindowPos" (ByVal hwnd As IntPtr, _
        ByVal hWndInsertAfter As IntPtr, ByVal x As Integer, _
        ByVal y As Integer, ByVal cx As Integer, _
        ByVal cy As Integer, ByVal wFlags As Integer) As Integer

    Public Const SWP_NOMOVE = &H2
    Public Const SWP_NOSIZE = &H1

End Class
```

Figure 11-17 | Add SWP_NOMOVE AND SWP_NOSIZE Constant

Double-click on the *Move* button, as shown below in Figure 11-18, to create the move_Click subroutine, and also to edit the button's code, as in Figure 11-19.

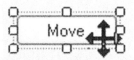

Figure 11-18 | Double Click Move Button

```
Private Sub move_Click(ByVal sender As System.Object, _
    ByVal e As System.EventArgs) Handles move.Click

End Sub
```

Figure 11-19 | move_Click Subroutine Created

Next you need to add the code to move_Click to start up Internet Explorer, as in Figure 11-20.

```
Private Sub move_Click(ByVal sender As System.Object, _
    ByVal e As System.EventArgs) Handles move.Click

    Dim p As Process
    p = Process.Start("iexplore.exe")
    p.WaitForInputIdle()
    System.Threading.Thread.Sleep(4000)

End Sub
```

Figure 11-20| Add Code To Start Internet Explorer

Add the code to move Internet Explorer so that its upper left hand corner is located at 0x, 0y on your desktop grid coordinates, as in Figure 11-21.

```
    System.Threading.Thread.Sleep(4000)

    SetWindowPos(p.MainWindowHandle, IntPtr.Zero, _
        0, 0, 0, 0, SWP_NOSIZE)
```

Figure 11-20| Add Code To Start Internet Explorer

The code is broken down here line by line:

C: Dim p As Process
    p = Process.Start("iexplore.exe")
    p.WaitForInputIdle()
D: Remotely Start Internet Explorer

C: System.Threading.Thread.Sleep(4000)
D: Wait for four seconds before proceeding

C: SetWindowPos(p.MainWindowHandle,IntPtr.Zero, 0, 0, 0, 0,SWP_NOSIZE)
D: Move Internet Explorer to 0x, 0y. The parameters you sent broken down in order
   - p.MainWindowHandle – Application handle
   - IntPtr.Zero, - Set value to zero
   - 0 – x coordinate used in moving Application
   - 0 – y coordinate used in moving Application
   - 0– Resize width of application in pixels, SWP_NOSIZE overrides this
   - 0 - Resize height of application in pixels, SWP_NOSIZE overrides this
   - SWP_NOSIZE– Inactivates the resizing of the application.

190

Now test what you have. Click the *Save All* button. Click either *Start Debugging*, or (*F5*). To make it a clean test shut down any Internet Explorer. Click on the *Move* button. The result will be Internet Explorer being opened, and then being moved to the desktop grid coordinated 0x, 0y, as in Figure 11-21 and 11-22.

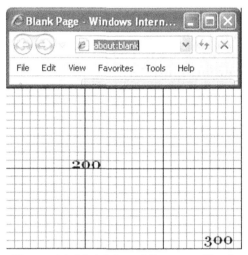

Figure 11-21 | Started Internet Explorer   Figure 11-22 | Moved Internet Explorer

Double-click on the *Move2* button, as shown below in Figure 11-23, to create the Move2_Click subroutine, and also edit the button's code, as in Figure 11-24.

Figure 11-23 | Double Click Move2 Button

```
Private Sub move2_Click(ByVal sender As System.Object, _
    ByVal e As System.EventArgs) Handles move2.Click
End Sub
```

Figure 11-24| move2_Click Subroutine Created

You have a combination of two steps for the Bot. The first step is to start and move Internet Explorer as in the previous example, which is shown in the code in Figure 11-25, below.

```
Private Sub move2_Click(ByVal sender As System.Object, _
    ByVal e As System.EventArgs) Handles move2.Click
    Dim p As Process
    p = Process.Start("iexplore.exe")
    p.WaitForInputIdle()
    System.Threading.Thread.Sleep(4000)
    SetWindowPos(p.MainWindowHandle, IntPtr.Zero, _
        0, 0, 0, 0, SWP_NOSIZE)
End Sub
```

Figure 11-25| move2_Click Subroutine Created

The second step is to start Windows Notepad and move it to 200x, 100y. Add the code for starting Notepad and moving it to grid coordinate 200x, 100y, as shown in Figure 11-26.

```
Private Sub move2_Click(ByVal sender As System.Object, _
    ByVal e As System.EventArgs) Handles move2.Click

    Dim p As Process
    p = Process.Start("iexplore.exe")
    p.WaitForInputIdle()
    System.Threading.Thread.Sleep(4000)
    SetWindowPos(p.MainWindowHandle, IntPtr.Zero, _
            0, 0, 0, 0, SWP_NOSIZE)
    p = Process.Start("notepad.exe")
    p.WaitForInputIdle()
    System.Threading.Thread.Sleep(4000)

    SetWindowPos(p.MainWindowHandle, IntPtr.Zero, _
            200, 100, 0, 0, SWP_NOSIZE)
End Sub
```

Figure 11-26 | move2_Click Subroutine Created

Now test what you have. Click the *Save All* button. Click either *Start Debugging*, or (*F5*). To make it a clean test shut down any Internet Explorer and Windows Notepad. Click on the *Move2* button on the moveRemoteApplicationsBot. The result will be Internet Explorer opening, then being moved to desktop grid coordinate 0x, 0y, and finally, Windows Notepad will be started and moved to grid coordinate 200x, 100y, as shown in Figure 11-27.

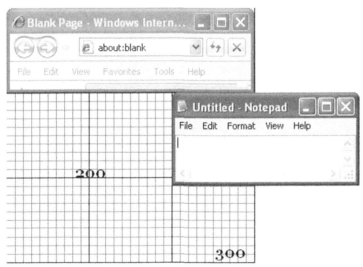

Figure 11-27 | Internet Explorer And Windows Notepad Started And Moved.

The Resize Move button will resize Windows Notepad to 200 Wide by 100 High and then move it to zero x and zero y on your desktop. Double-click on the *Resize Move* in the View Designer, as in Figure 11-28, to create resizeMove_Click subroutine, as in Figure 11-29.

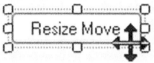

Figure 11-28 | Double Click Resize Move

```
Private Sub resizeMove_Click(ByVal sender As System.Object, _
      ByVal e As System.EventArgs) Handles resizeMove.Click

 End Sub
```

Figure 11-29| resizeMove_Click Subroutine Created

Now add the code to resize and move Windows Notepad, as in Figure 11-30.

```
Private Sub resizeMove_Click(ByVal sender As System.Object, _
      ByVal e As System.EventArgs) Handles resizeMove.Click

   Dim p As Process

   p = Process.Start("notepad.exe")

   p.WaitForInputIdle()

   System.Threading.Thread.Sleep(4000)

   SetWindowPos(p.MainWindowHandle, IntPtr.Zero, _
         0, 0, 200, 100, 0)
 End Sub
```

Figure 11-30| Resize And Move Windows Notepad Code

Notice: you do not use **SWP_NOSIZE** or **SWP_NOMOVE** in the last position. Simply send a zero, as in Figure 11-30, above.

Now test what you have. Click the *Save All* button. Click either *Start Debugging*, or (*F5*). To make it a clean test shut down any Windows Notepad. Click on the *Resize Move* button.

The result is that Windows Notepad is started and moved to grid coordinate 0x, 0y, then resized to 200 wide by 100 high, as in Figure 11-31.

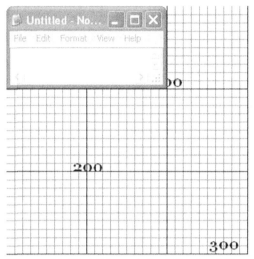

Figure 11-31 | Moved And Resized Results

Summary

It is very important to be able to move and resize an application to a specific location when the Bot testing is being visually inspected. You learned how to move one to many applications within a Bot. You also explored an example of how to combine both moving, and resizing, of an application.

Chapter 12:
Scheduled Tasks

It is extremely helpful to be able to create a Bot for which you don't have to present. You can click on a button to activate it. Visual Basic allows you to also create a Console Application to be used for creating a command-line application. Once you package the automation Bot into a Console Application, you can then use Windows Scheduled Task to run that application at either a specific time, or on a repetitive time schedule.

Creating Console Application

A Console Application is a program you simply run to start the automation, as compared to a Windows Forms Application where you have to click on a button to start the automation.

You will create two separate console applications:
- Start a new Notepad resize it to 200 Wide by 300 High and move it to 0x, 0y
- A Left Mouse click once a second until ALT Key is held down.

Setting Up The Project

Start a new project and choose **Console Application** and name it: **consoleNotepadBot** as in Figure 12-1. Make sure you select the *Console Application* template. This is different from what you have done in previous examples.

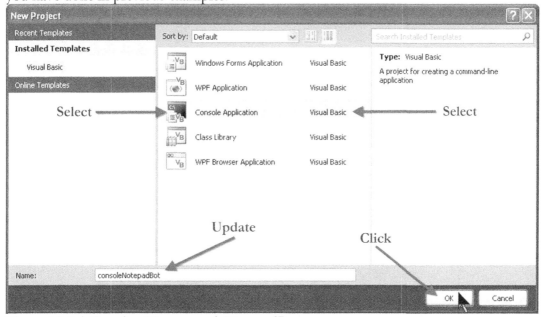

Figure 12-1 | Creating New consoleNotepadBot

Now click the *Save All* button, as in the below Figure 12-2.

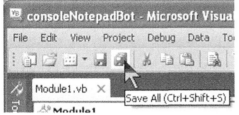

Figure 12-2 | Save All

Click *Save* to create directory structure for project, as in Figure 12-3.

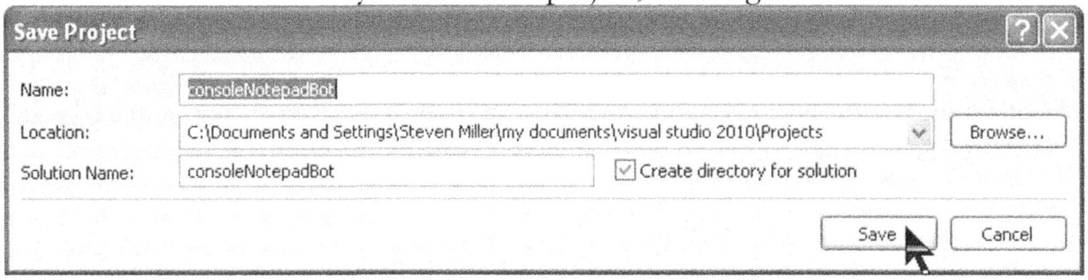

Figure 12-3| Saving And Creating Directory For Project

Laying Out The Form

There is no form when using a Console Application. You will produce an executable program that you will run from the command line.

Notice the Solution Explorer only has View Code and no Design View, as in Figure 12-4.

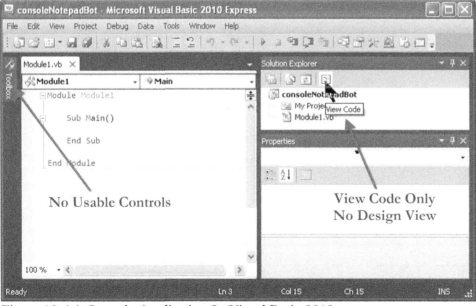

Figure 12-4 | Console Application In Visual Basic 2010

The Toolbox has no usable controls, so everything you create will have to be in the code, as shown in Figure 12-5.

Figure 12-5 | No Usable Controls In Toolbox Console Applications

Coding The Project

You can think of the Console Application as the same thing as having a one button Windows Forms Application, in which the button is automatically pressed when you run the application.

The default code you are given when you start a new Console Application is shown below in the example in Figure 12-5.

```
Module Module1
    Sub Main()
    End Sub
End Module
```

Figure 12-5 | Console Application Code

Sticking with the one button concept, the code between Sub Main() and End Sub is the location where you place the code for the automation. The space between Module Module1 and Sub Main() is where the libraries are located, as in Figure 12-6.

```
Module Module1
    ' Libraries Go Here
    Sub Main()
        ' Automation Code Goes Here
    End Sub
End Module
```

Figure 12-6 | Console Application Code

The first Console Application will start a new Windows Notepad, then resize it to 200 Wide by 300 High, and finally move it to 0x, 0y. This is the same code you used in the previous chapter and is the same as shown in Figure 11-30.

Using SetWindowPos requires you to include its library, which is shown in Figure 12-7.

```
Module Module1
  Public Declare Function SetWindowPos Lib "user32" Alias _
  "SetWindowPos" (ByVal hwnd As IntPtr, _
    ByVal hWndInsertAfter As IntPtr, ByVal x As Integer, _
    ByVal y As Integer, ByVal cx As Integer, _
    ByVal cy As Integer, ByVal wFlags As Integer) As Integer
  Sub Main()
    ' Automation Code Goes Here
  End Sub
End Module
```

Figure 12-7 | Console Application Library Code

Since you are using the exact same code from in the previous chapter, which is in Figure 11-30, simply copy and paste that code into Sub Main(), as in Figure 12-8.

```
Module Module1
  Public Declare Function SetWindowPos Lib "user32" Alias _
  "SetWindowPos" (ByVal hwnd As IntPtr, _
    ByVal hWndInsertAfter As IntPtr, ByVal x As Integer, _
    ByVal y As Integer, ByVal cx As Integer, _
    ByVal cy As Integer, ByVal wFlags As Integer) As Integer

  Sub Main()
    Dim p As Process
    p = Process.Start("notepad.exe")
    p.WaitForInputIdle()
    System.Threading.Thread.Sleep(4000)

    SetWindowPos(p.MainWindowHandle, IntPtr.Zero, _
        0, 0, 200, 100, 0)
  End Sub

End Module
```

Figure 12-8 | Windows Notepad Automation Bot Code

Now test what you have. Click the *Save All* button. Click either *Start Debugging*, or (*F5*). To make it a clean test shut down any Windows Notepad. Clicking Start Debugging, or (F5), will automatically run your Bot. A Command Prompt will open and run your command line application, as shown in Figure 12-9.

Figure 12-9 | Running Windows Notepad Console Application In Command Prompt.

The result is Windows Notepad being started, moved to grid coordinate 0x, 0y, and then resized to 200 wide by 100 high, as in Figure 12-10. Immediately after the Windows Notepad appears and has been moved and resized, the application will terminate and the Command Prompt will disappear.

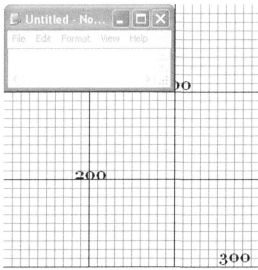

Figure 12-10 | Test Results Of Console Application Bot

You can also access your automation Bot directly by using the Command Prompt. Look back to Figure 12-3. You will see where your Console Application was created. If you do not remember where it was with your Console Application, you can click on *Tools -> Options*, as in Figure 12-11.

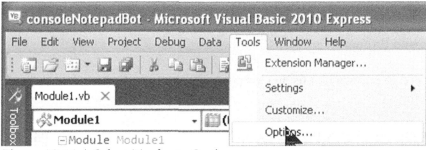

Figure 12-11 | Select Tools -> Options

This will open up the Options Menu. Click on *Project and Solutions*, and then the sub menu *General*. The Projects location will give you the path to the directory where your application's directory is saved.

Highlight the whole *Projects location.* Now right mouse click and *Copy*, as shown in the example below in Figure 12-12.

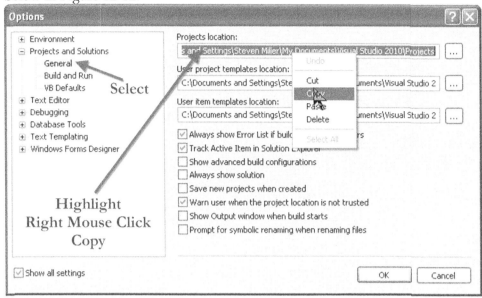

Figure 12-12 | Projects location For Your Console Application

My path is: C:\Documents and Settings\Steven Miller\My Documents\Visual Studio 2010\Projects. (Your path will be similar but not the same unless your user account is Steven Miller.)

Next, you need to start a Command Prompt. Click on *Start -> All Programs -> Accessories ->* and then *Command Prompt*, as in Figure 12-13.

Figure 12-13 | Start Command Prompt

The main command you need to know when using Command Prompt is **cd** which stands for change directory.

You need to change to the directory to the path in Projects location. The first step is to type **cd** in the command prompt, as in Figure 12-14.

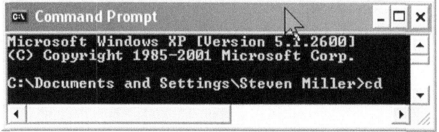

Figure 12-14 | Type cd (Change Directory) First In Command Prompt

Hit the spacebar to place a **space** after the cd command. Now take the whole Projects location path, as in Figure 12-12, and paste it, as in Figure 12-15. Make sure not to copy my Projects location path. You must use yours or it will not work.

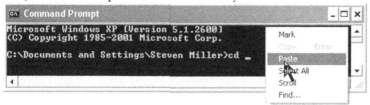

Figure 12-15 | Paste Projects Location Path After cd Command

Now press **Enter key** to change directories, as in Figure 12-16.

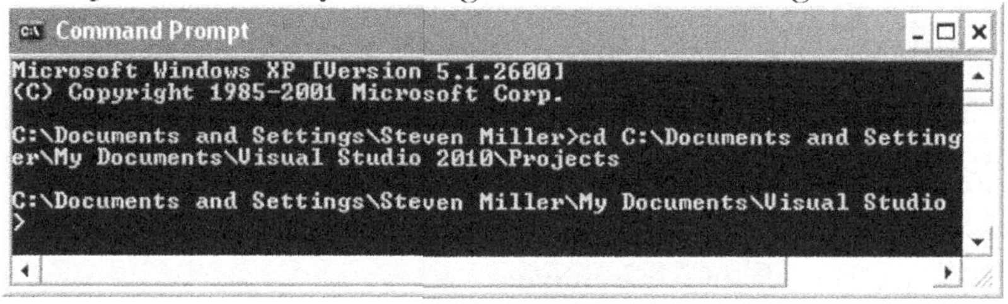

Figure 12-16 | Enter Key To Change Directories

The next command you need to know is **dir** which stands for directory and will show all the files and directories located there. Enter the **dir** command and press **Enter Key,** as shown below in the example in Figure 12-17.

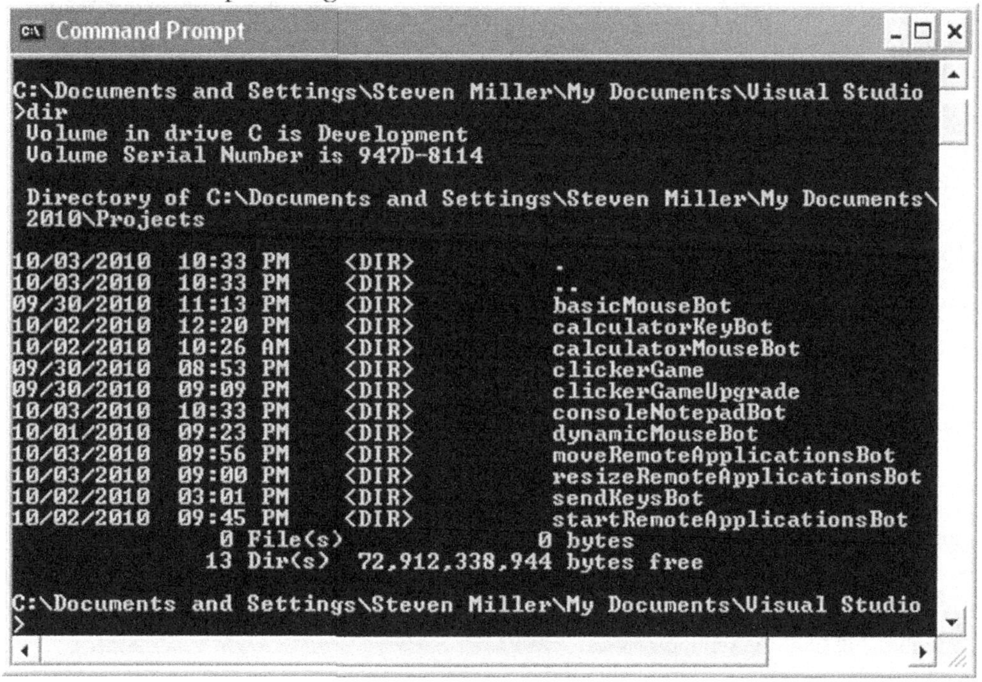

Figure 12-17 | dir Command List All Files And Directories Located In Current Directory

202

Figure 12-17 lists all of the projects, as well as any others, you have created. Now you need to enter the Application Console project. If you forgot the name, you can simply get it by looking at the title bar of the Microsoft Visual Basic 2010 Express where the name is consoleNotepadBot, as in Figure 12-18.

Figure 12-18 | Project Name consoleNotepadBot

Next, you need to enter the consoleNotepadBot directory by entering **cd consoleNotepadBot** and press the **Enter key**, as in Figure 12-19.

Figure 12-19 | Enter consoleNotepadBot Using cd Command

To see the contents of this directory type **dir** and **Enter key**, as in Figure 12-20.

Figure 12-20 | Show Directory Contents

Now enter consoleNotepadBot directory using **cd consoleNotepadBot** and **Enter Key,** as shown in Figure 12-21.

Figure 12-21 | Enter consoleNotepadBot Directory

To see the contents of this directory type **dir** and **Enter key**, as in Figure 12-22.

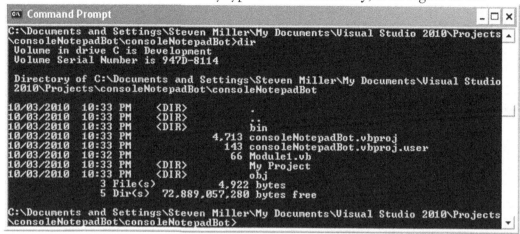

Figure 12-22 | Show Directory Contents

Enter the bin directory using **cd bin** and **Enter Key**, as in Figure 12-23.

Figure 12-23 | Enter bin Directory

To see the contents of this directory type **dir** and **Enter key**, as in Figure 12-24.

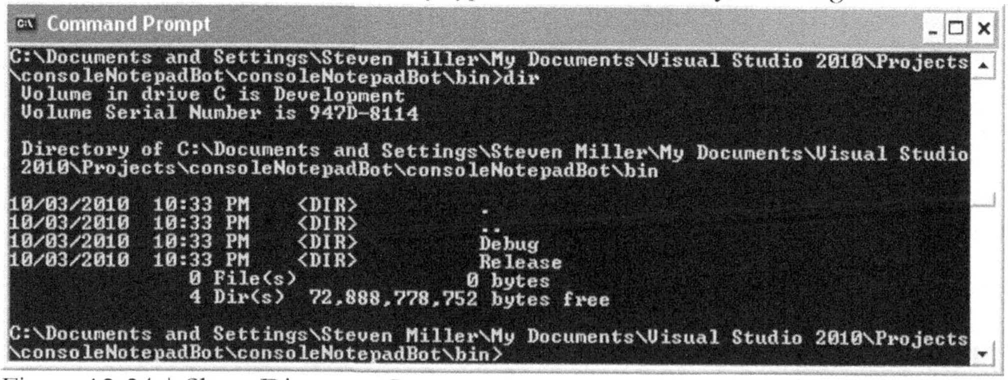

Figure 12-24 | Show Directory Contents

Next, enter Debug directory using **cd Debug** and **Enter key**, as in Figure 12-25.

Figure 12-25 | Enter Debug Directory

To see the contents of this directory type **dir** and **Enter key**, as in Figure 12-26.

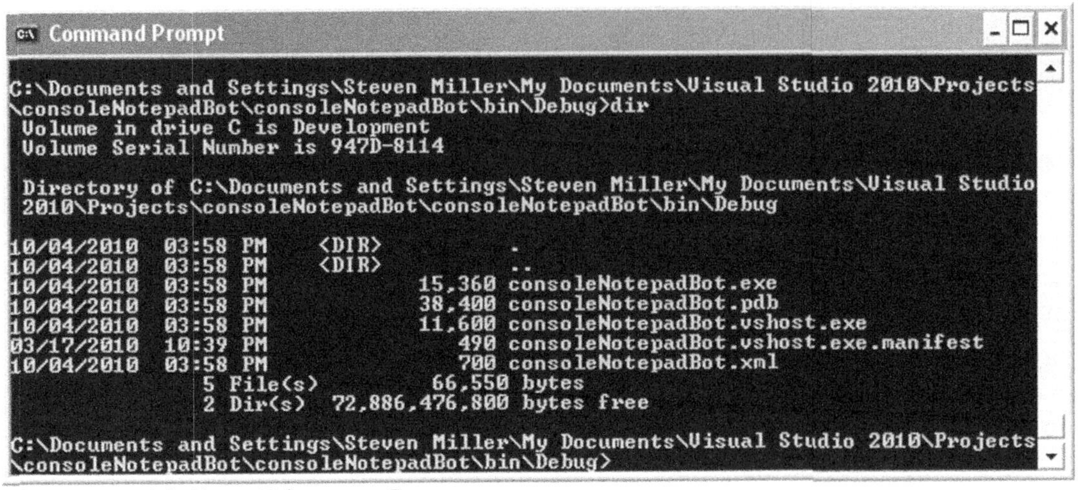

Figure 12-26 | Show Directory Contents

You are finally where you want to be. It is helpful to save this complete path for future reference.

Mine is: C:\Documents and Settings\Steven Miller\My Documents\Visual Studio 2010\Projects\consoleNotepadBot\consoleNotepadBot\bin\Debug.

Inside the Debug directory is the location of the executable file of the Console Application Bot.

Now test what you have by running the consoleNotepadBot.exe from the command line. To run the consoleNotepadBot application type in **consoleNotepadBot.exe** and **Enter key**, as in Figure 12-27. As the consoleNotepadbot application is running it will continue to show the command line of consoleNotepadbot.exe, as in Figure 12-27.

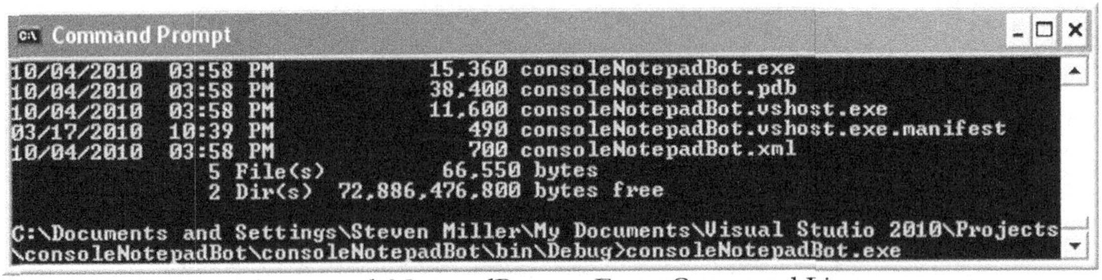

Figure 12-27 | Running consoleNotepadBot.exe From Command Line.

The Windows Notepad will start, be resized to 200 wide by 100 high, and then moved to grid coordinate 0x, 0y on the Windows desktop, as in Figure 12-28.

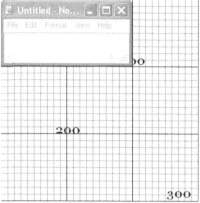

Figure 12-28 | Windows Notepad Started, Resized, and Moved Results

After the consoleNotepadbot.exe is done running it will drop out and place you at the next command prompt, as in Figure 12-29.

Figure 12-29 | Completed Run Of consoleNotepadBot.exe

Setting Up The Project

The next console Bot will show how to create a timer within the Console Application. Start a new project and choose *Console Application* and name it: **consoleMouseClickBot**, as in Figure 12-30.

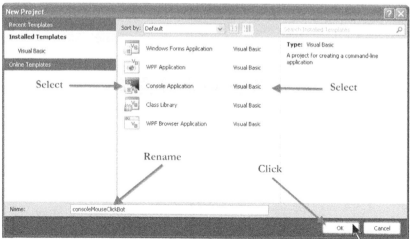

Figure 12-30 | Creating New consoleNotepadBot

Now click the *Save All* button, as in the below Figure 12-31.

Figure 12-31 | Save All

Click *Save* to create a directory structure for project, as in Figure 12-32.

Figure 12-32| Saving And Creating Directory For Project

Coding The Project

Again when you start a new Console Application you are given the default code, as shown below in Figure 12-33.

```
Module Module1
    Sub Main()
    End Sub
End Module
```

Figure 12-33| Console Application Code

This application will send left mouse clicks so you will need the mouse_event library and two constants, which are: MOUSEEVENTF_LEFTDOWN and MOUSEEVENTF_LEFTUP, as shown in Figure 12-34.

```
Module Module1

  Private Declare Sub mouse_event Lib "user32" (ByVal dwFlags As Integer, _
    ByVal dx As Integer, ByVal dy As Integer, ByVal cButtons As Integer, _
    ByVal dwExtraInfo As Integer)

  Private Const MOUSEEVENTF_LEFTDOWN = &H2
  Private Const MOUSEEVENTF_LEFTUP = &H4

  Sub Main()
  End Sub
End Module
```

Figure 12-34| mouse_event Library And Needed Constants

Now add the code for the main subroutine to send a mouse click once a second, as in Figure 12-35. To create a timer inside a Console Application use an endless loop with a means to terminate the loop.

```
Module Module1
    Private Declare Sub mouse_event Lib "user32" (ByVal dwFlags As Integer, _
        ByVal dx As Integer, ByVal dy As Integer, ByVal cButtons As Integer, _
        ByVal dwExtraInfo As Integer)

    Private Const MOUSEEVENTF_LEFTDOWN = &H2
    Private Const MOUSEEVENTF_LEFTUP = &H4

    Sub Main()
        Do While 1 > 0
            If (My.Computer.Keyboard.AltKeyDown) Then
                Exit Do
            End If
            mouse_event(MOUSEEVENTF_LEFTDOWN, 0, 0, 0, 0)
            System.Threading.Thread.Sleep(1000)
            mouse_event(MOUSEEVENTF_LEFTUP, 0, 0, 0, 0)
        Loop
    End Sub
End Module
```

Figure 12-35 | mouse_event Library And Needed Constants

Sub Main code broken down line by line:

C: Do While 1 > 0
D: Do loop that you purposely stick in an infinite loop. This means it will loop forever.

C: If (My.Computer.Keyboard.AltKeyDown) Then
        Exit Do
     End If
D: This is the only way you can stop the infinite loop. Each time you enter the loop it will look to see if the ALT key is pressed and if it is, it will exit you from the infinite loop.

C: mouse_event(MOUSEEVENTF_LEFTDOWN, 0, 0, 0, 0)
    System.Threading.Thread.Sleep(1000)
    mouse_event(MOUSEEVENTF_LEFTUP, 0, 0, 0, 0)
D: Perform a left mouse click with a one second delay

C: Loop
D: End of Do loop.

Now test what you have. First, start Windows Calculator up so you have something to click on in the test. Then Click the *Save All* button. Click either *Start Debugging*, or *(F5)*. Clicking Start Debugging or (F5) will automatic run your Bot like you would by running it as a command line application by starting a Command Prompt, as in Figure 12-36.

Figure 12-36 | Running consoleMouseClickBot In Command Prompt.

Move your mouse above any number on the Windows Calculator and allow it to run for a couple of seconds, as in Figure 12-37.

Figure 12-37 | consoleMouseClickBot Results

To terminate the left mouse clicks, hold down the **ALT key**. The consoleMouseClickBot will be closed and the Command Prompt window will be terminated.

Scheduled Tasks

The Microsoft Task Scheduler allows you to schedule your Console Application or system tools like the Windows Disk Defragmenter to run once, daily, weekly, monthly, or simply when you need them to. Windows Scheduled Tasks can be accessed using the following two methods. The first method is to open the Control Panel and locate the Scheduled Tasks, as shown in the example in Figure 12-38.

Figure 12-38 | Control Panel Then Double Click Scheduled Tasks

The second method is to click *Start -> All Programs -> Accessories -> System Tools ->* and then *Scheduled Tasks*, as in Figure 12-39.

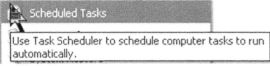

Figure 12-39 | System Tools -> Scheduled Tasks

Both methods will start the Scheduled Tasks, as in Figure 12-40.

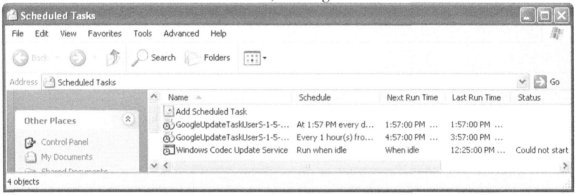

Figure 12-40 | Scheduled Tasks

You are going to schedule the consoleNotepadBot to running in a couple of minutes. Double click on *Add Scheduled Task*, as in Figure 12-41.

Figure 12-41 | Double Click Add Scheduled Task

This will then launch the Scheduled Task Wizard which allows you to schedule a task for Windows to perform, and then click *Next* as in Figure 12-42. The Wizard will ask you which program you want to run and then the time or time periods in which to run it.

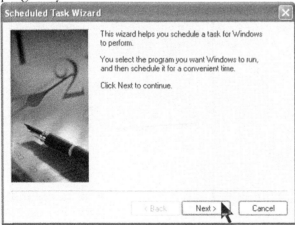

Figure 12-42 | Scheduled Task Wizard

210

The next step is to select the Application you wish to run. By default, a list of Applications can be chosen from the menu. Instead, click on the *Browse* button to find the application, as shown in the following example in Figure 12-43.

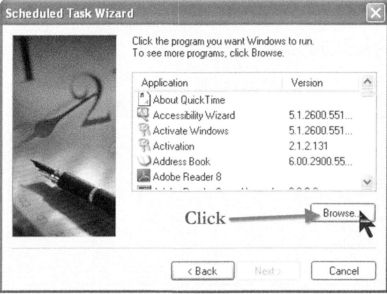

Figure 12-43 | Click Browse Button On Schedule Task Wizard

Next you see the directory structure. Remember the path for my coleNotepadBot was: C:\Documents and Settings\Steven Miller\My Documents\Visual Studio 2010\Projects\consoleNotepadBot\consoleNotepadBot\bin\Debug. Yours will be similar.

So click on *Document and Settings*, as in Figure 12-44

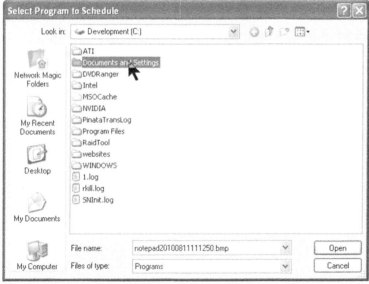

Figure 12-44 | Begin Accessing consoleNotepadBot Debug Directory

Continue to click until you are once again in the *Debug* directory, as in Figure 12-45.

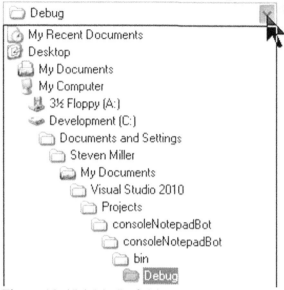

Figure 12-45 | My Path To consoleNotepadBot Debug Directory

If you're having trouble finding your path just do a search for consoleNotepadbot.exe. Finally, in the Debug directory select *consoleNotepadbot.exe* and select *Open* button, as Figure 12-46 shows, below.

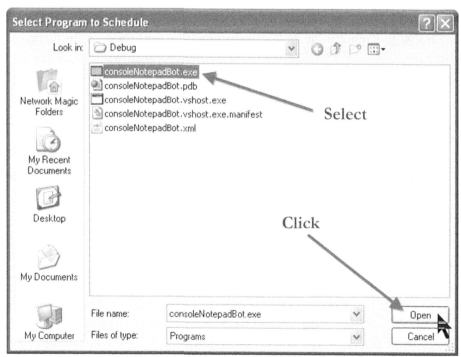

Figure 12-46 | Select consoleNotepadBot.exe In Debug Directory

You are then prompted to "Type a name for this task. The task can be the same name as the program name", to keep things simple, leave the program name as the task name.

Next, decide when to run it. It provides many options, as seen in Figure 12-47. The options prove extremely helpful for testing. To keep things simple choose **One time only**, as in Figure 12-47, and then click *Next*.

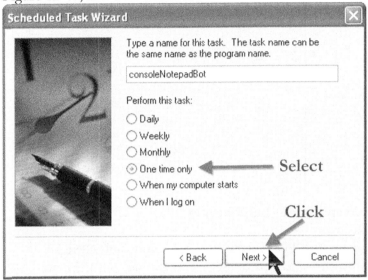

Figure 12-47 | Task Name And Select Timing

Now you are asked at what time to run the consoleNotePadBot.exe application. It shows the current time and date. Choose five minutes in the future from your current time, as in Figure 12-48, and then click *Next*.

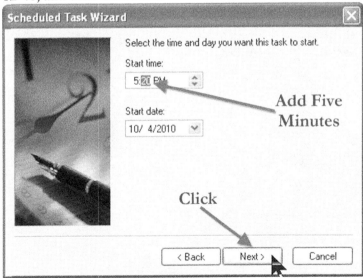

Figure 12-48 | Change The Time For Two Minutes In The Future

There are prompts for the user and password in order to run the task, as in Figure 12-49. Leave the user name as is, and the password blank. You may need to run it as administrator depending on the system.

Figure 12-49 | Choose user name

Make sure to check the box for **Open advanced properties for this task** and then click *Finish*, as in Figure 12-50.

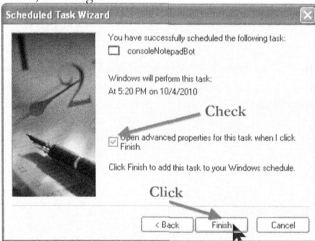

Figure 12-50 | Scheduled Task Wizard Success Screen

Without a password entered into the form in Figure 12-49 you may receive the warning shown in Figure 12-51. Ignore it and click *OK*. The password requirement will be removed in the Advanced Properties screen.

Figure 12-51 | Access is Denied Warning

214

On the Advanced Properties screen you need to check the box **Run only if logged on**, as in Figure 12-52. When you check the box the Set password… button is grayed out and a password is no longer needed.

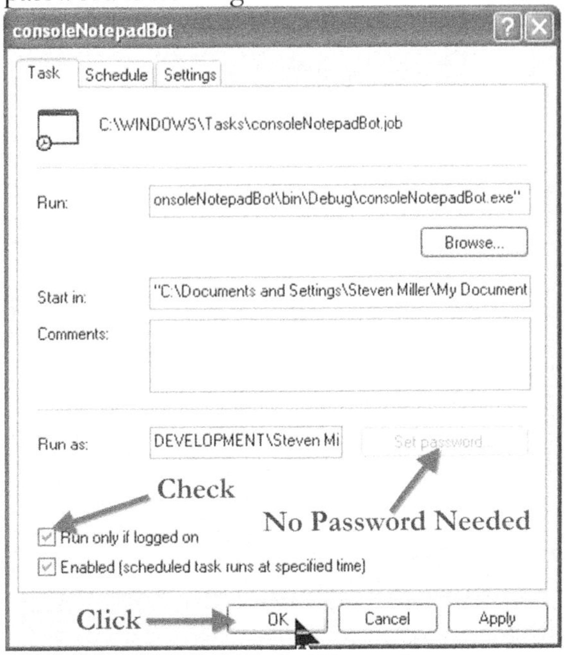

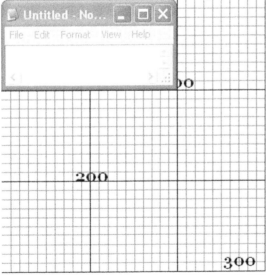

Figure 12-52 | Run only if logged on

Click *OK* and wait for the consoleNotepadBot to be started by Scheduled Task. The result will be that Windows Notepad will be started moved to grid coordinate 0x, 0y, and then resized to 200 wide by 100 high at the time specified in Scheduled Task, as in Figure 12-53.

Figure 12-53 | Test Results Of Scheduled Task And Console Application Bot

215

Summary

The combination of Console Applications and Scheduled Tasks is very powerful. Console Applications are needed when you want to run the automation Bot from the command line.

Command line execution of the automated bots enables you to include it in schedulers that call a single Bot, or multiple Bots, in a series.

Chapter 13:
Screen Capture Bot

A picture is said to be worth a thousand words. Therefore, an automated screen capture taken at 3:30 a.m. when you are sleeping soundly in order to create a picture of your desktop, or an application when it has detected an issue, must be worth at least two thousand.

A screen capture can be helpful when you need to see what is happening at a specific time. You can capture the whole desktop or a specific application.

Creating Screen Captures Bot Application

You will create three different buttons to demonstrate automating screen captures.

- Full Screen – Will perform a full screen capture and save it as a bitmap.
- Application – Will perform a application specific screen capture and save it as a bitmap.
- Every Second – Will perform a application specific screen capture and save it as bitmap with time stamp as the name.

Setting Up The Project

Start a new project and choose *Windows Form Application* and name it: **screenCaptureBot**, as in Figure 13-1.

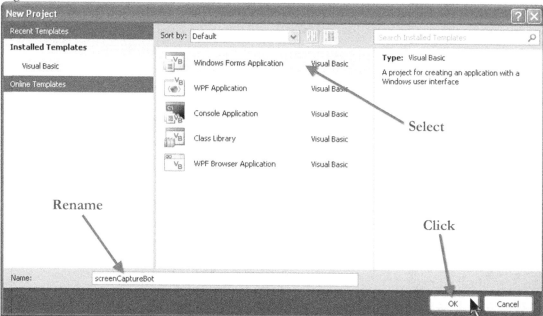

Figure 13-1 | Creating New screenCaptureBot

Now click the *Save All* button, as in the example below in Figure 13-2.

Figure 13-2 | Save All

Click *Save* to create the directory structure for project, as in Figure 13-3.

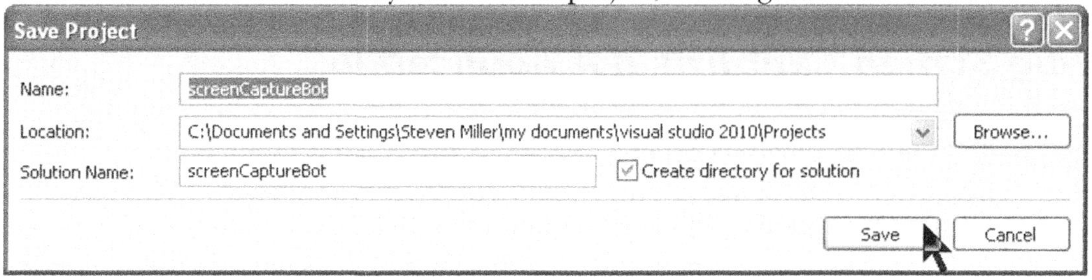

Figure 13-3 | Saving And Creating Directory For Project

Laying Out The Form

The first step is to resize the form and add three buttons to the form. Click on the *Toolbox* and drag three *buttons* onto the form, as in Figure 13-4.

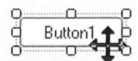

Figure 13-4 | Add Three Buttons And Resize Form

Select *Button1*, as in Figure 13-5, below. Then update Button1 Text Properties to **Full Screen** and the (Name) property to **fullscreen**, as in Figure 13-6 and Figure 13-7.

Figure 13-5 | Select Button1

Text	**Full Screen**	(Name)	**fullScreen**

Figure 13-6 | Text Property   Figure 13-7 | (Name) Property

Select *Button2*, as in Figure 13-8, below. Update Button2 Text Properties to **Application** and the (Name) property to **application**, as in Figure 13-9 and Figure 13-10.

Figure 13-8 | Select Button2

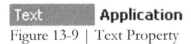

Figure 13-9 | Text Property

Figure 13-10 | (Name) Property

Select *Button3*, as in Figure 13-11, below. Update Button3 Text Properties to **Every Second** and the (Name) to **everySecond**, as in Figure 13-12 and Figure 13-13.

Figure 13-11 | Select Button3

Figure 13-12 | Text Property

Figure 13-13 | (Name) Property

Update the form title to Screen Capture Bot by clicking on the *form* any place there is no button. Select the *Properties* tab and update the Text property to **Screen Capture Bot**, as shown in Figure 13-14.

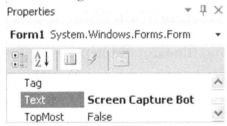

Figure 13-14 | Update Form Text Properpty

Coding The Project

You will start with the Full Screen capture. This will take a complete snapshot of your whole desktop, including multiple screens.

To keep things simple, finish the Full Screen button code first and then add the SetForegroundWindow library for the Application and Every Second button.

To perform the screen captures you will use SendKeys with PRTSC.   There is a difference between Windows Pressing Print Screen actions and the VB.Net Print Screen (PRTSC). In Windows Print Screen or CTRL+Print Screen will capture the entire screen while ALT +Print Screen will capture the application in focus. In contrast, PRTSC or ALT+PRTSC in VB.net

220

using the code SendKeys.SendWait("{PRTSC}") or SendKeys.SendWait("%{PRTSC}") will capture the application in focus.   CTRL+PRTSC using the code SendKeys.SendWait("^{PRTSC}") will capture a screenshot of the entire screen.

Double-click on the *Full Screen* button, as shown below in Figure 13-15, to create the fullScreen_Click subroutine, and also edit the button's code, as in Figure 13-16.

Figure 13-15 | Double Click Full Screen Button

```
Private Sub fullScreen_Click(ByVal sender As System.Object, _
     ByVal e As System.EventArgs) Handles fullScreen.Click

End Sub
```

Figure 13-16| fullScreen_Click Subroutine Created

Next you need to add the code to fullscreen_Click, as in Figure 13-17.

```
Private Sub fullScreen_Click(ByVal sender As System.Object, _
     ByVal e As System.EventArgs) Handles fullScreen.Click

    SendKeys.SendWait("^{PRTSC}")
    Dim clip As IDataObject = Clipboard.GetDataObject()
    If clip.GetDataPresent(GetType(System.Drawing.Bitmap)) Then
       Dim screenCapture As Bitmap = _
          CType(clip.GetData(GetType(System.Drawing.Bitmap)), Bitmap)
       screenCapture.Save("C:\fullScreenCapture.bmp")
    End If
    Clipboard.Clear()

End Sub
```

Figure 13-17| Add Code To Do Full Screen Capture

The code is broken down here line by line:

C: SendKeys.SendWait("^{PRTSC}")
D: Perform screen shot of entire desktop screen

C: Dim clip As IDataObject = Clipboard.GetDataObject()
D: Save Clipboard object in variable named clip

C: If clip.GetDataPresent(GetType(System.Drawing.Bitmap)) Then
D: Check to see if you captured anything before proceeding

221

C: Dim screenCapture As Bitmap = _
        CType(clip.GetData(GetType(System.Drawing.Bitmap)), Bitmap)
D: Store the contents of the Clipboard into a variable of type Bitmap

C: screenCapture.Save("C:\fullScreenCapture.bmp")
D: Save the full screen shot into the bitmap named fullScreenCapture.bmp into the root directory of C:\

C: End If
D: End If Statement

C: Clipboard.Clear()
D: Empty the Clipboard to free up memory

Now test what you have. The image is stored in the root directory of the C:\ drive. You can always change the location, if needed. You need to open up My Computer by clicking on *Start -> My Computer*, as in Figure 13-18. Double-click on your *C drive*, which may be similar to Figure 13-19 in the example below.

Figure 13-18 | Start -> My Computer

Figure 13-19 | Double Click C Drive

This will give you access to C:\ as in Figure 13-20. Now test what you have. Click the *Save All* button. Click either *Start Debugging*, or *(F5)*. Click on the *Full Screen* button.

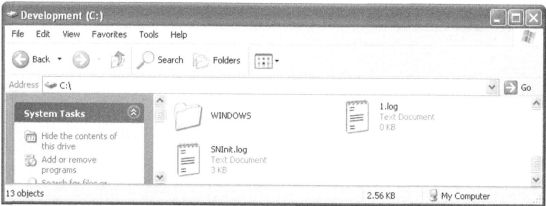

Figure 13-20 | C Drive Root Directory

The result will be a screen shot of your whole screen which will be saved into the file fullScreenCapture.bmp and will appear in the C:\ directory, as in Figure 13-21. Double-click on the *image* to preview your screen shot.

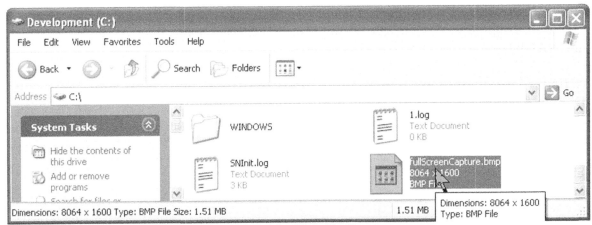

Figure 13-21 | fullScreenCapture.bmp Double Click To Preview

My test result shows the full screen capture of my desktop showing all four of my screens, as in Figure 13-22. It is important to know each time you click on the Full Screen button the fullScreenCapture.bmp is overwritten.

Figure 13-22 | My Full Screen Capture

The Application and Every Second button needs to set the focus on the application for which the screen shot will be taken. To set focus, add the library SetForegroundWindow.

Click on *Solution Explorer* then *View Code* to access the code, as in Figure 13-23.

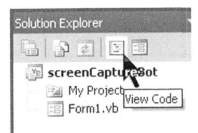

Figure 13-23 | Edit Code By Clicking View Code

Now add the SetForegroundWindow library code below Public Class Form1 and above Private Sub fullScreen_Click, as in Figure 13-24

```
Public Class Form1

    Private Declare Function SetForegroundWindow Lib "user32" _
        (ByVal handle As IntPtr) As Integer

    Private Sub fullScreen_Click(ByVal sender As System.Object, _
        ByVal e As System.EventArgs) Handles fullScreen.Click

        SendKeys.SendWait("^{PRTSC}")
        Dim clip As IDataObject = Clipboard.GetDataObject()
        If clip.GetDataPresent(GetType(System.Drawing.Bitmap)) Then
            Dim screenCapture As Bitmap = _
                CType(clip.GetData(GetType(System.Drawing.Bitmap)), Bitmap)
            screenCapture.Save("C:\fullScreenCapture.bmp")
```

Figure 13-24| Add SetForegroundWindow Library

Now click on the *Design Tab* to access the View Designer, as in Figure 13-25.

Figure 13-25 | Access View Designer

Double-click on the *Application* button, as shown below in Figure 13-26, and create the application_Click subroutine, and also edit the button's code, as in Figure 13-27.

Figure 13-26 | Double Click Full Screen Button

```
Private Sub application_Click(ByVal sender As System.Object, _
    ByVal e As System.EventArgs) Handles application.Click

End Sub
```

Figure 13-27| application_Click Subroutine Created

To capture the application in focus, use SendKeys.SendWait("%{PRTSC}"). Use Windows Notepad as the application upon which to set the focus. Add the code to application_Click, as shown in the example in Figure 13-28.

```
Private Sub application_Click(ByVal sender As System.Object, _
   ByVal e As System.EventArgs) Handles application.Click
   Dim ps() As Process = Process.GetProcessesByName("notepad")

   If ps.Length > 0 Then
      Dim p As Process = ps(0)
      Dim hWnd As IntPtr = p.MainWindowHandle
      SetForegroundWindow(hWnd)
      SendKeys.SendWait("%{PRTSC}")
      Dim clip As IDataObject = Clipboard.GetDataObject()
      If clip.GetDataPresent(GetType(System.Drawing.Bitmap)) Then
         Dim screenCapture As Bitmap = _
            CType(clip.GetData(GetType(System.Drawing.Bitmap)), Bitmap)
         screenCapture.Save("C:\notepad.bmp")
      End If
   End If

   Clipboard.Clear()

End Sub
```

Figure 13-28 | application_Click Subroutine Created

Now test what you have. Again, the image is stored in the root directory of the C:\ drive. First, start Windows Notepad and type something in it if you wish. Click the *Save All* button. Click either *Start Debugging*, or (*F5*). Click on the *Application* button. The result will be a screen shot of Windows Notepad saved into the file notepad.bmp and it will appear in the C:\ directory, as in Figure 13-29. Now double-click on the *image* to preview the screen shot.

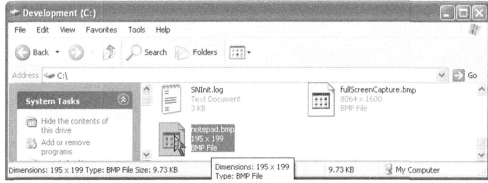

Figure 13-29 | notepad.bmp Result Double Click To Preview

My screen shot result is shown below in Figure 13-30.

Figure 13-30 | Notepad Screenshot Result

Click on the *Design Tab* to access the View Designer, as in Figure 13-31.

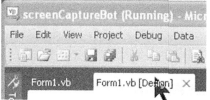

Figure 13-31 | Access View Designer

The goal here is to perform a screen shot of Windows Notepad once every second and save a unique image name for each screen shot. To do this, it is necessary to add a timer to the form. Click on *Toolbox* and click and drag a *Timer* onto the form, as in Figure 13-32.

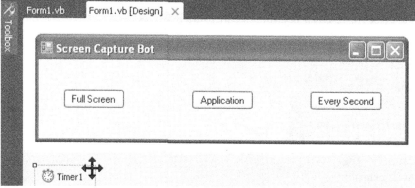

Figure 13-32 | Add Timer To Form

Make sure *Timer1* is selected, as in Figure 13-33, then change the Interval property to **1000** so it will fire once a second, as Figure 13-34.

Figure 13-33 | Select Timer1   Figure 13-34 | Update Interval Property

226

Double-click on the *Every Second* button, as in Figure 13-35, and create the everySecond_Click subroutine, and also to edit the code, as in Figure 13-36.

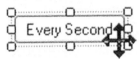

Figure 13-35 | Double Click Every Second Button

```
Private Sub everySecond_Click(ByVal sender As System.Object, _
    ByVal e As System.EventArgs) Handles everySecond.Click

End Sub
```

Figure 13-36 | application_Click Subroutine Created

Start the Timer1 inside the subroutine everySecond_Click add the code, as in Figure 13-37.

```
Private Sub everySecond_Click(ByVal sender As System.Object, _
    ByVal e As System.EventArgs) Handles everySecond.Click
    Timer1.Start()
End Sub
```

Figure 13-37 | Add Code To Start Timer1

You need a way to terminate the timer remotely. Again, utilize holding down the ALT key as a means to terminate Timer1 remotely. The only new code required in Timer1 is the ability to dynamically create file names. To create the dynamic names, use a time stamp as part of the name. This also provides the benefit of knowing exactly when the screen shot was taken.

Click on the *Design Tab* to access the View Designer, as in Figure 13-38.

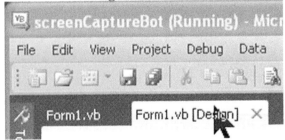

Figure 13-38 | Access View Designer

Double-click on *Timer1* to create the Timer1_Click subroutine, as in Figure 13-39.

Figure 13-39 | Double Click Timer1

The Timer1_Click subroutine has been created, and can be edited, as shown in Figure 13-40.

```
Private Sub Timer1_Tick(ByVal sender As System.Object, _
    ByVal e As System.EventArgs) Handles Timer1.Tick

End Sub
```

Figure 13-40 | Timer1_Click Subroutine Created

Add the code to exit Timer1 when the ALT key is held down, as in Figure 13-41. Timers can behave oddly when you set their property interval to one second, for example, because the code in the Timer subroutine takes more than a second. Therefore, I suggest the code in the Else statement stop the timer when you begin, and restart it when you exit as, as in the example shown in Figure 13-41.

```
Private Sub Timer1_Tick(ByVal sender As System.Object, _
    ByVal e As System.EventArgs) Handles Timer1.Tick
    If (My.Computer.Keyboard.AltKeyDown) Then
        Timer1.Stop()
    Else
        Timer1.Stop()
        Timer1.Start()
    End If
End Sub
```

Figure 13-41 | Exit Timer1 Code

You can reuse most of the code that you used for the Application button. What you need to do is update the line screenCapture.Save("C:\notepad.bmp") to be dynamic. You will create a dynamic name with a timestamp with the format yyyyMMddhhmmss which is **Y**ear, **M**onth, **D**ay, **H**our, **M**inute, and **S**econd.

Add code to set focus on Windows Notepad, take a screen shot, and then add the new code to provide a dynamic name using a timestamp, as in Figure 13-42.

```
Private Sub Timer1_Tick(ByVal sender As System.Object, _
    ByVal e As System.EventArgs) Handles Timer1.Tick
    If (My.Computer.Keyboard.AltKeyDown) Then
        Timer1.Stop()
    Else
        Timer1.Stop()
        Dim ps() As Process = Process.GetProcessesByName("notepad")
        If ps.Length > 0 Then
            Dim p As Process = ps(0)
            Dim hWnd As IntPtr = p.MainWindowHandle
            SetForegroundWindow(hWnd)
            SendKeys.SendWait("%{PRTSC}")
            Dim clip As IDataObject = Clipboard.GetDataObject()
            If clip.GetDataPresent(GetType(System.Drawing.Bitmap)) Then
```

```
            Dim screenCapture As Bitmap = _
                CType(clip.GetData(GetType(System.Drawing.Bitmap)), Bitmap)
            Dim timeStamp As String = _
                DateTime.Now.ToString("yyyyMMddhhmmss")
            Dim screenCaptureName As String = _
                "C:\notepad" & timeStamp & ".bmp"
            screenCapture.Save(screenCaptureName)
          End If
        End If
        Clipboard.Clear()
        Timer1.Start()
      End If
    End Sub
End Class
```

Figure 13-42 | Exit Timer1 Code

Now test what you have. Once again the images will be stored in the root directory of the C:\ drive. First start Windows Notepad and make sure it is cleared out. Click the *Save All* button. Click either *Start Debugging*, or (F5).

Click on the *Every Second* button and immediately begin typing in Windows Notepad. After a few seconds, hold down the **ALT key** to terminate the Bot.

The result will be a series of screenshots of your Windows Notepad saved into multiple files using the format notepadyyyyMMddhhmmss.bmp and they will appear in the C:\ directory. Double-click an *image* to preview your screenshots, as in Figure 13-43.

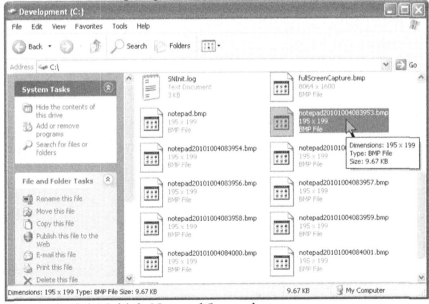

Figure 13-43 | Multiple Notepad Screenshots

Double click on *images* to preview them, as shown in the example in Figure 13-44.

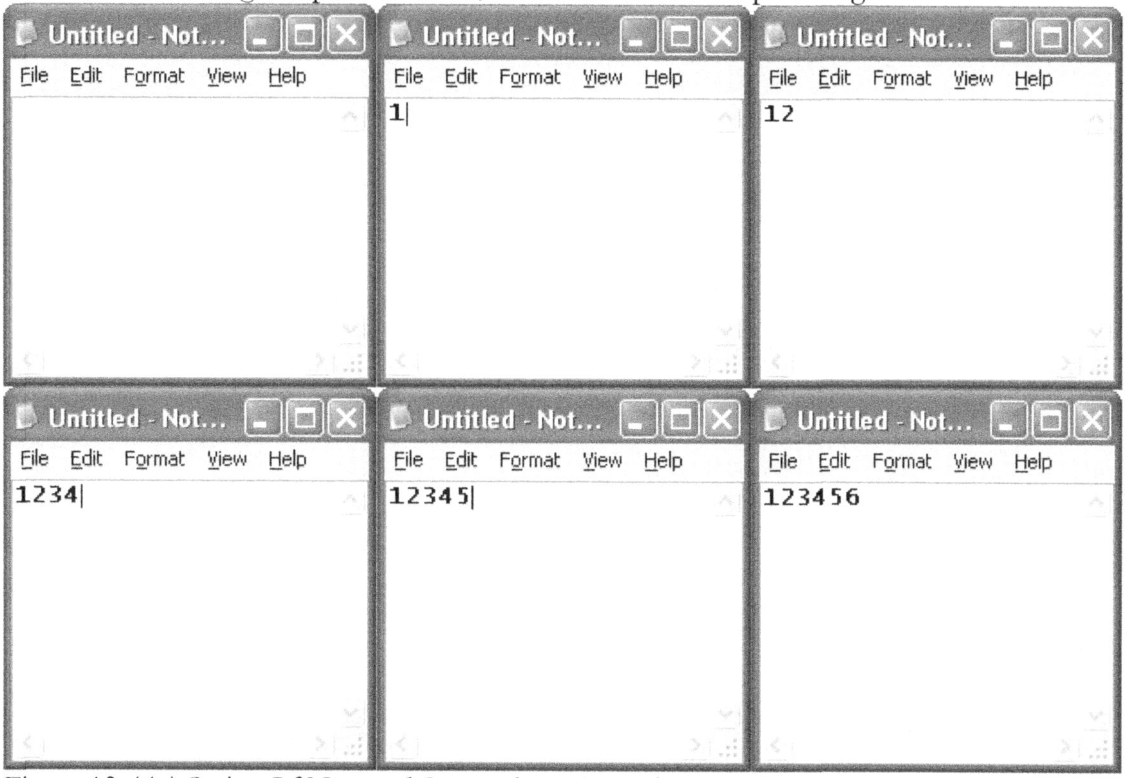

Figure 13-44 | Series Of Notepad Screenshots Once A Second

Summary

You have covered how to capture a screenshot of the entire desktop or a screenshot of the active application. This provides you the ability to capture visual data of the specific application you are testing.

Chapter 14:
Pixel Recognition Botting

Using pixel recognition is the way in which you see an application or a game. When you see the world through your eyes you see the whole room. The starting point for seeing as a Bot is one pixel. You build up from there with pattern matching via a combination of pixels. Pixel recognition tends to be more important when creating automation bots for games, but it can also be useful for applications.

The Pixel Recognition Bot will play 3D Pinball for Windows. In fact, this was actually the game that sent me down the path of learning Bot automation. My experience has shown that none of the off-the-shelf automation tools (costing $35-$20,000 plus), could intelligently automate the replay of a Windows 3D Pinball Game. Most could not even replay the timing of the paddles since they do not capture the timing between the key press down and up.

Creating Pixel Recognition Bot

You will focus pixel recognition in two areas:
- Plunger
- Paddles

Look to see if the ball is currently located near the plunger or the paddles. Depending on ball's location, you would either pull the plunger or fire a paddle.

Setting Up The Project

Start a new project and choose *Windows Form Application* and name it: **pixelRecognitionBot**, as in Figure 14-1.

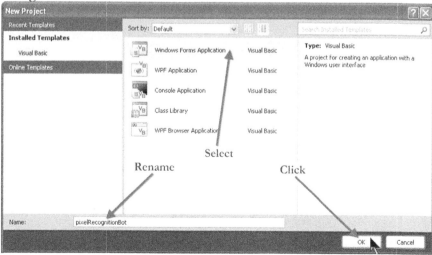

Figure 14-1 | Creating New pixelRecognitionBot

Now click the *Save All* button, as in the example shown below in Figure 14-2.

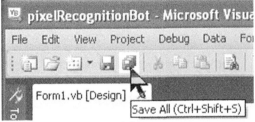

Figure 14-2 | Save All

Click *Save* to create directory structure for project, as in Figure 14-3.

Figure 14-3 | Saving And Creating Directory For Project

Laying Out The Form

You only need one button for the Pixel Recognition Bot. Click on *Toolbox* and drag a *Button* onto the form. Then, resize the form, as in Figure 14-4 below.

Figure 14-4 | Add One Button To Form

Select *Button1*, as in Figure 14-5 below. Then update Button1 Text Properties to **Play** and the (Name) property to **play**, as in Figure 14-6 and Figure 14-7.

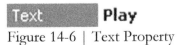

Figure 14-5 | Select Button1

Figure 14-6 | Text Property

Figure 14-7 | (Name) Property

Update the form title to Pixel Recognition Bot by clicking on the *form* any place there is no button. Select the *Properties* tab and update the Text property to **Pixel Recognition Bot**, as in Figure 14-8.

Figure 14-8 | Update Form Properties Text

When you watch TV, your the human eye can detect somewhere between 60 frames per second and 120 frames per second. So, at 100 FPS you notice differences in images 10 milliseconds apart. When you use pixel recognition in Windows 3D Pinball, you need to approach it in a similar fashion. You will sample a certain number of milliseconds apart. To do that you will need to add a timer to fire a certain number of milliseconds apart so that you can read the screen and determine a course of action.

Click on the *Toolbox* and drag a *Timer* on to the form, as in Figure 14-9. The default of 100 milliseconds will be sufficiant.

Figure 14-9 | Add Timer To Form

Coding The Project

Double-click on the Play button, as in Figure 14-10, and create the play_Click subroutine, and also to edit the code for the Play button, as in Figure 14-11.

Figure 14-10 | Double-Click Play Button

```
Private Sub play_Click(ByVal sender As System.Object, _
      ByVal e As System.EventArgs) Handles play.Click

 End Sub
```

Figure 14-11 | play_Click Subroutine Created

234

Add the code to start Timer1 inside the subroutine play_Click, as in Figure 14-12.

Private Sub play_Click(ByVal sender As System.Object, _
    ByVal e As System.EventArgs) Handles play.Click

Timer1.Start()

End Sub

Figure 14-12| Add Code To Start Timer1

Since you will be sending keystrokes and taking screenshots of Windows 3d Pinball, you will need to get its process name.

Start Windows 3-D Pinball, as in Figure 14-13.

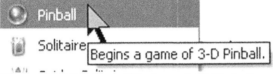

Figure 14-13 | Start Windows 3-D Pinball

Again, to get the process name press *CTRL+ALT+DEL* and locate **3D Pinball for Windows – Space Cadet** application and select, then *right mouse* click and choose **Go To Process**, as shown in Figure 14-14.

Figure 14-14 | Pinball Select Go To Process

235

The image name for 3-D Windows Pinball is pinball.exe, as in Figure 14-15.   You remove the .exe and have the process name of **pinball**.

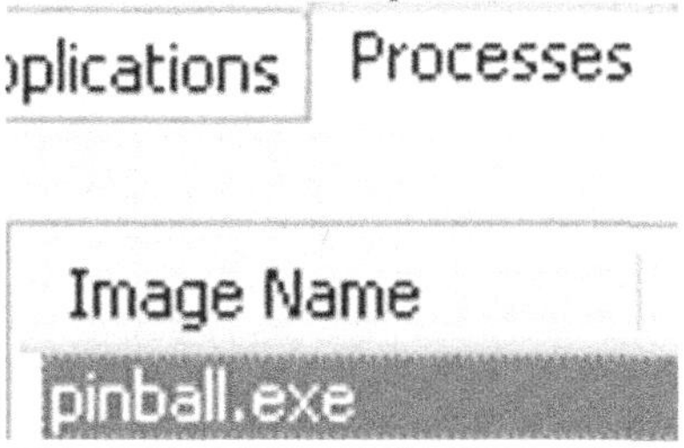

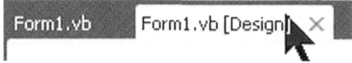

Figure 14-15 | pinball.exe Image Name Process Name pinball

Now click on the *Design tab* to access the View Designer, as in Figure 14-16, below.

Figure 14-16 | Click Design Tab To Access View Designer

Double-click on the *Timer1* button, as in Figure 14-17, and create the Timer1_Click subroutine, and also to edit the code, as in Figure 14-18.

Figure 14-17 | Double Click Timer1

```
Private Sub Timer1_Tick(ByVal sender As System.Object, _
    ByVal e As System.EventArgs) Handles Timer1.Tick

  End Sub
```

Figure 14-18|Timer1_Click Subroutine Created

Add the code to exit Timer1 when the ALT key is held down, as in Figure 14-19.

```
Private Sub Timer1_Tick(ByVal sender As System.Object, _
    ByVal e As System.EventArgs) Handles Timer1.Tick
    If (My.Computer.Keyboard.AltKeyDown) Then
      Timer1.Stop()
    Else
      Timer1.Stop()

      Timer1.Start()
    End If
  End Sub
```

Figure 14-19|Exit Timer1 Code

If the ALT has not been pressed down you will enter the Else code block. Now you need to check to see if Windows 3-D Pinball is currently open, as in Figure 14-20.

```
Private Sub Timer1_Tick(ByVal sender As System.Object, _
    ByVal e As System.EventArgs) Handles Timer1.Tick
    If (My.Computer.Keyboard.AltKeyDown) Then
        Timer1.Stop()
    Else
      Timer1.Stop()

        Dim ps() As Process = Process.GetProcessesByName("pinball")

        If ps.Length > 0 Then
            Dim p As Process = ps(0)
            Dim hWnd As IntPtr = p.MainWindowHandle
        End If

        Timer1.Start()

    End If
  End Sub
```

Figure 14-20 | Check If 3-D Pinball Is Running

If Windows 3-D Pinball is currently running, set focus on the application. To do that, include the SetForegroundWindow library.

Add the SetForegroundWindow library code below Public Class Form1, as shown below in the example in Figure 14-21.

```
Public Class Form1

    Private Declare Function SetForegroundWindow Lib "user32" _
        (ByVal handle As IntPtr) As Integer
```

Figure 14-21 | Add SetForegroundWindow Library

Next, add the code to set focus on the 3-D Pinball application right after storing the MainWindowHandle, as in Figure 14-22.

```
Private Sub Timer1_Tick(ByVal sender As System.Object, _
    ByVal e As System.EventArgs) Handles Timer1.Tick

    If (My.Computer.Keyboard.AltKeyDown) Then
        Timer1.Stop()
    Else

        Timer1.Stop()
        Dim ps() As Process = Process.GetProcessesByName("pinball")
```

```
        If ps.Length > 0 Then
           Dim p As Process = ps(0)
           Dim hWnd As IntPtr = p.MainWindowHandle
           SetForegroundWindow(hWnd)
        End If


        Timer1.Start()


     End If
  End Sub
```

Figure 14-22 | Set Focus On Pinball Application

Now add the code to capture a screen shot of Windows 3-D pinball, as in Figure 14-23. Add Clipboard.Clear() to remove the image from memory when you are done using it, as in Figure 14-23.

```
If (My.Computer.Keyboard.AltKeyDown) Then
   Timer1.Stop()
Else
   Timer1.Stop()
   Dim ps() As Process = Process.GetProcessesByName("pinball")

   If ps.Length > 0 Then
      Dim p As Process = ps(0)
      Dim hWnd As IntPtr = p.MainWindowHandle
      SetForegroundWindow(hWnd)
      SendKeys.SendWait("%{PRTSC}")
      Dim clip As IDataObject = Clipboard.GetDataObject()

      If clip.GetDataPresent(GetType(System.Drawing.Bitmap)) Then
         Dim screenCapture As Bitmap = _
            CType(clip.GetData(GetType(System.Drawing.Bitmap)), Bitmap)
      End If

   End If

   Clipboard.Clear()
   Timer1.Start()

End If
```

Figure 14-23 | Perform Screen Capture On Windows 3-D Pinball

238

Because it is not necessary to actually save the image to the hard drive, simply access the image and its properties from the variable screenCapture of type Bitmap.

The next step is to prevent a bug from occurring with the Pixel Recognition Bot. When selecting a menu item, as in Figure 14-24, the size of the application is shrinked down to the size of the pull down menu. False readings will occur since a screen shot will only provide the size of the pull down menu. Therefore, to prevent the Bot from doing any further processing check to see if the size is not the full size of 3d Pinball for Windows.

Figure 14-24 | Pull Down Menu

Determine the full size of 3d Pinball for Windows by starting the Automation Tool Helper. Make sure 3-D Pinball for Windows is still running. Then enter **pinball** into the Process Name field on the Automation Tool Helper and click *Read Applications* Button, as in Figure 14-25. As noted below, the full size of Pinball is 606 pixels wide by 468 pixels high.

Automation Tool Helper By Steve Miller

Designed For The Book: Bot Programming: Intelligent Automation For Windows Applicatio

Screen Capture

Process Name

pinball

Read Applications

Pixel Color

BMP Image

X Coord   0   Y Coord

RGB HEX

Get Color   Get Color Saves To Clipboard

ID	App Na...	xPos	yPos	Height	Width
3D Pinball for Windows - Space Cadet	4468	4	7	468	606

Figure 14-25 | pinball Process Name Information

It is not necessary to check both the height and width. Obviously, if it is the full size of either height or width you know you have 3-D Pinball in play mode. Simply check the width of the screenCapture to verify that it is 606 pixels wide.

To capture the screenshot use Dim screenCapture As Bitmap. Variables of type Bitmap have the method Width that allows you to get the width of the screenshot you have stored into screenCapture variable.

Add the code shown below in Figure 14-26 to get the screenCapture width and to check to verify if it is 606 pixels wide.

```
Timer1.Stop()
Dim ps() As Process = Process.GetProcessesByName("pinball")
       System.Threading.Thread.Sleep(2000)

If ps.Length > 0 Then

    Dim p As Process = ps(0)
    Dim hWnd As IntPtr = p.MainWindowHandle
    SetForegroundWindow(hWnd)

    SendKeys.SendWait("%{PRTSC}")
    Dim clip As IDataObject = Clipboard.GetDataObject()

    If clip.GetDataPresent(GetType(System.Drawing.Bitmap)) Then
      Dim screenCapture As Bitmap = _
        CType(clip.GetData(GetType(System.Drawing.Bitmap)), Bitmap)
        Dim widthWindow As Integer = screenCapture.Width()
        If (widthWindow = 606) Then

        End If
    End If

End If

Clipboard.Clear()
Timer1.Start()
```

Figure 14-26 | Get screenCapture Width And Check If Pinball is 606 Pixels Wide

3D Pinball Plunger

That brings you to the point where being the process of doing pixel recognition. Start by looking closely at the plunger with, and without, a ball, as in Figure 14-27 and Figure 14-28.

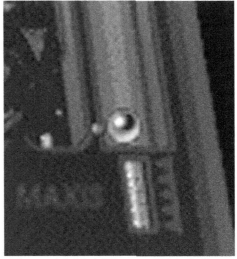

Figure 14-27 | Plunger Without Ball   Figure 14-28 | Plunger With Ball

The basic principle for pixel recognition is to look for a color at a specific pixel, or the opposite, and check if a pixel is not a color. When you compare the images above, any pixel where the ball is located will work to identify when to pull the plunger.

To identify a specific pixel and its color, use the Automation tool Helper and Windows Paint. Make sure Windows Pinball is running and a ball is located on the plunger, as in Figure 14-28. Also, verify that Automation Tool Helper has the Process Name **pinball,** and then click *Read Applications* to update the information. Now, click the *name* in the *ID* field to perform a screen capture of Pinball, as in Figure 14-29. It will save a copy of the bitmap in the same directory as the Automation Tool Helper.

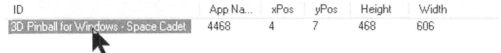

ID	App Na...	xPos	yPos	Height	Width
3D Pinball for Windows - Space Cadet	4468	4	7	468	606

Figure 14-29 | Screen Capture Of Pinball

The name of the image fill will be captureyyyyMMddhhmmss.bmp, as in Figure 14-30.

Figure 14-30 | Screen Capture Of Pinball

When you click on name in the *ID* field the name of the most recent Bitmap Image is written to the BMP Image field in the Pixel Color area and a preview of the screen shot is shown at the bottom of the Automation Tool Helper, as in Figure 14-31.

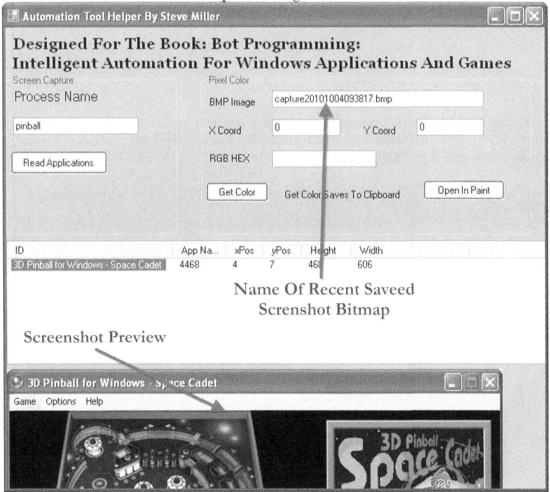

Figure 14-31 | BMP Image Name Written, Screen Preview, and Screen Shot Saved

To look at a specific pixel requires the assistance of Windows Paint. To open the most recent screenshot into Windows Paint click on the *Open In Paint* button, as in Figure 14-32.

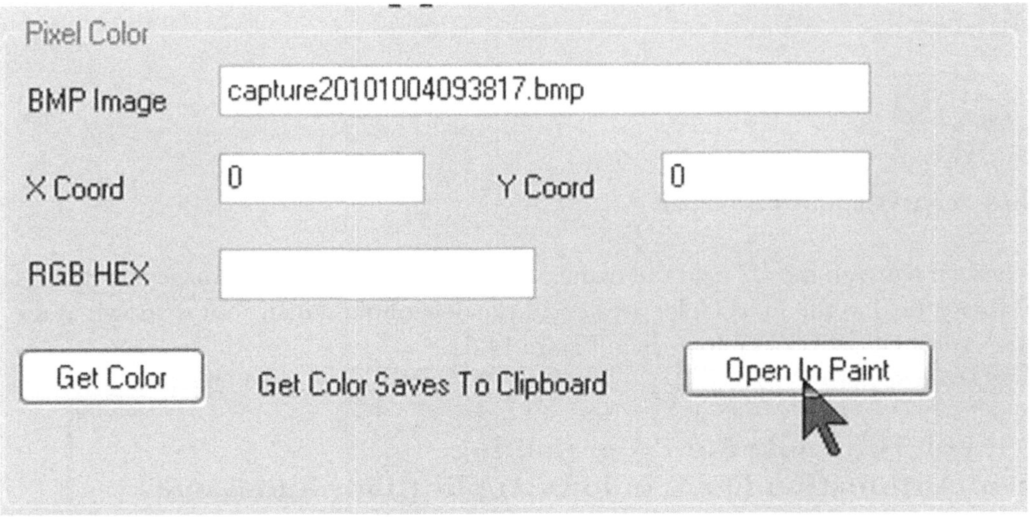

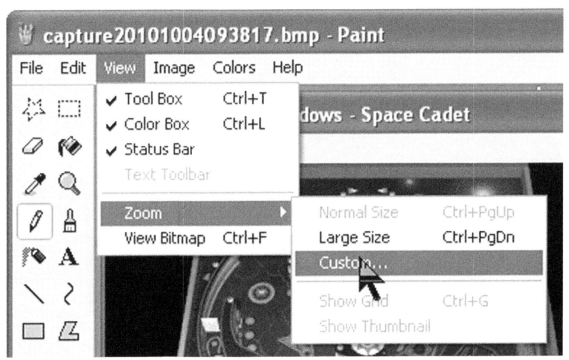

Figure 14-32 | Open Screenshot In Paint

Paint will open up the screenshot bitmap in the BMP Image text box. Utilize the Zoom to determine which pixel to use when determining if the Bot needs to pull the plunger. Choose the Custom zoom option by clicking *View -> Zoom -> Custom*, as in Figure 14-33.

Figure 14-33 | Select Custom Zoom

Choose Zoom to be 800% and then click *Ok* button, as in Figure 14-34.

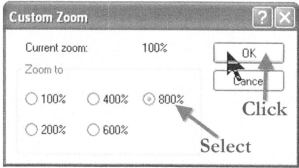

Figure 14-34 | Select 800 Percent Zoom

With Paint zooming in 800% on the most recent screenshot, move the pencil point to right above the ball and choose a pixel for the pixel recognition. The best way to decide which pixel to use is one in which the color is obviously different from when the ball is not present. (Refer to Figure 14-27 to see an image without a ball.) Once a suitable location is found, point the pencil on that mark. Look to the lower right of Paint to see the x, y pixel location, as in Figure 14-35. You may choose whichever location you want. I chose this location because there are no white colored pixels when the ball is not present.

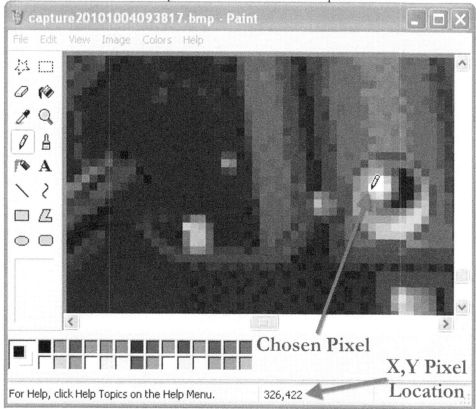

Figure 14-35| Determine Pixel Location In 800% Zoom

This gives you 326x and 422y as the position relative to the application's upper left hand corner.

Now determine what the color of that pixel is within Visual Basic. Make sure to do this for your particular system since colors can vary on different systems.

Take the **326** and place it in the X Coord field and **422** in the Y Coord field in the Automation Tool Helper, as in Figure 14-36.

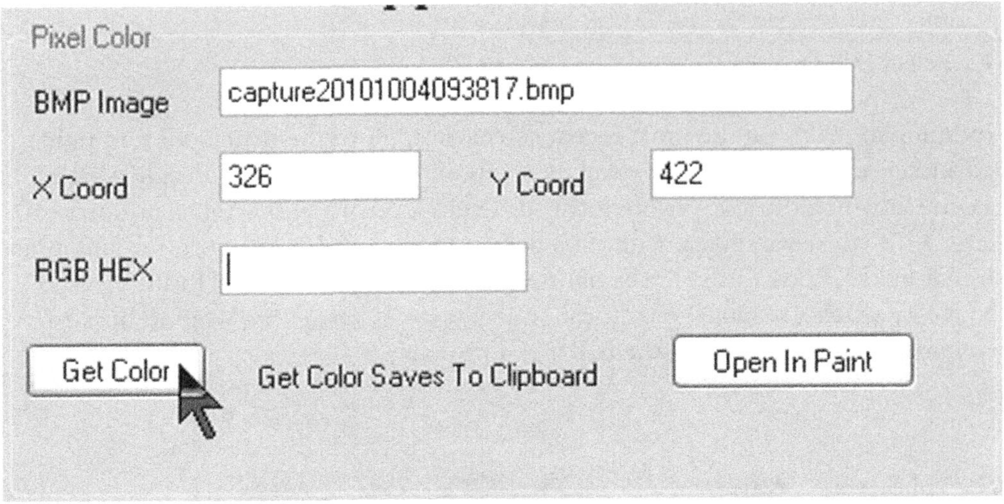

Figure 14-36 | Get Color Of A Specific Pixel

Click on the *Get Color* button, as in Figure 14-37. This will give you the Red Green Blue Hex value for that single pixel. The value is stored into the RGB Hex field. On my system, the color of the pixel 326x, 422y on the application 3D Pinball is FFFFFFFF. That value is translated to the color White in the RGB color system.

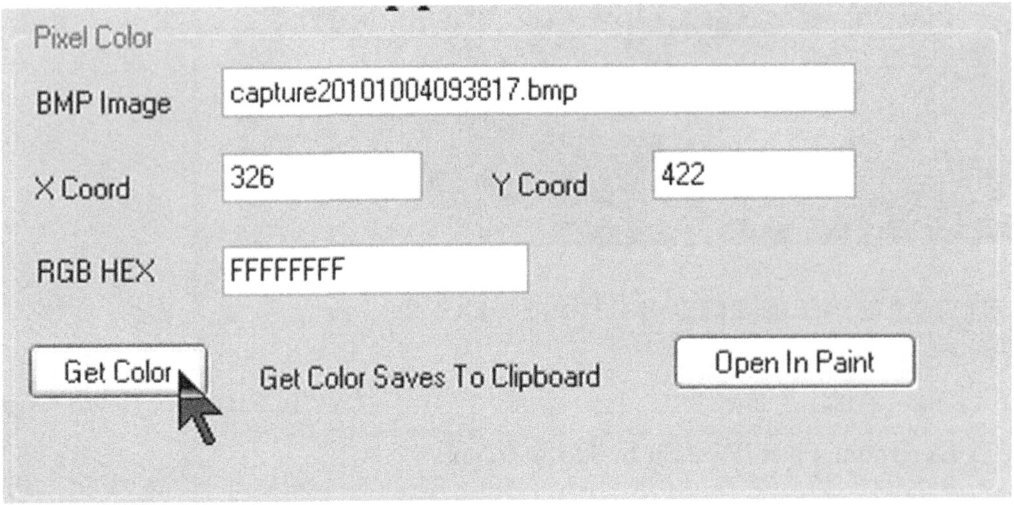

Figure 14-37 | Pixel Color is FFFFFFFF

The RGB Hex colors can get very complex (such as FF101828), which can be prone to causing errors if you attempt to retype them by hand. For that reason, when clicking on Get Color, the value is also stored into the clipboard memory so that it can be pasted directly into your code, as in Figure 14-38 and Figure 14-39. Select the location to paste, and either right mouse click -> *Paste*, or use the short cut keys *CTRL+V*.

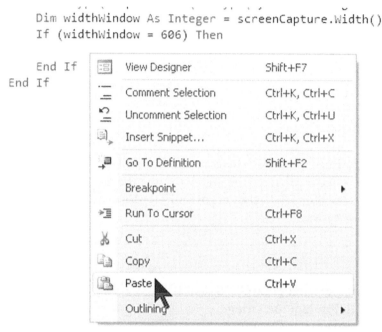

```
Dim widthWindow As Integer = screenCapture.Width()
If (widthWindow = 606) Then
```

View Designer	Shift+F7
Comment Selection	Ctrl+K, Ctrl+C
Uncomment Selection	Ctrl+K, Ctrl+U
Insert Snippet...	Ctrl+K, Ctrl+X
Go To Definition	Shift+F2
Breakpoint	▶
Run To Cursor	Ctrl+F8
Cut	Ctrl+X
Copy	Ctrl+C
Paste	Ctrl+V
Outlining	▶

Figure 14-38 | Select Location To Paste And Right Mouse Click -> Paste

```
If (widthWindow = 606) Then
    FFFFFFFF
End If
```
Figure 14-39 | Pixel Color Value Pasted Into Code

When capturing multiple pixel values, creating a spread sheet or simple notes will prevent a lot of bugs later.

The RGB color received in RGB Hex field is broken down into four different sets of two values. The first set is always FF. The second is the red color value in Hex. The third is the green color value in Hex. The fourth is the blue value in Hex. The color value of FF101828 is broken down as FF (default set), 10 (Red), 18 (Green), 28 (Blue).

The next step is to check the pixelRecognitionBot screenshot at pixel 326x and 422y. The color is FFFFFFFF. If the Bot detects the color of FFFFFFFF at 326x and 422y the Bot needs to pull the plunger.

When capturing the screenshot, use Dim screenCapture As Bitmap. The variable of type Bitmap has the method GetPixel (x Coord, y Coord). This allows for determining the specific color of an individual pixel within a screenshot. Add the code to get the color of the pixel at 326x and 422y, then check to see if it is the color "FFFFFFFF", as in Figure 14-40.

```
If (widthWindow = 606) Then
    Dim ball As Color = screenCapture.GetPixel(326, 422)
    Dim ballColor As String = Hex(ball.ToArgb)
    If (ballColor = "FFFFFFFF") Then

    End If
End If
```

Figure 14-40 | Check If Pinball Pixel 326x 422y IS Color FFFFFFFF

If the Pinball pixel 326x 422y is FFFFFFFF, then send the command to pull the plunger back. Use keybd_event and MapVirtualKey since it provides the ability to time the down and up timing of sending the keystroke. Add the libraries keybd_event and MapVirtualKey right under Public Class Form1, as in Figure 14-41.

```
Public Class Form1

    Private Declare Sub keybd_event Lib "user32.dll" (ByVal bVk As Byte, _
        ByVal bScan As Byte, ByVal dwFlags As Integer, _
        ByVal dwExtraInfo As Integer)
    Private Declare Function MapVirtualKey Lib "user32" Alias "MapVirtualKeyA" _
        (ByVal wCode As Integer, ByVal wMapType As Integer) As Integer

    Private Declare Function SetForegroundWindow Lib "user32" _
        (ByVal handle As IntPtr) As Integer
```

Figure 14-41 | Add Libraries keybd_event and MapVirtualKey

The next step is to determine the player control for the 3-D Pinball for Windows game. Click on *Options* Menu then choose *Players Controls*, as in Figure 14-42.

Figure 14-42 | Select Options -> Player Controls

The 3D Pinball: Player Control is shown below, in Figure 14-43. When the ball is present above the plunger you need to send the keystroke **Spacebar**.

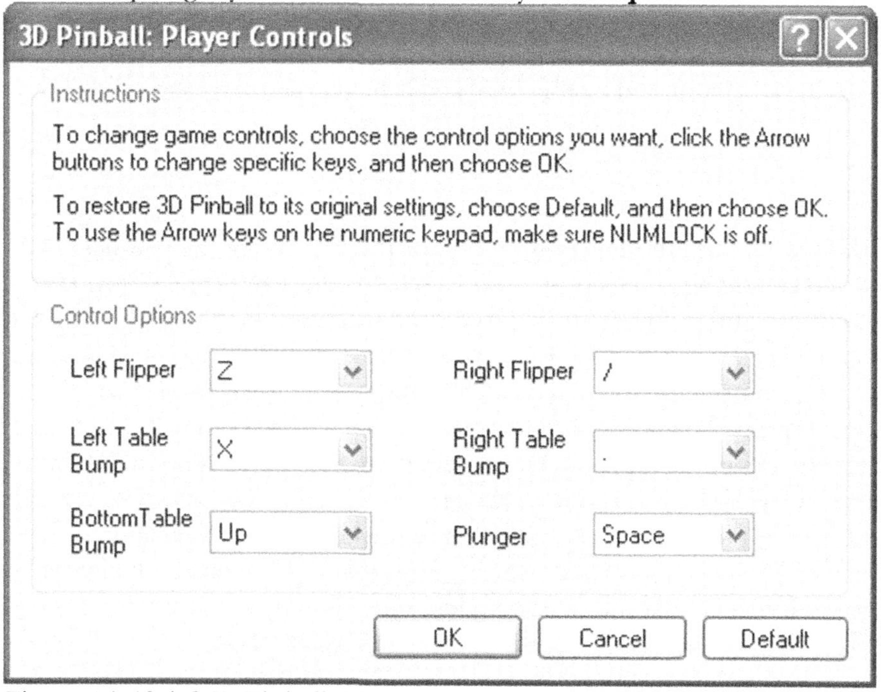

Figure 14-43 | 3-D Pinball: Player Controls

The Spacebar translates with MapVirtualKey to Keys.Space, as in Figure 14-44.

```
MapVirtualKey(Keys.Space|, 0), 0, 0)
```

MapVirtualKey(**wCode As Integer**, wMapType As Integer) As Integer

▣ Space	System.Windows.Forms.Keys.Space = 32
	The SPACEBAR key.

Figure 14-44 | Spacebar Translates To Keys.Space

Practice pulling the plunger on Pinball and mentally counting how long it takes to pull the plunger until it is released. Some time between one to three seconds works. Take the middle ground and use two seconds as the time to use to pull the plunger before releasing it. Add the code to send the down Spacebar keystroke followed by a two second delay, then send up Spacebar keystroke, as in Figure 14-45.

```
If (pixelColor = "FFFFFFFF") Then
    keybd_event(Keys.Space, MapVirtualKey(Keys.Space, 0), 0, 0)
    System.Threading.Thread.Sleep(2000)
    keybd_event(Keys.Space, MapVirtualKey(Keys.Space, 0), 2, 0)
End If
```

Figure 14-45| Send Keystrokes To Pull Plunger

Now test what you have. Click the *Save All* button. Click either *Start Debugging*, or (*F5*). Make sure 3D Pinball for Windows is running, then select the Game menu and choose New Game, or F2. Make sure the ball is above the plunger. Click on the *Play* button. The result will be the plunger pulling back for two seconds and then launching the ball. This process will continue until all three balls have been played or the ALT key is held down.

3D Paddles

The next step is to determine where to put detection points for the ball above the paddles. A question to think about when an adding a detection point is: what is the size of the object that is being detected? The ball is the object you are trying to detect, so determine the width of the ball so that the detection points can be spaced appropriately. Think of it like creating a strainer to catch the ball. On the computer screen, the ball creates a unique issue with respect to screen-shots and detections points. The left and right edges of the ball are comprised of just a few pixels. The detection points could completely miss 'seeing' the ball, depending on when the screen-shot captured the image. However, due to the greater number of pixels the detections points can read from top-to-bottom of the ball, the screen-shot has a greater probality of recognizing the ball in any single screen-shot. With that consideration, I suggest calculating the width of the ball several pixels in from the left and right edges, as shown in the example in Figure 14-45. Use paint to get the x coordinates, as in Figure 14-46.

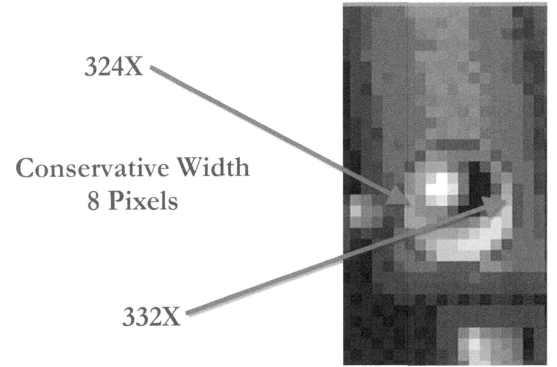

Figure 14-46 | Conservative Calculation of Pixel Width

At a minimum, place the detection points eight pixels apart. Choosing where to place the detection points is usually best determined by practicing with the game and thinking about the optimal place to perform an action. Then place the detecting points in a location that allows for detecting an object and that would also lead to optimal performace.

To keep it simple in this example you will place the detection points along a straight line, as in Figure 14-47.

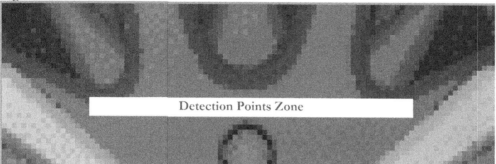

Figure 14-47 | Detection Points Zone

Here I started to create the detection points going from left to right in the detection zone, as in Figure 14-47, below. Use Paint to capture the grid coordinate for the first point, as shown in Figure 14-48. This gives the position of 147x and 430y.

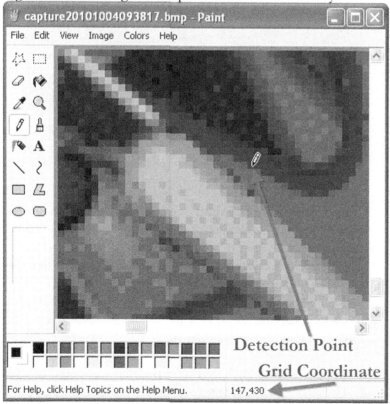

Figure 14-48 | Capture Grid Coordinates For Detection Point

Again, to keep things simple for the example, place all the detection points along the horizontal line with detection point's eight pixels apart. Now create the detection points list. With the detection points on a horizontal line, this means the 430y will be constant. Simply add an additional eight to each of the x coordinate until reaching the right side of the detection zone.

Detection Points List
- 147x, 430y
- 155x, 430y
- 163x, 430y
- 171x, 430y
- 179x, 430y
- 187x, 430y
- 195x, 430y
- 203x, 430y
- 211x, 430y
- 219x, 430y

The visual representation of the detection point list can be seen in Figure 14-49.

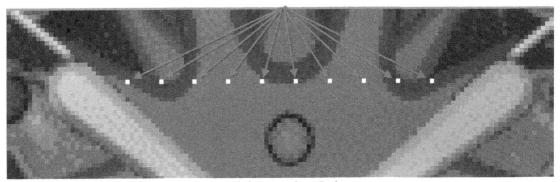

Figure 14-49 | Visual Representation Of Detection Points

The programming logic behind the detection is that once there is positive detection, the Bot will act accordingly and stop any future detection. To accomplish that in programming logic, use If, Else If, Else If layout. This will stop any further detection after the first positive detection, and help to prevent a false positive detection. A false positive might occur like this: A detection causes the left flipper to fire. The movement of the left flipper passes through the detection grid, which again fires the left flipper, and which results in the left flipper getting stuck in the up position. There will still be issues such as this when reducing the Timer1 Interval property, but the above approach should help minimize it.

The next step is to determine which flipper to fire at each detection point. Both could be fired, but I think that is less then optimal. The ball bounces around and could increase false positives.

Start with the paddle firing examples below, shown in Figure 14-50. Try to optimize these detection points later for practice.

147x, 430y	Left Paddle		187x, 430y	Both Paddles
155x, 430y	Left Paddle		195x, 430y	Right Paddle
163x, 430y	Left Paddle		203x, 430y	Right Paddle
171x, 430y	Left Paddle		211x, 430y	Right Paddle
179x, 430y	Both Paddles		219x, 430y	Right Paddle

Figure 14-50 | Detection Points List

When detecting for the plunger, determine the value of a pixel with the ball present. Alternatively, you could have determined the color of a pixel when the ball is not present, then check to see if the value is not that color to pull the plunger. In that case it is really a matter of preference on how to do the detection. Note: When doing detections for the flippers you do not know exactly where the ball will be. Therefore, get the color of the pixel without the ball, and then in the code check if that color has changed.

The Automation Tool Helper has been built to quickly help determine the pixel colors of when the ball is not present for the list of detection points. It is important to complete this step. Depending on your operating system and version on Pinball, these results may vary.

To use the Automation Tool Helper either enter in a bitmap name into the BMP Image field, or perform another screen capture using the Process Name pinball and have it auto-filled in.

Enter in the grid coordinates of each of the detection point individually to create a list with the pixel color for each detection pixel, as shown below in Figure 14-51.

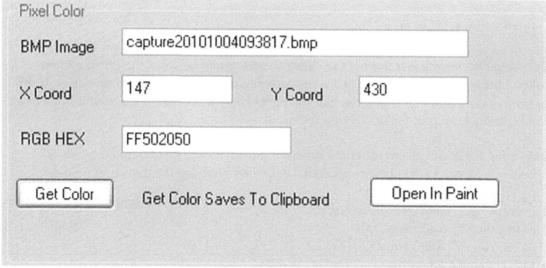

Figure 14-51 | Get RGB Hex Color For Detection Pixel

Complete that and update the Detection Points list to include the RGB Hex color as below.

- 147x, 430y   Left Paddle   FF502050
- 155x, 430y   Left Paddle   FF502050
- 163x, 430y   Left Paddle   FF604078
- 171x, 430y   Left Paddle   FF684884
- 179x, 430y   Both Paddles   FF684884
- 187x, 430y   Both Paddles   FF502050
- 195x, 430y   Right Paddle   FF684884
- 203x, 430y   Right Paddle   FF684884
- 211x, 430y   Right Paddle   FF382038
- 219x, 430y   Right Paddle   FF382038

Now refer back to the Player Controls, as in Figure 14-52. The default setting with left flipper is the letter Z, and the right flipper is the forward slash.

Figure 14-52 | 3-D Pinball: Player Controls

This Bot would be worthless if not for the ability to add timing between the down and up keystroke. This is because Pinball does not properly register a keystroke with no delay. If the delay is set to zero with the plunger, the ball will never launch. Timing is key to the Bot's basic usage and extremely helpful for optimizing the results.

The code using for keybd_event to send a Z keystrokewith a delay of 200 milliseconds is shown below in Figure 14-53. Insert this code later when verifying the detection points.

```
keybd_event(Keys.Z, MapVirtualKey(Keys.Z, 0), 0, 0)
 System.Threading.Thread.Sleep(200)
 keybd_event(Keys.Z, MapVirtualKey(Keys.Z, 0), 2, 0)
```

Figure 14-53| Send Z Keystroke To Fire Left Paddle

The right paddle uses the forward slash by default. Accessing the forward slash and back slash is a little counter intuitive since the MapVirtualKey is actually the character above it on the keyboard. Therefore, the forward slash is the question mark and the backslash is the pipe. In order to access the question mark or the pipe, use Keys.ShiftKey, as in Figure 8-46.

The code using keybd_event to send a / keystroke with a delay of 200 milliseconds, is shown in Figure 14-54. Insert this code later when verifying the detection points.

```
keybd_event(Keys.OemQuestion, MapVirtualKey(Keys.OemQuestion, 0), 0, 0)
System.Threading.Thread.Sleep(200)
keybd_event(Keys.OemQuestion, MapVirtualKey(Keys.OemQuestion, 0), 2, 0)
```

Figure 14-54| Send / Keystroke To Fire Right Paddle

To fire both paddles using the keybd_event and send a Z and / keystroke, use the code in Figure 14-55. Insert this code later when verifying the detection points.

```
keybd_event(Keys.OemQuestion, MapVirtualKey(Keys.OemQuestion, 0), 0, 0)
keybd_event(Keys.Z, MapVirtualKey(Keys.Z, 0), 0, 0)
System.Threading.Thread.Sleep(200)
keybd_event(Keys.Z, MapVirtualKey(Keys.Z, 0), 0, 0)
keybd_event(Keys.OemQuestion, MapVirtualKey(Keys.OemQuestion, 0), 2, 0)
```

Figure 14-55| Send Z and / Keystroke To Fire Both Paddles

The next step is to add code to determine the RGB Hex color of all of the detection points. Process detection points color right after the area where the ball color was determined, as shown in the example in Figure 14-56.

```
If (widthWindow = 606) Then
Dim ball As Color = screenCapture.GetPixel(326, 422)
Dim ballColor As String = Hex(ball.ToArgb)
' Add detection points color processing here
If (ballColor = "FFFFFFFF") Then
```

Figure 14-56| Send Z and / Keystroke To Fire Both Paddles

Continue to work left to right for the determination on the current color at the detection point. To determine the color at detection point located at 147x and 430y, use the code in Figure 14-55. When dealing with a lot of detection points it become helpful to include the grid coordinate in the name, as shown below in Figure 14-57.

```
Dim d147x430y As Color = screenCapture.GetPixel(147, 430)
Dim d147x430yColor As String = Hex(d147x430y.ToArgb)
```

Figure 14-57| Determine 147x and 430y Pixel Color

254

The completed list of coding the color determination for detection points, in Figure 14-58.

```
If (widthWindow = 606) Then
    Dim ball As Color = screenCapture.GetPixel(326, 422)
    Dim ballColor As String = Hex(ball.ToArgb)

    Dim d147x430y As Color = screenCapture.GetPixel(147, 430)
    Dim d147x430yColor As String = Hex(d147x430y.ToArgb)
    Dim d155x430y As Color = screenCapture.GetPixel(155, 430)
    Dim d155x430yColor As String = Hex(d155x430y.ToArgb)
    Dim d163x430y As Color = screenCapture.GetPixel(163, 430)
    Dim d163x430yColor As String = Hex(d163x430y.ToArgb)
    Dim d171x430y As Color = screenCapture.GetPixel(171, 430)
    Dim d171x430yColor As String = Hex(d171x430y.ToArgb)
    Dim d179x430y As Color = screenCapture.GetPixel(179, 430)
    Dim d179x430yColor As String = Hex(d179x430y.ToArgb)
    Dim d187x430y As Color = screenCapture.GetPixel(187, 430)
    Dim d187x430yColor As String = Hex(d187x430y.ToArgb)
    Dim d195x430y As Color = screenCapture.GetPixel(195, 430)
    Dim d195x430yColor As String = Hex(d195x430y.ToArgb)
    Dim d203x430y As Color = screenCapture.GetPixel(203, 430)
    Dim d203x430yColor As String = Hex(d203x430y.ToArgb)
    Dim d211x430y As Color = screenCapture.GetPixel(211, 430)
    Dim d211x430yColor As String = Hex(d211x430y.ToArgb)
    Dim d219x430y As Color = screenCapture.GetPixel(219, 430)
    Dim d219x430yColor As String = Hex(d219x430y.ToArgb)

    If (ballColor = "FFFFFFFF") Then
```

Figure 14-58 | Complete List Of Determined Pixel Current Color

Now check to see if the ball has passed over one of the detection points. Do that by adding Else If statement after checking the ballColor, as in Figure 14-59.

```
If (ballColor = "FFFFFFFF") Then
    keybd_event(Keys.Space, MapVirtualKey(Keys.Space, 0), 0, 0)
    System.Threading.Thread.Sleep(2000)
    keybd_event(Keys.Space, MapVirtualKey(Keys.Space, 0), 2, 0)
ElseIf (d147x430yColor <> "FF502050") Then
    keybd_event(Keys.Z, MapVirtualKey(Keys.Z, 0), 0, 0)
    System.Threading.Thread.Sleep(200)
    keybd_event(Keys.Z, MapVirtualKey(Keys.Z, 0), 2, 0)
End If
```

Figure 14-59 | Check If Current Color Is Not A Match To Detection Point Color Without Ball

The ElseIf code broken down line by line:

C: ElseIf (d147x430yColor <> "FF502050") Then
D: Check if the current color of the pixel is not the same as the previously record color of the pixel when the ball was not present. The symbol <> represents the logical comparison of IS NOT. If the color matches you proceed to the next Else If or End If statement. If the color does not match you execute the code block to fire the appropriate flipper or flippers.

C: keybd_event(Keys.Z, MapVirtualKey(Keys.Z, 0), 0, 0)
D: Fire the left flipper to the up position

C: System.Threading.Thread.Sleep(200)
D: Hold the left flipper in the up position for 200 milliseconds

C: keybd_event(Keys.Z, MapVirtualKey(Keys.Z, 0), 2, 0)
D: Release the Z key and allow the flipper to return to its resting state

C: End If or possibly another Else If
D: After finishing the above code block you exit the series of If, Else If, Else If … statements. This helps prevent any false positives.

Complete the coding to check the remaining detection pixels and fire the appropriate paddle or paddles, as in Figure 14-60. Please take your time to make sure you have the proper values for your system.

```
If (ballColor = "FFFFFFFF") Then
    keybd_event(Keys.Space, MapVirtualKey(Keys.Space, 0), 0, 0)
    System.Threading.Thread.Sleep(2000)
    keybd_event(Keys.Space, MapVirtualKey(Keys.Space, 0), 2, 0)
ElseIf (d147x430yColor <> "FF502050") Then
    keybd_event(Keys.Z, MapVirtualKey(Keys.Z, 0), 0, 0)
    System.Threading.Thread.Sleep(200)
    keybd_event(Keys.Z, MapVirtualKey(Keys.Z, 0), 2, 0)
ElseIf (d155x430yColor <> "FF502050") Then
    keybd_event(Keys.Z, MapVirtualKey(Keys.Z, 0), 0, 0)
    System.Threading.Thread.Sleep(200)
    keybd_event(Keys.Z, MapVirtualKey(Keys.Z, 0), 2, 0)
ElseIf (d163x430yColor <> "FF604078") Then
    keybd_event(Keys.Z, MapVirtualKey(Keys.Z, 0), 0, 0)
    System.Threading.Thread.Sleep(200)
    keybd_event(Keys.Z, MapVirtualKey(Keys.Z, 0), 2, 0)
ElseIf (d171x430yColor <> "FF684884") Then
    keybd_event(Keys.Z, MapVirtualKey(Keys.Z, 0), 0, 0)
    System.Threading.Thread.Sleep(200)
```

```
    keybd_event(Keys.Z, MapVirtualKey(Keys.Z, 0), 2, 0)
ElseIf (d179x430yColor <> "FF684884") Then
    keybd_event(Keys.Z, MapVirtualKey(Keys.Z, 0), 0, 0)
    System.Threading.Thread.Sleep(200)
    keybd_event(Keys.Z, MapVirtualKey(Keys.Z, 0), 2, 0)
ElseIf (d187x430yColor <> "FF502050") Then
    keybd_event(Keys.Z, MapVirtualKey(Keys.Z, 0), 0, 0)
    System.Threading.Thread.Sleep(200)
    keybd_event(Keys.Z, MapVirtualKey(Keys.Z, 0), 2, 0)
ElseIf (d195x430yColor <> "FF684884") Then
    keybd_event(Keys.Z, MapVirtualKey(Keys.Z, 0), 0, 0)
    System.Threading.Thread.Sleep(200)
    keybd_event(Keys.Z, MapVirtualKey(Keys.Z, 0), 2, 0)
ElseIf (d203x430yColor <> "FF684884") Then
    keybd_event(Keys.Z, MapVirtualKey(Keys.Z, 0), 0, 0)
    System.Threading.Thread.Sleep(200)
    keybd_event(Keys.Z, MapVirtualKey(Keys.Z, 0), 2, 0)
ElseIf (d211x430yColor <> "FF382038") Then
    keybd_event(Keys.Z, MapVirtualKey(Keys.Z, 0), 0, 0)
    System.Threading.Thread.Sleep(200)
    keybd_event(Keys.Z, MapVirtualKey(Keys.Z, 0), 2, 0)
ElseIf (d219x430yColor <> "FF382038") Then
    keybd_event(Keys.Z, MapVirtualKey(Keys.Z, 0), 0, 0)
    System.Threading.Thread.Sleep(200)
    keybd_event(Keys.Z, MapVirtualKey(Keys.Z, 0), 2, 0)
End If
```

Figure 14-60 | Detection Pixel Check With Paddle Firing

Now test what you have. Make sure 3D Pinball for Windows is started with a new game by pressing *F2*. To ensure a high score clear the High Scores by clicking on *Game -> High Scores*, as shown below in the example of Figure 14-61.

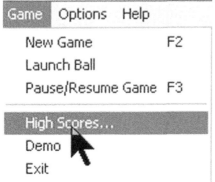

Figure 14-61 | Game -> High Scores

Click on the *Clear* button, as in Figure 14-62, and finally click *OK*, as in Figure 14-63. Now click the *Save All* button. Click either *Start Debugging*, or (*F5*).

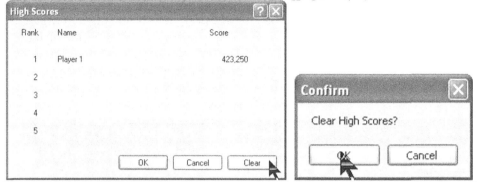

Figure 14-62 | Click On Clear Button   Figure 14-63 | Ok Confirm Clear High Scores

Press the *Play* button and let it play one complete game. When the High Scores window pops up, hold down the *ALT* button to terminate the Bot automation. Since the Bot is still processing, it will make it difficult to enter in a High Score. The pop-up window of the High Scores gives a great opportunity to deal with pop-up windows in a game or application. There are four important things that happen when the High Scores window pops up. The first is that just before the High Scores window pops up the ball count goes blanks. The blank ball count indicates the game is over. The second is that if the new score is greater than any of the top five scores, then the High Score window pops up. The third is the child window's title name is High Scores. And finally the player name is highlighted by default, as shown in the example in Figure 14-64, below.

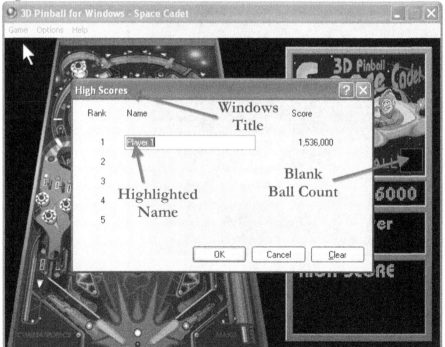

Figure 14-64 | Detailed Analysis Of High Score Pop-up Window

258

Upgrading To Enter High Score

The next task is to automate the handling on the High Scores pop-up and starting a new game for indefinite game play. There needs to be a way to determine when the ball count is blank. It takes a little work, but acquire four different screen shots to determine a pixel that is "on" with ball 1, 2, and 3, but "off" when blank. When comparing the ball count images side by side, notice that their base and top are at the same height, as in Figure 14-65. Any pixel near the bottom center should work.

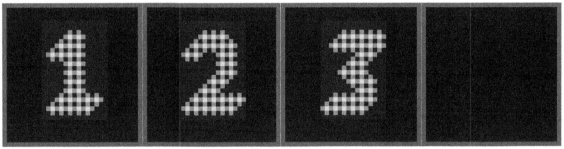

Figure 14-65 | Ball Count Snap Shot

The second to the bottom row rotates between two blue colors while the bottom rotates between blue and black. So, it seems best to pick a pixel in second row from the bottom, at a place near the center. That gives a grid coordinate of 561x and 220y, as in Figure 14-66.

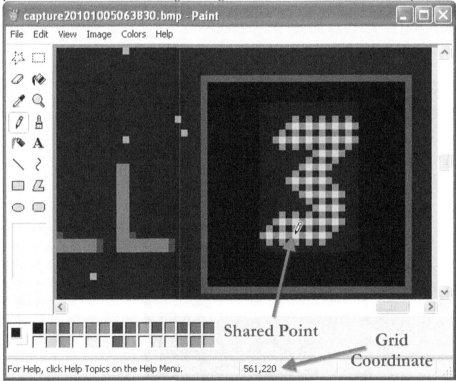

Figure 14-66 | Determine A Pixel Shared By Ball 1, 2, And 3

Confirm the color at 561x and 220y with a ball count of one, two, three, and blank. Shown below is a bitmap image that captured a screenshot with the ball count of three, and the grid coordinate **561**x and **220**y into the Automation Tool Helper to get the color for that pixel. This is shown in Figure 14-67, below.

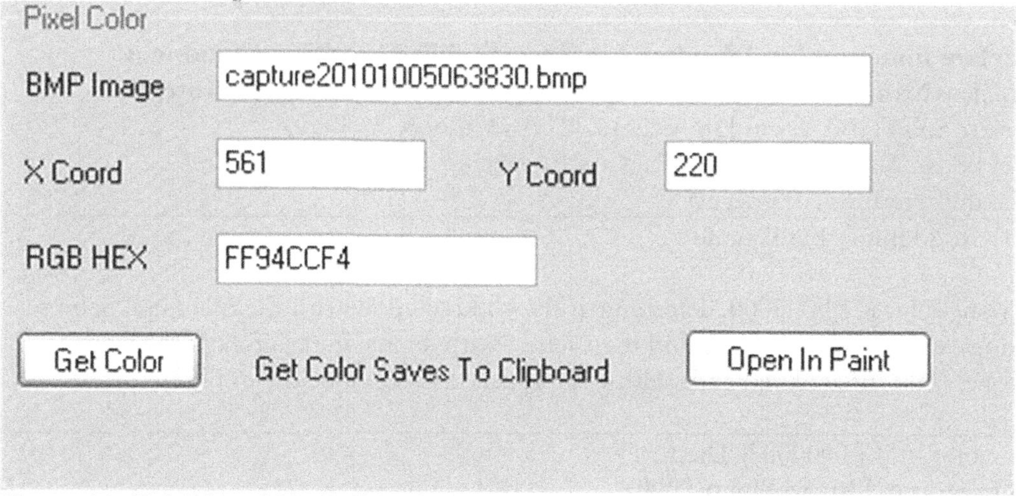

Figure 14-67 | 561x, 220y Ball 3 Pixel Color

Continue to do the same for Ball 1, 2, and blank to create a list as follows:

- Ball 1 (561x, 220y)   FF7858DC
- Ball 2 (561x, 220y)   FF94CCF4
- Ball 3 (561x, 220y)   FF94CCF4
- Blank (561x, 220y)   FF000000

The results show that using pixel 561x and 220y can determine if there are balls still in play, or if the game is over.

The first step in checking for the high score will be to determine if the pixel 561x and 220y has the value FF000000. The next question is: Where to put the check in the If ElseIf Elseif ... statement? Since this indicates the game is over, there is no reason to perform any of the other checks. The example is shown below in Figure 14-68.

```
Dim d219x430y As Color = screenCapture.GetPixel(219, 430)
Dim d219x430yColor As String = Hex(d219x430y.ToArgb)
Dim ballCount As Color = screenCapture.GetPixel(561, 220)
Dim ballCountColor As String = Hex(ballCount.ToArgb)
If (ballCountColor = "FF000000") Then

ElseIf (ballColor = "FFFFFFFF") Then
    keybd_event(Keys.Space, MapVirtualKey(Keys.Space, 0), 0, 0)
    System.Threading.Thread.Sleep(2000)
    keybd_event(Keys.Space, MapVirtualKey(Keys.Space, 0), 2, 0)
```

Figure 14-68| Add Check For Ball Count

To uniquely identify the child window High Scores you will use the library FindWindow. Add the library FindWindow directly under Public Class Form1, as in Figure 14-69.

```
Public Class Form1

  Private Declare Function FindWindow Lib "user32.dll" Alias "FindWindowA" _
    (ByVal lpClassName As String, ByVal lpWindowName As String) As Integer
  Private Declare Sub keybd_event Lib "user32.dll" (ByVal bVk As Byte, _
      ByVal bScan As Byte, ByVal dwFlags As Integer, _
      ByVal dwExtraInfo As Integer)
```

Figure 14-69 | Add Library FindWindow

If the Ball Count color is FF000000, determine if the child window with the title High Scores exists. If it does, ensure focus is on it, and then send yourpersonal initials followed by an Enter keystroke. Add the updated code with your initials, as shown below in Figure 14-70.

```
If (ballCountColor = "FF000000") Then
   System.Threading.Thread.Sleep(5000)
   Dim windowHandle As Integer
   windowHandle = FindWindow(vbNullString, "High Scores")
   If windowHandle <> 0 Then
     SetForegroundWindow(windowHandle)
     keybd_event(Keys.S, MapVirtualKey(Keys.S, 0), 0, 0)
     System.Threading.Thread.Sleep(100)
     keybd_event(Keys.S, MapVirtualKey(Keys.S, 0), 2, 0)
     System.Threading.Thread.Sleep(100)
     keybd_event(Keys.C, MapVirtualKey(Keys.C, 0), 0, 0)
     System.Threading.Thread.Sleep(100)
     keybd_event(Keys.C, MapVirtualKey(Keys.C, 0), 2, 0)
     System.Threading.Thread.Sleep(100)
     keybd_event(Keys.M, MapVirtualKey(Keys.M, 0), 0, 0)
     System.Threading.Thread.Sleep(100)
     keybd_event(Keys.M, MapVirtualKey(Keys.M, 0), 2, 0)
     System.Threading.Thread.Sleep(100)
     keybd_event(Keys.Enter, MapVirtualKey(Keys.Enter, 0), 0, 0)
     System.Threading.Thread.Sleep(100)
     keybd_event(Keys.Enter, MapVirtualKey(Keys.Enter, 0), 2, 0)
   End If
ElseIf (ballColor = "FFFFFFFF") Then
```

Figure 14-70 | Check For High Score Window And Enter Initials Followed By Enter Key

The inside ballCountColor check code block broken down line by line:

C: System.Threading.Thread.Sleep(5000)
D: Allow the High Score window time to pop-up

C: Dim windowHandle As Integer
   windowHandle = FindWindow(vbNullString, "High Scores")
D: Get handle to child window with title High Score

C: If windowHandle <> 0 Then
D: See if a window with the title High Score exists

C: SetForegroundWindow(windowHandle)
D: Ensure focus is set on window with windowHandle

```
C:    keybd_event(Keys.S, MapVirtualKey(Keys.S, 0), 0, 0)
      System.Threading.Thread.Sleep(100)
      keybd_event(Keys.S, MapVirtualKey(Keys.S, 0), 2, 0)
      System.Threading.Thread.Sleep(100)
      keybd_event(Keys.C, MapVirtualKey(Keys.C, 0), 0, 0)
      System.Threading.Thread.Sleep(100)
      keybd_event(Keys.C, MapVirtualKey(Keys.C, 0), 2, 0)
      System.Threading.Thread.Sleep(100)
      keybd_event(Keys.M, MapVirtualKey(Keys.M, 0), 0, 0)
      System.Threading.Thread.Sleep(100)
      keybd_event(Keys.M, MapVirtualKey(Keys.M, 0), 2, 0)
      System.Threading.Thread.Sleep(100)
      keybd_event(Keys.Enter, MapVirtualKey(Keys.Enter, 0), 0, 0)
      System.Threading.Thread.Sleep(100)
      keybd_event(Keys.Enter, MapVirtualKey(Keys.Enter, 0), 2, 0)
```
D: Send initials followed by Enter keystroke

C: End If
D: Terminate End If code block

Now test what you have. Make sure 3D Pinball for Windows is started with a new game by pressing *F2*. To ensure a high score, clear the High Scores by clicking on *Game -> High Scores*. Then click on the *Clear* button and finally click *OK*. Now click the *Save All* button. Click either *Start Debugging*, or (*F5*) and press *Play* on pixelRecognitionBot.

262

After a game has completed it should pause five seconds before typing in your personal initials and hitting Enter, as in Figure 14-71.

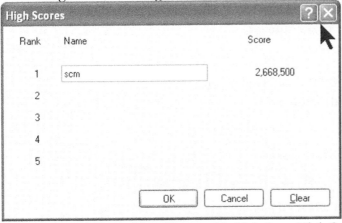

Figure 14-71 | Enter Your Personal Initials Into High Scores Window

Continuously Start New Game For Indefinite Testing Periods

It can be helpful to allow an automation Bot to run in an indefinite loop in order to help catch those bugs that only pop up at random time periods. This is the perfect type of Bot to start before leaving work at the end of the day.

It is time to restart a new game when the ballCountColor is equal to FF000000. The code is already in place to check if ballCountColor is equal to FF000000, but first, make sure the High Scores window does not exist. To do that place the restart code in an else code block after checking for if High Score window exists, as in Figure 14-72.

```
If (ballCountColor = "FF000000") Then
    System.Threading.Thread.Sleep(5000)
    Dim windowHandle As Integer
    windowHandle = FindWindow(vbNullString, "High Scores")
    If windowHandle <> 0 Then
        SetForegroundWindow(windowHandle)
        keybd_event(Keys.S, MapVirtualKey(Keys.S, 0), 0, 0)
        System.Threading.Thread.Sleep(100)
        keybd_event(Keys.S, MapVirtualKey(Keys.S, 0), 2, 0)
        System.Threading.Thread.Sleep(100)
        keybd_event(Keys.C, MapVirtualKey(Keys.C, 0), 0, 0)
        System.Threading.Thread.Sleep(100)
        keybd_event(Keys.C, MapVirtualKey(Keys.C, 0), 2, 0)
        System.Threading.Thread.Sleep(100)
        keybd_event(Keys.M, MapVirtualKey(Keys.M, 0), 0, 0)
        System.Threading.Thread.Sleep(100)
```

```
        keybd_event(Keys.M, MapVirtualKey(Keys.M, 0), 2, 0)
        System.Threading.Thread.Sleep(100)
        keybd_event(Keys.Enter, MapVirtualKey(Keys.Enter, 0), 0, 0)
        System.Threading.Thread.Sleep(100)
        keybd_event(Keys.Enter, MapVirtualKey(Keys.Enter, 0), 2, 0)
      Else
        'Start New Game
        keybd_event(Keys.F2, MapVirtualKey(Keys.F2, 0), 0, 0)
        System.Threading.Thread.Sleep(100)
        keybd_event(Keys.F2, MapVirtualKey(Keys.F2, 0), 2, 0)
      End If
ElseIf (ballColor = "FFFFFFFF") Then
```

Figure 14-72 | Continuously Restart Game After Game Completes

Now test what you have. Make sure 3D Pinball for Windows is started with a new game by pressing *F2*. Now click the *Save All* button. Click either *Start Debugging*, or (*F5*) and press *Play*. After a game has finished it should pause five seconds and enter initials if High Score then restart a new game.

When time allows, let the Bot to play overnight in order to see how high the scores can get, as I did in the example in Figure 14-73, below.

Figure 14-73 | High Score List

Summary

The ability to do pixel recognition is important when creating intelligent bots for Windows games. Sometimes pixel recognition might require more than one pixel to make a determination, and it that case **AND** both pixels together in the code, as in Figure 14-74.

```
If (pixel1Color = "FF000000" AND pixel2Color = "FF010204") Then
  ' Do Code
End If
```

Figure 14-74| Check For Multiple Pixels

Chapter 15:
Leveling Up By Moving Characters In Games

Game testers can spend an immense amount of time just reaching levels. Some software companies opt to code in short cuts or cheat codes as a means to speed up testing, but that practices always seems to undermine the game play when released. Automation Bots can assist in the tester's daily grind and also free up their time to focus more on specific testing, rather then just having to repeat the same test over and over.

Creating A Game Level Bot

You will be testing the Flash game Hero's Arms developed by Berzerk Studio in 2009, hosted on the site MaxGames.com. Use the Mozilla Firefox web browser on which to play the game. Hero's Arms is a good old fashion Zelda-like adventure game and will work well to show Bot automation to create character movement.

Hero's Arms Instructions:
- Press W, A, S, D Keys To Move Around
- Press The N Key To Attack
- Press The M Key to Perform A Magical Attack
- Press Space Bar To Bring Up The Inventory
--- OR ---
- Press The Directional Arrow Keys To Move Around
- Press The Z Key To Attack
- Press The x Key To Perform A Magical Attack
- Press Space bar To Bring Up The Inventory

Create two different buttons to demonstrate character movement and action:
- Rectangle Pattern
- Board Transition

Setting Up The Project

Start a new project and select *Windows Form Application* and name it: **gameLevelBot**, as in the example shown in Figure 15-1.

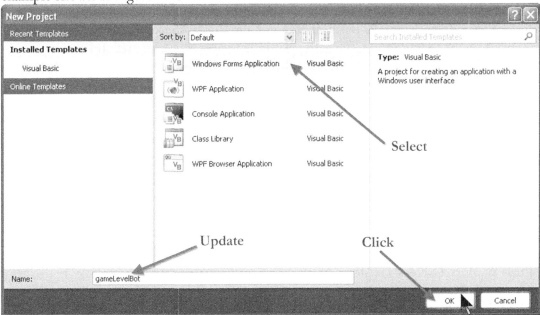

Figure 15-1 | Creating New gameLevelBot

Now click the *Save All* button, as in the below Figure 15-2.

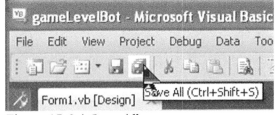

Figure 15-2 | Save All

Click *Save* to create directory structure for project, as in Figure 15-3.

Save Project		
Name:	gameLevelBot	
Location:	C:\Documents and Settings\Steven Miller\my documents\visual studio 2010\Projects	Browse...
Solution Name:	gameLevelBot	☑ Create directory for solution

Figure 15-3| Saving And Creating Directory For Project

Laying Out The Form

Two buttons are required for the Pixel Recognition Bot. Click on *Toolbox* and drag two *buttons* onto the form. Resize the form, as shown in Figure 15-4, below.

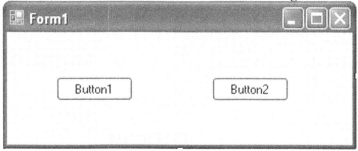

Figure 15-4 | Add Two Buttons To Form

Select *Button1*, as in Figure 15-5. Update Button1 Text Properties to **Rectangle Pattern** and the (Name) property to **rectanglePattern**, as in Figure 15-6 and Figure 15-7.

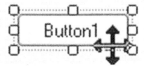

Figure 15-5 | Select Button1

Text	**Rectangle Pattern**

Figure 15-6 | Text Property

(Name)	**rectanglePattern**

Figure 15-7| (Name) Property

Now select *Button2*, as in Figure 15-8. Update Button2 Text Properties to **Board Transition** and the (Name) property to **boardTransition**, as in Figure 15-9 and 15-10.

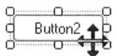

Figure 15-8 | Select Button2

Text	**Board Transition**

Figure 15-9 | Text Property

(Name)	**boardTransition**

Figure 15-10| (Name) Property

Click on the *Toolbox* and drag two *timers* onto the form, as in Figure 15-11. The default of 100 milliseconds will be fine.

Figure 15-11 | Add Timer To Form

Select *Timer1*, as in Figure 15-12. Then update the Timer1 (Name) property to **rectangleTimer**, as in Figure 15-13.

Figure 15-12 | Select Timer1   Figure 15-13 | Update (Name) Property

Select *Timer1*, as in Figure 15-14. Update the Timer1 (Name) property to **transitionTimer**, as in Figure 15-15.

Figure 15-14 | Select Timer2   Figure 15-15 | Update (Name) Property

Update the form title to Game Level Bot by clicking on the *form* anyplace there is no button. Select the *Properties* tab and update the Text property to **Game Level Bot**, as in Figure 15-16.

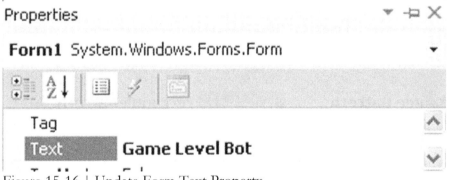

Figure 15-16 | Update Form Text Property

Next, determine a standard web browser size for the game. This is extremely important since pixel recognition will determine courses of action. Note: It is very important not to use the scroll bars since any move will completely change the pixel recognition.

Start Mozilla Firefox and open up the URL

http://www.maxgames.com/play/heros-arms.html

Click on the *Play* button on the flash game, as in Figure 15-17.

Figure 15-17 | Click Play To Begin

Now resize the web browser by clicking on the *lower right hand corner* and dragging it so the whole Flash game screen is visible, as shown in Figure 15-18.

Figure 15-18 | Resize Web Browser For Flash Game To Fit

Now determine the process name for Firefox by starting Windows Task Manager and holding down CTRL+ALT+DEL, selecting Firefox and right mouse clicking, and then choosing **Go To Process**, as in Figure 15-19. Determine the process name to be **firefox** from the highlighted Image Name and simply remove the .exe, as in Figure 15-20.

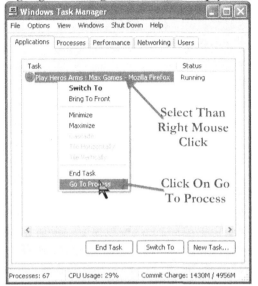

Figure 15-19 | Select Firefox And Go To Process   Figure 15-20 | firefox Process Name

Make sure only one window of Firefox web browser is running with the Flash game Hero's Arms.   Start the Automation Tool Helper and enter the Process Name firefox. Read the Height and Width for the Id with Play Heros Arms: Max Game – Mozilla Firefox, as shown below in the example in Figure 15-21. Your Height and Width may be different, but just make sure the whole Flash game screen in the Firefox web browser is visible. My Height is **1061** pixels and the Width is **785** pixels.

Figure 15-21 | Firefox Height And Width to Show Hero's Arms Game Screen

The next step is the hard part. Yep-you need to play the game a little to understand what you are trying to automate with a Bot. Click *Start* and then click *CREATE PLAYER* and enter a name and then click on the *fist*, as in Figure 15-22, Figure 15-23, and Figure 15-24.

Figure 15-22 | Click START

Figure 15-23 | Click CREATE PLAYER

Figure 15-24 | Enter Name And Click On Fist

Your player will then be created and you can click on the *player* to start the game, as shown below in Figure 15-25.

Figure 15-25 | Click On Player To Start

Watch or Skip the introduction, then review the Controls, as in Figure 15-26.

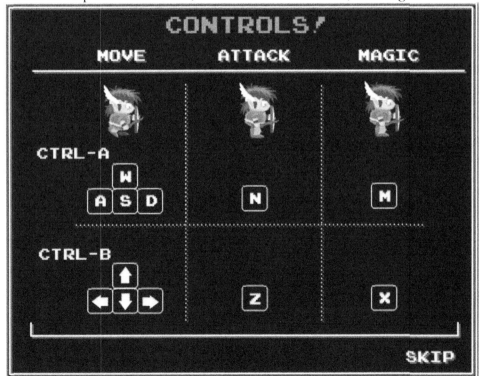

Figure 15-26 | Hero's Arms Controls

The two statues provide life and magic regeneration, shown in Figure 15-27.

Figure 15-27 | Life And Magic Regeneration

Now move to the left and up to pass through the fence gate, as in Figure 15-28.

Figure 15-28 | Pass Through Fence Gate

274

Move up past the tree, and up to the left near the stump, as in Figure 15-29. It is this area in which you will implement a rectangle pattern for the character to gain experience. Patterns are most effective when the enemy automatically moves towards the character to attack. The bugs in this game do not do that, but this still works as a great training ground for adding this type of code.

Figure 15-29 | Area For Rectangle Pattern

Now move your character up until he runs into the trees and the move him to the left into the clearing, as in Figure 15-30.

Figure 15-30 | Up To Tree Then Left To Clearing

The next area is a board transition area. Move your character up until it transitions into the next board and the mouse approaches, as in Figure 15-31.

Figure 15-31 | Transition Into Next Board With Mouse

The benefit of a transition is when the enemies automatically responds each time you transition into that area. Use the clearing in the forest with the mouse for the board transition area.

Coding The Project

The Rectangle Pattern button will move the character:
- Left six seconds
- Up twelve seconds
- Right six seconds
- Down twelve seconds

During the movement, attack once every 200 milliseconds.

Double-click on the *Rectangle Pattern* button, as in Figure 15-32, to create the pattern_Click subroutine, and also to edit the code for the Rectangle button, as in figure 15-33.

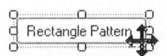

Figure 15-32 | Double Click Rectangle Pattern Button

```
Private Sub rectanglePattern_Click(ByVal sender As System.Object,_
    ByVal e As System.EventArgs) Handles rectanglePattern.Click

End Sub
```

Figure 15_33| rectanglePattern_Click Subroutine Created

Simply start rectangleTimer inside the subroutine rectanglepattern_Click by adding the code, as shown below in the example in Figure 15-34.

```
Private Sub rectanglePattern_Click(ByVal sender As System.Object, _
    ByVal e As System.EventArgs) Handles rectanglePattern.Click

    rectangleTimer.Start()

End Sub
```

Figure 15-34| Add Code To Start rectangleTimer

Return to the View Designer by clicking on the *Form Design* tab, as in Figure 15-35.

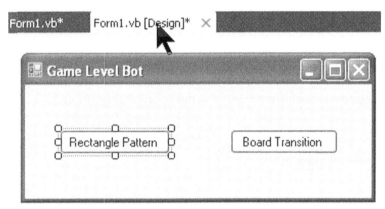

Figure 15-35 | Enter View Design

Double-click on the *rectangle Timer* button, as in Figure 15-36, to create the rectangle Timer_Tick subroutine, and also to edit the code for the rectangle Timer button, as in Figure 15-37.

Figure 15-36 | Double Click rectangleTimer

```
Private Sub rectangleTimer_Tick(ByVal sender As System.Object, _
    ByVal e As System.EventArgs) Handles rectangleTimer.Tick

End Sub
```

Figure 15-37| rectangleTimer_Tick Subroutine Created

The next step is to ensure focus is set on Firefox and sending keystrokes with timing. To do that, first add the libraries keybd_event, MapVirtualKey, SetForegroundWindow, and SetWindowPos and the constant SWP_NOMOVE just below Public Class Form1, as shown below in the example in Figure 15-38.

```
Public Class Form1
Private Declare Sub keybd_event Lib "user32.dll" (ByVal bVk As Byte, _
    ByVal bScan As Byte, ByVal dwFlags As Integer, _
    ByVal dwExtraInfo As Integer)

Private Declare Function MapVirtualKey Lib "user32" Alias "MapVirtualKeyA" _
    (ByVal wCode As Integer, ByVal wMapType As Integer) As Integer

Private Declare Function SetForegroundWindow Lib "user32" _
    (ByVal handle As IntPtr) As Integer

Public Declare Function SetWindowPos Lib "user32" Alias _
    "SetWindowPos" (ByVal hwnd As IntPtr, _
      ByVal hWndInsertAfter As IntPtr, ByVal x As Integer, _
      ByVal y As Integer, ByVal cx As Integer, _
      ByVal cy As Integer, ByVal wFlags As Integer) As Integer

Public Const SWP_NOMOVE = &H2
```

Figure 15-38| Add Libraries And Constant

Now set the focus on the Firefox web browser by adding code to the rectangleTimer subroutine, as shown in Figure 15-39.

```
Private Sub rectangleTimer_Tick(ByVal sender As System.Object, _
    ByVal e As System.EventArgs) Handles rectangleTimer.Tick

    Dim ps() As Process = Process.GetProcessesByName("firefox")
    If ps.Length > 0 Then
      Dim p As Process = ps(0)
      Dim hWnd As IntPtr = p.MainWindowHandle
      SetForegroundWindow(hWnd)
    End If
End Sub
```

Figure 15-39|Set Focus On Firefox Web Browser

278

NOTE: IMPORTANT THAT YOU USE THE CTRL KEY! There is a bug which, if the ALT key and any arrow direction are used, the player gets stuck walking in that direction.

Inside rectangleTimer you need to add the ability to exit rectangleTimer when the CTRL key is held down, as in Figure 15-40.

```
rectangleTimer.Stop()
Dim ps() As Process = Process.GetProcessesByName("firefox")
If ps.Length > 0 Then
   Dim p As Process = ps(0)
   Dim hWnd As IntPtr = p.MainWindowHandle
   SetForegroundWindow(hWnd)
   If (My.Computer.Keyboard.CtrlKeyDown) Then
      ' Do Not Start
   Else
      rectangleTimer.Start()
   End If
End If
```

Figure 15-40 | Exit rectangleTimer Code

The next step is to make sure the Firefox Web Browser is the specific size required before doing any pixel recognition. Add SetWindowPos with your specific width and height to ensure the full Flash game screen can be seen. My width was 785 and height was 1061. Add a 50 millisecond delay to allow the resize to settle down, as shown below in Figure 15-41.

```
rectangleTimer.Stop()
Dim ps() As Process = Process.GetProcessesByName("firefox")
If ps.Length > 0 Then
   Dim p As Process = ps(0)
   Dim hWnd As IntPtr = p.MainWindowHandle
   SetForegroundWindow(hWnd)
   SetWindowPos(hWnd, IntPtr.Zero, 0, 0, _
    785, 1061, SWP_NOMOVE)
   System.Threading.Thread.Sleep(50)
   If (My.Computer.Keyboard.CtrlKeyDown) Then
      ' Do Not Start
   Else
      rectangleTimer.Start()
   End If
End If
```

Figure 15-41 | ForceFirefox Web Browser Size

Now test what you have. Make sure Firefox is running with Heros Arms. Click the *Save All* button. Click either *Start Debugging,* or (*F5*). Clicking on the *Rectangle Pattern* button will resize Firefox to the size your specified to show the whole game. Attempt to resize Firefox again by hand. The Bot should keep resizing it. When done, hold down the CTRL key to terminate the rectangleTimer. Close the gameLevelBot and return to View Code.

The next step is to have the character walk in a rectangular patter while attacking every 200 milliseconds. I am going to use the arrow keys to move the character and the Z key to attack. Add the following code to move the character using the arrow keys and attack using the Z key, as shown below in the example in Figure 15-42.

```
If ps.Length > 0 Then
  Dim p As Process = ps(0)
  Dim hWnd As IntPtr = p.MainWindowHandle
  SetForegroundWindow(hWnd)
  SetWindowPos(hWnd, IntPtr.Zero, 0, 0, _
  785, 1061, SWP_NOMOVE)
  System.Threading.Thread.Sleep(50)
  ' Move Left Three Seconds
  keybd_event(Keys.Left, MapVirtualKey(Keys.Left, 0), 0, 0)
  For index = 1 To 30 Step 1
    keybd_event(Keys.Z, MapVirtualKey(Keys.Z, 0), 0, 0)
    System.Threading.Thread.Sleep(50)
    keybd_event(Keys.Z, MapVirtualKey(Keys.Z, 0), 2, 0)
    System.Threading.Thread.Sleep(150)
  Next
  keybd_event(Keys.Left, MapVirtualKey(Keys.Left, 0), 2, 0)
  ' Move Up Six Seconds
  keybd_event(Keys.Up, MapVirtualKey(Keys.Up, 0), 0, 0)
  For index = 1 To 60 Step 1
    keybd_event(Keys.Z, MapVirtualKey(Keys.Z, 0), 0, 0)
    System.Threading.Thread.Sleep(50)
    keybd_event(Keys.Z, MapVirtualKey(Keys.Z, 0), 2, 0)
    System.Threading.Thread.Sleep(150)
  Next
  keybd_event(Keys.Up, MapVirtualKey(Keys.Up, 0), 2, 0)
  ' Move Right Three Seconds
  keybd_event(Keys.Right, MapVirtualKey(Keys.Right, 0), 0, 0)
  For index = 1 To 30 Step 1
    keybd_event(Keys.Z, MapVirtualKey(Keys.Z, 0), 0, 0)
    System.Threading.Thread.Sleep(50)
    keybd_event(Keys.Z, MapVirtualKey(Keys.Z, 0), 2, 0)
    System.Threading.Thread.Sleep(150)
  Next
  keybd_event(Keys.Right, MapVirtualKey(Keys.Right, 0), 2, 0)
```

280

```
' Move Down Six Seconds
keybd_event(Keys.Down, MapVirtualKey(Keys.Down, 0), 0, 0)
For index = 1 To 60 Step 1
    keybd_event(Keys.Z, MapVirtualKey(Keys.Z, 0), 0, 0)
    System.Threading.Thread.Sleep(50)
    keybd_event(Keys.Z, MapVirtualKey(Keys.Z, 0), 2, 0)
    System.Threading.Thread.Sleep(150)
Next
keybd_event(Keys.Down, MapVirtualKey(Keys.Down, 0), 2, 0)
If (My.Computer.Keyboard.CtrlKeyDown) Then
    ' Do Not Start
```

Figure 15-42 | Move Character In Rectangular Pattern

New code broken down line by line:

C: System.Threading.Thread.Sleep(50)
D: Need to allow system to settle down before sending keystroke. If the first keystroke is not working, increase this time.

C: keybd_event(Keys.Left, MapVirtualKey(Keys.Left, 0), 0, 0)
D: Press down left arrow key

C: For index = 1 To 30 Step 1
        keybd_event(Keys.Z, MapVirtualKey(Keys.Z, 0), 0, 0)
        System.Threading.Thread.Sleep(50)
        keybd_event(Keys.Z, MapVirtualKey(Keys.Z, 0), 2, 0)
        System.Threading.Thread.Sleep(150)
    Next
D: Loop 30 times to give a total of 30 times 200 milliseconds or six seconds. Press down the Z key for 50 milliseconds then release Z key and wait 150 milliseconds.

C: keybd_event(Keys.Left, MapVirtualKey(Keys.Left, 0), 2, 0)
D: Release the left arrow key

C: keybd_event(Keys.Up, MapVirtualKey(Keys.Up, 0), 0, 0)
D: Press down up arrow key

C: For index = 1 To 60 Step 1
        keybd_event(Keys.Z, MapVirtualKey(Keys.Z, 0), 0, 0)
        System.Threading.Thread.Sleep(50)
        keybd_event(Keys.Z, MapVirtualKey(Keys.Z, 0), 2, 0)
        System.Threading.Thread.Sleep(150)
    Next
D: Loop for a total of twelve seconds pressing down the Z key each time.

C: keybd_event(Keys.Up, MapVirtualKey(Keys.Up, 0), 2, 0)
D: Release the up arrow key

C: keybd_event(Keys.Right, MapVirtualKey(Keys.Right, 0), 0, 0)
D: Press right arrow key

```
C:   For index = 1 To 30 Step 1
        keybd_event(Keys.Z, MapVirtualKey(Keys.Z, 0), 0, 0)
        System.Threading.Thread.Sleep(50)
        keybd_event(Keys.Z, MapVirtualKey(Keys.Z, 0), 2, 0)
        System.Threading.Thread.Sleep(150)
     Next
```
D: Loop for a total of six seconds pressing down the Z key each time.

C: keybd_event(Keys.Right, MapVirtualKey(Keys.Right, 0), 2, 0)
D: Release the right arrow key
C: keybd_event(Keys.Down, MapVirtualKey(Keys.Down, 0), 0, 0)
D: Press down arrow key

```
C:   For index = 1 To 60 Step 1
        keybd_event(Keys.Z, MapVirtualKey(Keys.Z, 0), 0, 0)
        System.Threading.Thread.Sleep(50)
        keybd_event(Keys.Z, MapVirtualKey(Keys.Z, 0), 2, 0)
        System.Threading.Thread.Sleep(150)
     Next
```
D: Loop for a total of twelve seconds pressing down the Z key each time.

C: keybd_event(Keys.Down, MapVirtualKey(Keys.Down, 0), 2, 0)
D: Release the down arrow key

The code block shown above runs for 36 seconds. To terminate the Bot quickly, I suggest clicking on the Stop Debugging (**CTRL+ALT+BREAK***)* to terminate the Bot, as in Figure 15-43.

Figure 15-43 | Stop Debugging

Now test what you have. Make sure Firefox is running with Heros Arms. Move your character to just below the stump, north of the fence opening, as in Figure 15-44. Now click the *Save All* button. Click either *Start Debugging* ,or (*F5*) and click *Rectangle Pattern* button. The character should move and attack to the left for six seconds, then up for twelve seconds, right for six seconds and finally down for twelve seconds. Allow a couple of loops, then press Stop Debugging.

Figure 15-44 | Character Start Point

The last thing to do is to check if the character is almost dead. If the character is almost dead, terminate the rectangleTimer to help preserve his life until he can be manually returned for life regeneration. Open the Automation Tool Helper with the Hero's Arms game open in Firefox. Type **firefox** into the Process Name and click the button *Read Applications*. Then click on the ID "*Play Heros Arms: Max Games –Mozilla Firefox*" to perform a screen capture, as shown below in the example in Figure 15-45.

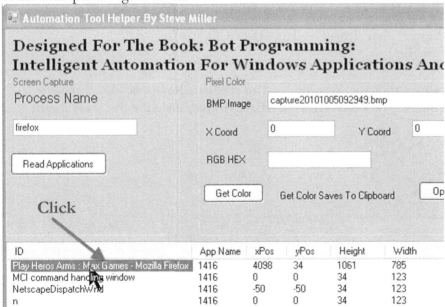

Figure 15-45 | Click On ID To Perform Screen Capture

283

With the screen capture bitmap preloaded into the BMP Image click on *Open In Paint* button and then custom zoom to 800 percent. Consider a drop below one bar of health almost dead. It is best to choose a pixel that is also surrounded by pixels of the same color, to allow for discrepancies when browsing. This is important since some website banners come in slightly different sizes and this could give false positives. Make sure to perform this on your specific computer. In Windows Paint I choose 372x and 501y as my pixel, as shown in Figure 15-46.

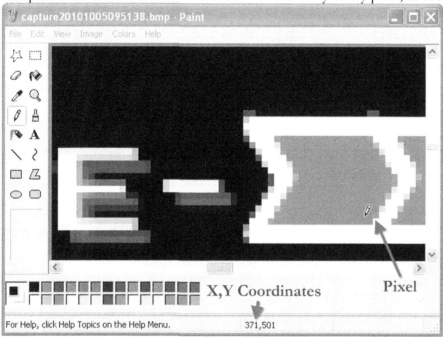

Figure 15-46 | Choose Almost Dead Pixel

Now enter your pixel coordinates into the Automation Tool Helper to get the RGB HEX color, as in Figure 15-47. My result returns FFFF0000, which is red.

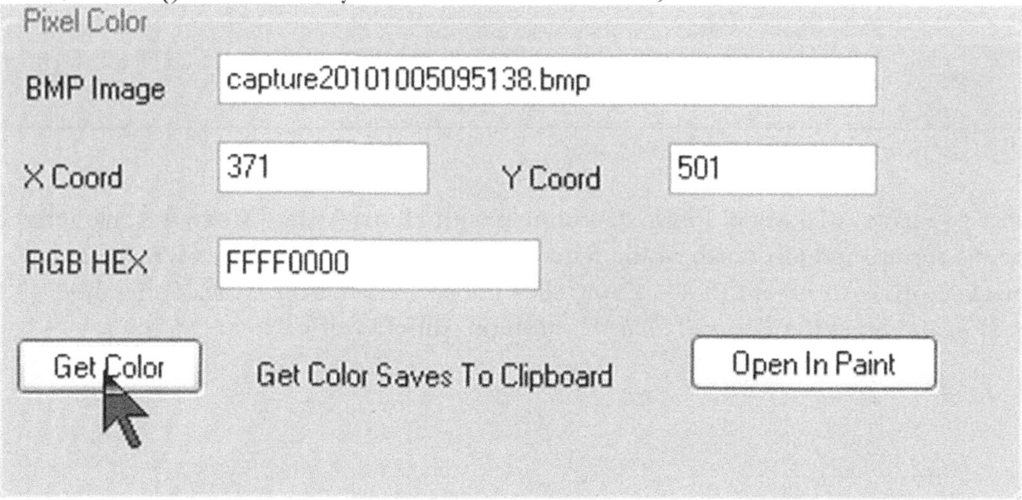

Figure 15-47 | Get Color Of Pixel 371x And 501y

284

After the game character completes a whole rectangle path, determine if the pixel 371x and 501y is no longer FFFF0000. If it is no longer FFFF0000 you will not start the rectangleTimer before exiting the rectangleTimer_Tick subroutine. Currently, the rectangleTimer.Start() is located in the Else statement when you check for the CTRL to bypass starting the timer. Inside the Else statement, update the code to check the 372x and 501y pixel for the color FFFF0000. If it finds a match then restart the timer, as shown below in Figure 15-48.

Currently the end of the rectangleTimer_Tick subroutine looks like Figure 15-48 below.

```
If (My.Computer.Keyboard.CtrlKeyDown) Then
    ' Do Not Start
Else

    SendKeys.SendWait("%{PRTSC}")
    Dim clip As IDataObject = Clipboard.GetDataObject()
    If clip.GetDataPresent(GetType(System.Drawing.Bitmap)) Then

        Dim screenCapture As Bitmap = _
            CType(clip.GetData(GetType(System.Drawing.Bitmap)), Bitmap)
        Dim almostDead As Color = screenCapture.GetPixel(371, 501)
        Dim almostDeadColor As String = Hex(almostDead.ToArgb)

        If (almostDeadColor = "FFFF0000") Then
            rectangleTimer.Start()
        End If

        Clipboard.Clear()

    End If

End If
```

Figure 15-48| Check For Almost Dead Character

Now test what you have. Make sure Firefox is running with Heros Arms. Move the character to just below the stump, and just north of the fence opening and ensure the character's life is below the pixel cutoff, as in Figure 15-49. Now click the *Save All* button. Click either *Start Debugging*, or (*F5*) and press the *Rectangle Pattern* button on gameLevelBot.

The character should move and attack to the left for six seconds, up for twelve seconds, right for six seconds, and finally down for twelve seconds. Then, the character should stop after the first complete loop due to the low life, as shown in the example in Figure 15-50.

Figure 15-49 | Low Life Character Life

Figure 15-50 | Stopped Due To Low

With that finished, begin on the Board Transition. Double-click on the Board Transition button, as in Figure 15-51, to create the boardTransition_Clicksubroutine, and also to be able to edit the code for the Board transition button, as in Figure 15-52.

Figure 15-51 | Double Click Rectangle Pattern Button

```
Private Sub boardTransition_Click(ByVal sender As System.Object, _
     ByVal e As System.EventArgs) Handles boardTransition.Click

End Sub
```

Figure 15-52 | boardTransition_Click Subroutine Created

Start the transitionTimer inside the subroutine boardTransition_Click by adding the code shown in the example in Figure 15-53.

```
Private Sub boardTransition_Click(ByVal sender As System.Object, _
     ByVal e As System.EventArgs) Handles boardTransition.Click
     transitionTimer.Start()
End Sub
```

Figure 15-53| Add Code To Start boardTransition_Click

Return to the View Designer by clicking on the *Form Design* tab, as in Figure 15-54.

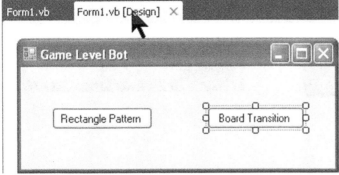

Figure 15-54 | Enter View Design

Double-click in the *transitionTimer* button, as in Figure 15-55, to create the transitionTimer_Ticksubroutine, and also to be able to edit the code for the transition Timer, as in Figure 15-56.

Figure 15-55 | Double Click transitionTimer

```
Private Sub transitionTimer_Tick(ByVal sender As System.Object, _
    ByVal e As System.EventArgs) Handles transitionTimer.Tick

End Sub
```

Figure 15-56 | transitionTimer_Tick Subroutine Created

Reuse the previous code to resize the Firefox browser.

Next, set the focus on the Firefox web browser, as shown in Figure 15-57.

```
Private Sub transitionTimer_Tick(ByVal sender As System.Object, _
    ByVal e As System.EventArgs) Handles transitionTimer.Tick

    Dim ps() As Process = Process.GetProcessesByName("firefox")
    If ps.Length > 0 Then
        Dim p As Process = ps(0)
        Dim hWnd As IntPtr = p.MainWindowHandle
        SetForegroundWindow(hWnd)
    End If

End Sub
```

Figure 15-57 | Set Focus On Firefox Web Browser

287

NOTE: IMPORTANT THAT YOU USE THE CTRL KEY! There is a bug which, if the ALT key and any arrow direction are used, the player gets stuck walking in that direction.

Inside transitionTimer, add the ability to exit transitionTimer when the CTRL key is held down, as in Figure 15-58.

```
transitionTimer.Stop()
Dim ps() As Process = Process.GetProcessesByName("firefox")
If ps.Length > 0 Then
    Dim p As Process = ps(0)
    Dim hWnd As IntPtr = p.MainWindowHandle
    SetForegroundWindow(hWnd)

    If (My.Computer.Keyboard.CtrlKeyDown) Then
        ' Do Not Start
    Else
        transitionTimer.Start()
    End If
End If
```

Figure 15-58 | Exit transitionTimer Code

The next step is to make sure the Firefox Web Browser is the specific size needed before doing any pixel recognition. Add SetWindowPos with your width and height to ensure the full Flash game screen can be seen. I set the width was 785 and height was 1061. Added a 50 millisecond delay to allow the resize to settle down, as in Figure 15-59.

```
transitionTimer.Stop()
Dim ps() As Process = Process.GetProcessesByName("firefox")
If ps.Length > 0 Then
    Dim p As Process = ps(0)
    Dim hWnd As IntPtr = p.MainWindowHandle
    SetForegroundWindow(hWnd)

    SetWindowPos(hWnd, IntPtr.Zero, 0, 0, _
        785, 1061, SWP_NOMOVE)

    System.Threading.Thread.Sleep(50)

    If (My.Computer.Keyboard.CtrlKeyDown) Then
        ' Do Not Start
    Else
        transitionTimer.Start()
    End If
End If
```

Figure 15-59 | ForceFirefox Web Browser Size

The next step is to layout the character movement pattern. The character always enters the board on the left side next to the shrub, with the mouse up and to the right. Note: It is always important to play a little **before** automating, so you know how the game works.

In the Hero's Arms game, when transitioning from one board to another the enemies are reset. This provides a great opportunity to find a location in which to gain experience without risking the loss of the character's life.

For your benefit, the path below is what I mapped out for the character to help in the visualization of what the automation Bot will do, as in Figure 15-60.

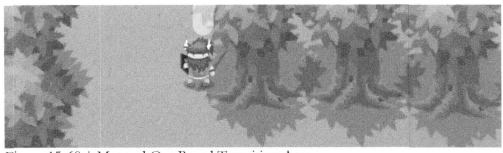

Figure 15-60 | Mapped Out Board Transition Area

The character will start in the lower part and move up for two seconds; pause; attack in place for seven seconds; then move up one second; move a quarter of a second to the right; and finally, move down for two seconds.

Add the code to move and cause the character to attack, as shown in Figure 15-61.

```
If ps.Length > 0 Then
    Dim p As Process = ps(0)
    Dim hWnd As IntPtr = p.MainWindowHandle
    SetForegroundWindow(hWnd)
    SetWindowPos(hWnd, IntPtr.Zero, 0, 0, _
        785, 1061, SWP_NOMOVE)
    System.Threading.Thread.Sleep(50)
    ' Move Up Two Seconds
    keybd_event(Keys.Up, MapVirtualKey(Keys.Up, 0), 0, 0)
    System.Threading.Thread.Sleep(2000)
    keybd_event(Keys.Up, MapVirtualKey(Keys.Up, 0), 2, 0)
    ' Attack For Seven Seconds
    For index = 1 To 70 Step 1
        keybd_event(Keys.Z, MapVirtualKey(Keys.Z, 0), 0, 0)
        System.Threading.Thread.Sleep(50)
        keybd_event(Keys.Z, MapVirtualKey(Keys.Z, 0), 2, 0)
        System.Threading.Thread.Sleep(50)
    Next
    ' Move Up One Second
    keybd_event(Keys.Up, MapVirtualKey(Keys.Up, 0), 0, 0)
    System.Threading.Thread.Sleep(1000)
    keybd_event(Keys.Up, MapVirtualKey(Keys.Up, 0), 2, 0)
    ' Move Right Quarter Second
    keybd_event(Keys.Right, MapVirtualKey(Keys.Right, 0), 0, 0)
    System.Threading.Thread.Sleep(250)
    keybd_event(Keys.Right, MapVirtualKey(Keys.Right, 0), 2, 0)
    ' Move Down Two Seconds
    keybd_event(Keys.Down, MapVirtualKey(Keys.Down, 0), 0, 0)
    System.Threading.Thread.Sleep(2000)
    keybd_event(Keys.Down, MapVirtualKey(Keys.Down, 0), 2, 0)
    ' Pause To Allow Board Transition To Complete
    System.Threading.Thread.Sleep(1000)
    If (My.Computer.Keyboard.CtrlKeyDown) Then
        ' Do Not Start
    Else
        transitionTimer.Start()
    End If
End If
```

Figure 15-61 | Add Code To Move And Have Character Attack

When moving a character, one issue is the fact that they gradually float. What is meant by 'float' is that if they move up three seconds and then back three seconds, after a while they are no longer in the same spot that they started. This is ever present when fighting enemies since the enemies' appearances tend to be random and this slows down a character's movement. One way to deal with floating is to have the character bump into a barrier. This will serve as a grounding point. The code in Figure 15-61 shows how to do this by moving up a total of three seconds, bumping into the hedge, and only moving back two seconds. This will serve to cancel out any floating of the character.

Another issue to be aware of is the time it takes a character to transition from one board to another. This can vary each time a character transitions, which can cause excessive floating in a character movement pattern. I have found it useful to add a delay after crossing the transition, as in shown in the previous example of Figure 15-61.

Now test what you have. Make sure Firefox is running with Heros Arms. Move your character to the tree clearing just below the transition area with the enemy mouse character, as in Figure 15-62. Now click the *Save All* button. Click either *Start Debugging,* or (*F5*) and press *Board Transition* button. The character should move up two seconds, attack for seven seconds, move up for one second, move right for a quarter of a second, down for two seconds, and pause for one second.

Figure 15-62 | Starting Point For Board Transition Bot

The finally piece is to check for an almost dead character and stop him in the safest place until he can be healed. Use the same pixel and code as in the Rectangle Pattern to determine whether the character is almost dead.

After the game character completes a board transition path, determine if the pixel 371x and 501y is still FFFF0000. If it is no longer FFFF0000 you will not start the transitionTimer before exiting the transitionTimer_Tick subroutine. Currently the transitionTimer.Start() is located in the Else statement when you check for the CTRL to bypass starting the timer.

Inside the Else statement, update the code to check the 372x and 501y pixel for the color FFFF0000. If it finds a match then restart the timer, as shown below in Figure 15-63.

```
If (My.Computer.Keyboard.CtrlKeyDown) Then
  ' Do Not Start
Else
  SendKeys.SendWait("%{PRTSC}")
  Dim clip As IDataObject = Clipboard.GetDataObject()
  If clip.GetDataPresent(GetType(System.Drawing.Bitmap)) Then
    Dim screenCapture As Bitmap = _
      CType(clip.GetData(GetType(System.Drawing.Bitmap)), Bitmap)
    Dim almostDead As Color = screenCapture.GetPixel(371, 501)
    Dim almostDeadColor As String = Hex(almostDead.ToArgb)
    If (almostDeadColor = "FFFF0000") Then
      transitionTimer.Start()
    End If
    Clipboard.Clear()
  End If

End If
```

Figure 15-63 | Check For Almost Dead Character

Now test what you have. Make sure Firefox is running with Heros Arms. Move your character to the tree clearing just below the transition area with the mouse, as in Figure 15-62. Now click the *Save All* button. Click either *Start Debugging*, or (*F5*) and press *Board Transition* button. The character should move up two seconds, attack for seven seconds, move up for one second, move right for a quarter of a second, down for two seconds, and pause for one second. If the Life bar drops to less than one quarter the character stops in the starting position, shown below in Figure 15-64.

Figure 15-64 | Starting Point For Board Transition Bot

Summary

The amount of time that creating a Bot can save a tester is huge when they create level bots to assist in the grind of gaining experience, money, and items. In this game, if the life reaches zero and the character has a Band-Aid, full health is restored. If, for example, a sample game allowed drinking a potion to regain health, then instead of not starting the timer the character would drink a potion, then continue and restart the timer.

Chapter 16:
Handling Multiple Scenes In Games

Many games have characters in multiple scenes that switch the player's control.   The automation Bot then needs to adjust when different scenes and controls are present.

Creating Handling Multiple Scenes Bot

Test the Flash game World of Pain: Chapter 2 developed by matakukos in 2009, hosted on the site MaxGames.com. Use the Mozilla Firefox web browser on which to play the game. World of Pain: Chapter 2 is a Role-playing Game (RPG) where the character is enhanced by fighting enemies and gaining experience.   As the character walks around on the map, they are randomly transported into a new fight scene. This will work great to demonstrate handling an automation Bot when encountering multiple scences.

World Of Pain: Chapter 2 Instructions:

- Press W, A, S, D Or Arrow Keys To Move Around
- Press The Shift Key To Run
- Press Left Mouse To Select
- Press Space Bar To Open Chest And Talk To People

Setting Up The Project

Start a new project and choose *Windows Form Application* and name it: **multipleScencesBot,** as in Figure 16-1.

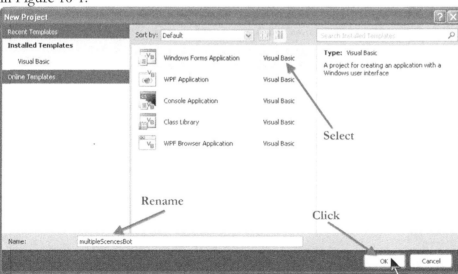

Figure 16-1 | Creating New multipleScenesBot

Now click the *Save All* button, as in the below Figure 16-2.

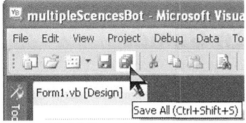

Figure 16-2 | Save All

Click *Save* to create directory structure for project, as in Figure 16-3.

Figure 16-3| Saving And Creating Directory For Project

Laying Out The Form

Only one button is needed for the Pixel Recognition Bot. Click on *Toolbox* and drag a *Button* on to the form. Resize the *form*, as in Figure 16-4 below.

Figure 16-4 | Add One Button To Form

Select *Button1*, as in Figure 16-5 below. Then update Button1 Text Properties to **Bot** and the (Name) property to **bot**, as in Figure 16-6 and Figure 16-7.

Figure 16-5 | Select Button1

Figure 16-6 | Text Property   Figure 16-7| (Name) Property

Update the form title to Multiple Scences Bot by clicking on the form anyplace there is no button. Select the *Properties* tab and update the Text property to **Multiple Scences Bot**, as shown in the example in Figure 16-8.

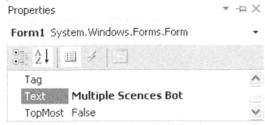

Figure 16-8 | Update Form Text Property

Click on the *Toolbox* and drag a *Timer* on to the form, as in Figure 16-9. The default of 100 milliseconds will be fine.

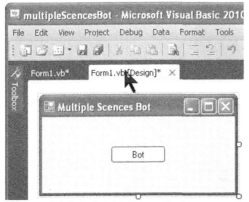

Figure 16-9 | Add Timer To Form

Next, determine a standard web browser size for the game. This is extremely important since pixel recognition will determine courses of action. Note: It is very important not to use the scroll bars since any move will completely change the pixel recognition.

Start Mozilla Firefox and open up the URL

http://www.maxgames.com/play/world-of-pain-2.html

Click on the *START* button, as in Figure 16-10.

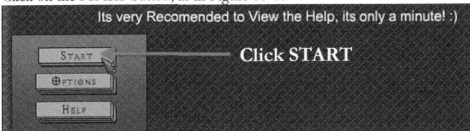

Figure 16-10 | Click Start Button

Click on any *NEW GAME* button, as in Figure 16-11.

Figure 16-11 | Click NEW GAME Button

Enter in your characters name; choose a gender and difficulty level, then click on the *START* button, as in Figure 16-12.

Figure 16-12 | Setup Character

Next, there is an information panel on the game and it is necessary to click on the *blinking Char box* to setup the character's statistics, as in Figure 16-13.

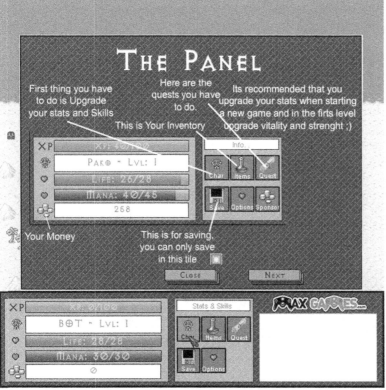

Figure 16-13 | Information Panel And Click On Blinking Char Box

There are additional Attribute points and Skill points. Under the Skill Points add one point to the HEAL skill so that the character can be healed if needed, and the two points to STRENGTH attribute, as in Figure 16-14. Click on the *Save* Icon to save these attributes. Then click on the *CLOSE* button below the character's image in the upper left hand corner.

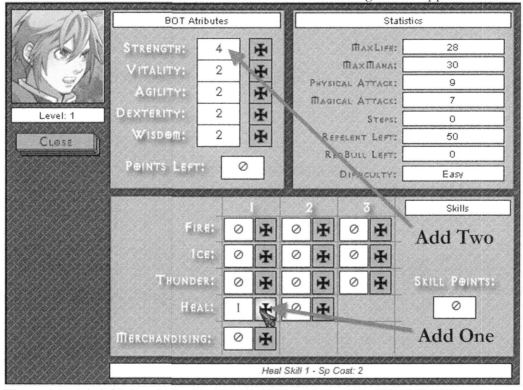

Figure 16-14 | Add One Point To HEAL Skill And Two To STRENGTH

Now click *NEXT* on The Panel to read more information about the game, as in Figure 16-15. When reading about the game is completed, click the *CLOSE* button, shown in Figure 16-16.

Figure 16-15 | Click Next Button   Figure 16-16 | Close When Done

Resize the Firefox web browser to ensure the full World of Pain 2 game screen is visible. Open up the Automation Tool Helper, enter in the Process Name firefox, and click the *Read Application* button to get the Height and Width of the browser, as in Figure 16-17. Mine shows a height of 1091 pixels by width of 791 pixels. Make sure to do this for your web browser to get the values that work on your computer.

ID	App Name	xPos	yPos	Height	Width
Play World Of Pain 2 : Max Games - Mozilla ...	1416	3889	84	1091	791

Figure 16-17 | firefox Application Information

There are two scenes that will utilize the Bot. The first scene is the desert island where the character is moved around using the arrow keys, as in Figure 16-18.

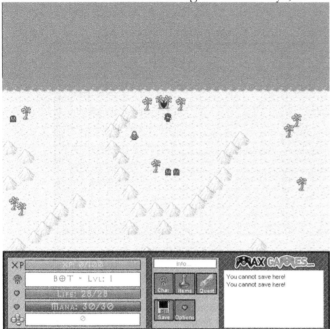

Figure 16-18 | Desert Island Map

The second is the fight scene, as shown here in Figure 16-19.

Figure 16-19 | Fight Scene

It is necessary to determine in which scene you are. To do this, look for a pixel or combination of pixels, which are constant and unique within a scene. In other words, they will not randomly appear in the other scene. When I compare the two scenes, the red heart near the life meter should work as a good identifier betweeen the two. Perform a screen shot of the desert island scene, open it in paint, and then zoom in to 800 percent, as in Figure 16-20. Once again, the goal is to find a pixel that is unique but also has the same color surrounding it to ensure a little buffer when determining a pixel's color.

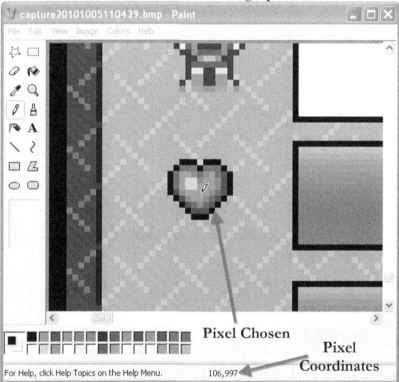

Figure 16-20 | Choose A Pixel To Determine Which Scene

Go back to the Automation Tool Helper and enter in your chosen pixel coordinates to get the color, as in Figure 16-21. Mine gave me the pixel color of FFF85010.

Figure 16-21 | Get Chosen Pixel Color

300

Coding The Project

Code the character to walk back and forth until a random enemy pops the character into fight mode. Once in fight mode, attack the enemy when the fight meter says ready. If the life meter reads less than ten, click on *Heal1* to increase the life. You are starting at the first level. It is typically better to complete a couple of levels by hand to ensure a cushion of health when running the automation Bot.

Double-click on the *Bot* button, as in Figure 16-22, to create the bot_Click subroutine, and also to edit the code for the rectangle Bot button, as in Figure 16-33.

Figure 16-22 | Double Click Bot Button

```
Private Sub bot_Click(ByVal sender As System.Object, _
    ByVal e As System.EventArgs) Handles bot.Click

End Sub
```

Figure 16-23| bot_Click Subroutine Created

Add code to start Timer1 by adding the code, in Figure 16-24.

```
Private Sub bot_Click(ByVal sender As System.Object, _
    ByVal e As System.EventArgs) Handles bot.Click

    Timer1.Start()

End Sub
```

Figure 16-24| Add Code To Start Timer1

Return to the View Designer by clicking on the *Form Design* tab, shown in Figure 16-25.

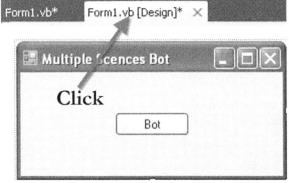

Figure 16-25 | Enter View Design

Double-click on the *Timer1* button, as in Figure 16-26, to create the rectangle Timer1_Tick subroutine, and also to edit the code for the rectangle *Timer1* button, as in Figure 16-27.

Figure 16-26 | Double Click Timer1

```
Private Sub Timer1_Tick(ByVal sender As System.Object, _
    ByVal e As System.EventArgs) Handles Timer1.Tick

End Sub
```

Figure 16-27| Timer1_Tick Subroutine Created

The next step is to ensure focus is set on Firefox and that it is resized to the specified size. To do that, first add the libraries SetForegroundWindow and SetWindowPos and the constant SWP_NOMOVE as below Public Class Form1, as in Figure 16-28.

```
Public Class Form1

    Private Declare Function SetForegroundWindow Lib "user32" _
        (ByVal handle As IntPtr) As Integer

    Public Declare Function SetWindowPos Lib "user32" Alias _
        "SetWindowPos" (ByVal hwnd As IntPtr, _
        ByVal hWndInsertAfter As IntPtr, ByVal x As Integer, _
        ByVal y As Integer, ByVal cx As Integer, _
        ByVal cy As Integer, ByVal wFlags As Integer) As Integer

    Public Const SWP_NOMOVE = &H2
```

Figure 16-28| Add Focus And Resize Libraries And Constant

Add the libraries to allow for sending keystrokes for the character's movement. To do that, add keybd_event and MapVirtualKey libraries, as shown in Figure 16-29.

```
Public Class Form1

    Private Declare Sub keybd_event Lib "user32.dll" (ByVal bVk As Byte, _
    ByVal bScan As Byte, ByVal dwFlags As Integer, _
    ByVal dwExtraInfo As Integer)

    Private Declare Function MapVirtualKey Lib "user32" Alias "MapVirtualKeyA" _
        (ByVal wCode As Integer, ByVal wMapType As Integer) As Integer

    Private Declare Function SetForegroundWindow Lib "user32" _
```

Figure 16-29| Add Keystroke Libraries

To click on *Attack* and *Heal 1*, application specific mouse clicks are required. To do that, add the libraries mouse_event and GetWindowRect along with the constants MOUSEEVENTF_LEFTDOWN and MOUSEEVENTF_LEFTUP and the data structure RECT, as shown in the example in Figure 16-30.

```
Public Class Form1
  Private Declare Sub mouse_event Lib "user32" (ByVal dwFlags As Integer, _
    ByVal dx As Integer, ByVal dy As Integer, ByVal cButtons As Integer, _
    ByVal dwExtraInfo As Integer)

  Private Const MOUSEEVENTF_LEFTDOWN = &H2
  Private Const MOUSEEVENTF_LEFTUP = &H4

  Private Structure RECT
    Public Left As Int32
    Public Top As Int32
    Public Right As Int32
    Public Bottom As Int32
  End Structure

  Private Declare Function GetWindowRect Lib "user32" Alias _
    "GetWindowRect" (ByVal hwnd As IntPtr, ByRef lpRect As RECT) As Integer

  Private Declare Sub keybd_event Lib "user32.dll" (ByVal bVk As Byte, _
```

Figure 16-30 | Add Application Specific Mouse Clicks

The next piece should look familiar. It is the same beginning as with Game Level Bot. When creating automation Bots it is easy to create templates that save time by reusing code. Appendix A includes code templates to help assist you in reusing code.

Set the focus on the Firefox web browser by adding the code shown below to the subroutine Timer1_Tick, as in Figure 16-31.

```
Private Sub Timer1_Tick(ByVal sender As System.Object, _
    ByVal e As System.EventArgs) Handles Timer1.Tick

    Dim ps() As Process = Process.GetProcessesByName("firefox")
    If ps.Length > 0 Then
      Dim p As Process = ps(0)
      Dim hWnd As IntPtr = p.MainWindowHandle
      SetForegroundWindow(hWnd)
    End If

End Sub
```

Figure 16-31 | Set Focus On Firefox Web Browser

Inside Timer1_Tick you need to add the ability to not restart Timer1 when the CTRL key is held down, as in Figure 16-32.
NOTE: IMPORTANT THAT YOU USE THE CTRL KEY! There is a bug that if the ALT key and any arrow direction are used, the player gets stuck walking in that direction.

```
Private Sub Timer1_Tick(ByVal sender As System.Object, _
    ByVal e As System.EventArgs) Handles Timer1.Tick
    Timer1.Stop()
    Dim ps() As Process = Process.GetProcessesByName("firefox")
    If ps.Length > 0 Then
        Dim p As Process = ps(0)
        Dim hWnd As IntPtr = p.MainWindowHandle
        SetForegroundWindow(hWnd)
        If (My.Computer.Keyboard.CtrlKeyDown) Then
            ' Do Not Start
        Else
            Timer1.Start()
        End If
    End If
End Sub
```
Figure 16-32 | Stop Timer1 If Alt Key Held Down

The next step is to make sure the Firefox Web Browser is the specific size needed before doing any pixel recognition. Add SetWindowPos with the width and height to ensure the full Flash game screen can be seen. My width was 791 and height was 1091, as coded in Figure 16-33. Also add a delay of 50 milliseconds to allow the system to settle down before making any more moves or decisions in the game.

```
If ps.Length > 0 Then
    Dim p As Process = ps(0)
    Dim hWnd As IntPtr = p.MainWindowHandle
    SetForegroundWindow(hWnd)
    SetWindowPos(hWnd, IntPtr.Zero, 0, 0, _
        791, 1091, SWP_NOMOVE)
    System.Threading.Thread.Sleep(50)

    If (My.Computer.Keyboard.CtrlKeyDown) Then
        ' Do Not Start
    Else
        Timer1.Start()
    End If
End If
```
Figure 16-33 | ForceFirefox Web Browser Size

Now determine which scene your character is in and then act accordingly. Refer back to Figure 16-20 and Figure 16-21 to get the pixel coordinates and color for the heart icon which is to the left of the Life meter. My pixel was 106x and 1003y, with a pixel color of FFF85010. Your code needs to perform a screen shot and get the pixel color for 106x and 1003y (or your specific pixel) and compare it with the color FFF85010 or (your specific color). Add the check after resizing the browser and delaying for 50 milliseconds, as in Figure 16-34.

```
Private Sub Timer1_Tick(ByVal sender As System.Object, _
   ByVal e As System.EventArgs) Handles Timer1.Tick
   Timer1.Stop()
   Dim ps() As Process = Process.GetProcessesByName("firefox")
   If ps.Length > 0 Then
      Dim p As Process = ps(0)
      Dim hWnd As IntPtr = p.MainWindowHandle
      SetForegroundWindow(hWnd)
      SetWindowPos(hWnd, IntPtr.Zero, 0, 0, _
         791, 1091, SWP_NOMOVE)
      System.Threading.Thread.Sleep(50)
      SendKeys.SendWait("%{PRTSC}")
      Dim clip As IDataObject = Clipboard.GetDataObject()
      If clip.GetDataPresent(GetType(System.Drawing.Bitmap)) Then
         Dim screenCapture As Bitmap = _
            CType(clip.GetData(GetType(System.Drawing.Bitmap)), Bitmap)
         Dim heart As Color = screenCapture.GetPixel(106, 1003)
         Dim heartColor As String = Hex(heart.ToArgb)
         If (heartColor = "FFF85010") Then

            ' Desert Island Scene

         Else

            ' Fight Scene

         End If
      End If
      If (My.Computer.Keyboard.CtrlKeyDown) Then
         ' Do Not Start
      Else
         Timer1.Start()
      End If
   End If
End Sub
```

Figure 16-34 | Take Screenshot To Determine Which Scene The Character Is In

When the character is in the desert island scene, simply move him in an up and down direction until he encounters a fight. To keep track of the last direction traveled, add a global variable named **direction** of type Boolean.   If direction is set to False, travel south until the time expires or he meets an enemy. If the direction is set to True, travel north until the time expires or he meets an enemy. Add the variable direction of type Boolean with an initial value of False in the global name space just below Public Class Form1, as in Figure 16-35.

```
Public Class Form1

    Dim direction As Boolean = False

    Private Declare Sub mouse_event Lib "user32" (ByVal dwFlags As Integer, _
```

Figure 16-35 Add Global Variable direction Of Type Boolean

If your character is in the desert island scene, he will travel in the direction dictated by the direction variable. The character will travel three seconds, then flip the direction value to False if it was True, and True if it was False. Add the code in the If block of the heartColor = "FFF85010", as in Figure 16-36.

```
If (heartColor = "FFF85010") Then
    ' Desert Island Scene

    If (direction = True) Then

        keybd_event(Keys.Up, MapVirtualKey(Keys.Up, 0), 0, 0)
        System.Threading.Thread.Sleep(3000)
        keybd_event(Keys.Up, MapVirtualKey(Keys.Up, 0), 2, 0)
        direction = False

    Else

        keybd_event(Keys.Down, MapVirtualKey(Keys.Down, 0), 0, 0)
        System.Threading.Thread.Sleep(3000)
        keybd_event(Keys.Down, MapVirtualKey(Keys.Down, 0), 2, 0)
        direction = True

    End If

Else
    ' Fight Scene
End If
```

Figure 16-36 Add Global Variable direction Of Type Boolean

Now test what you have. Make sure Firefox is running with World of Pain: Chapter 2. Move the character to right, as in Figure 16-37. Now click the *Save All* button. Click either *Start Debugging*, or (*F5*) and press the *Bot* button. The character should move down for three seconds, then up for three seconds. When finished, hold down the CTRL key.

Figure 16-37 | Move Character To The Right

Next, the character needs to fight enemies when they randomly pop up. To do that, take a screen shot of when the fight bar says "Wait". Open the Automation Tool Helper and enter **firefox** as the Process Name and click *Read Application* with the game World of Pain 2 open. Move the character until a fight scene pops up and take a screenshot by clinking on the *ID*, as in the example in Figure 16-38.

ID	App Name	xPos	yPos	Height	Width
Play World Of Pain 2 : Max Games - Mozilla ...	1416	3889	84	1091	791
MCI command handling window	1416	0	0	34	123
NetscapeDispatchWnd	1416	-50	-50	34	123

Figure 16-38 | Click On ID To Take Screenshot

Then click *Open In Paint* and zoom in to 800 percent and get a grayish pixel at the end of the Wait bar, as in Figure 16-39. The pixel coordinates I received below were 394x and 885y.

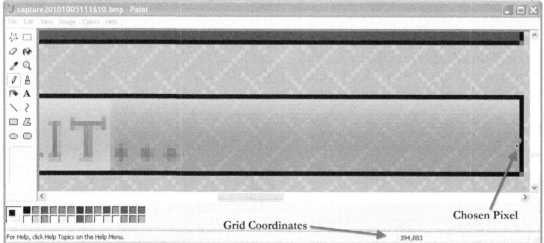

Figure 16-39 | Find Grayish Pixel At End Of Wait Bar

I entered **394**x and **883**y into Automation Tool Helper to get the color, as in Figure 16-40.

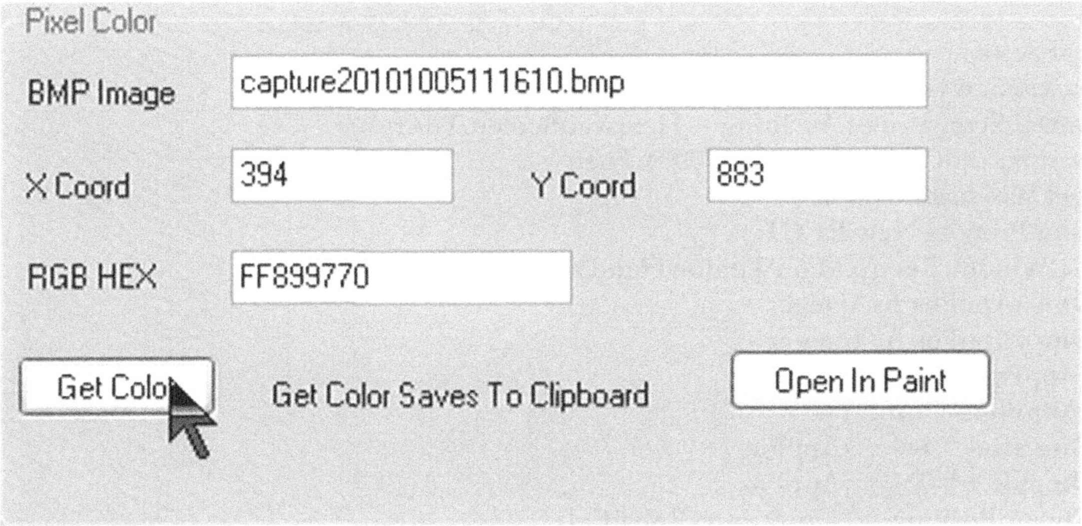

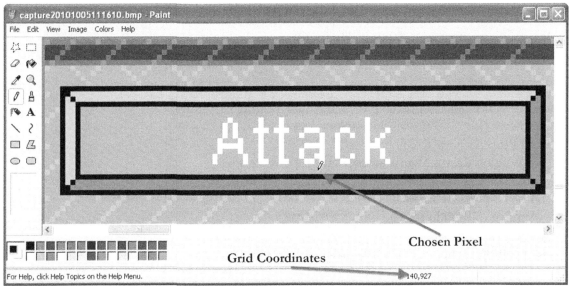

Figure 16-40 | Capture Pixel Color For 394x and 888y

The pixel color I capture at 394x and 888y was FF899770. Yours may be different on your particular system, and you should use your specific coordinates and pixel color.

If the character is in a fight scene and the color is not FF899770, then click on the *Attack* button. Find the middle of the *Attack* button to get a grid coordinate, as in Figure 16-41. The pixel grid coordinate I have is 140x and 927y.

Figure 16-41 | Find Pixel Grid Coordinate In Middle Of Attack Button.

308

Add the code into the Else code block below the Fight Scene comment, as in Figure 16-42.

```
Else
  ' Fight Scene
  Dim waitScreen As Color = screenCapture.GetPixel(394, 888)
  Dim waitScreenColor As String = Hex(waitScreen.ToArgb)
  If (waitScreenColor <> "FF899770") Then
    'get Window Position
    Dim Prop As New RECT()
    GetWindowRect(p.MainWindowHandle.ToInt32, Prop)
    Dim xAppPos As Integer
    Dim yAppPos As Integer
    xAppPos = Prop.Left
    yAppPos = Prop.Top
    Dim xRel = 140 + xAppPos
    Dim yRel = 927 + yAppPos
    Cursor.Position = New Point(xRel, yRel)
    mouse_event(MOUSEEVENTF_LEFTDOWN, xRel, yRel, 0, 0)
    System.Threading.Thread.Sleep(50)
    mouse_event(MOUSEEVENTF_LEFTUP, xRel, yRel, 0, 0)
  End If
End If
```

Figure 16-42 Add Global Variable direction Of Type Boolean

New code broken down line by line:

C: Dim waitScreen As Color = screenCapture.GetPixel(394, 888)
   Dim waitScreenColor As String = Hex(waitScreen.ToArgb)
D: Get color of the end of a WAIT bar pixel

C: If (waitScreenColor <> "FF899770") Then
D: If color is not grayish proceed to click Attack button.

C: Dim Prop As New RECT()
     GetWindowRect(p.MainWindowHandle.ToInt32, Prop)
     Dim xAppPos As Integer
     Dim yAppPos As Integer
     xAppPos = Prop.Left
     yAppPos = Prop.Top
D: Get position on upper left hand corner of Firefox

C: Dim xRel = 140 + xAppPos
     Dim yRel = 927 + yAppPos
D: Calculate relative x and y position of middle of Attack button

C: Cursor.Position = New Point(xRel, yRel)
     mouse_event(MOUSEEVENTF_LEFTDOWN, xRel, yRel, 0, 0)
     System.Threading.Thread.Sleep(50)
     mouse_event(MOUSEEVENTF_LEFTUP, xRel, yRel, 0, 0)
     End If
D: Send left mouse click to relative position of Firefox 140x and 937y on Attack button

Now test what you have. Make sure Firefox is running with World of Pain: Chapter 2. Move the character to right, as in Figure 16-43.   Now click the *Save All* button. Click either *Start Debugging,* or *(F5)* and press the *Bot* button. The character should move down for three seconds, then up for three seconds. When the fight screen pops up the character should attack when the WAIT bar turns to READY. When finished, hold down the CTRL key.

Figure 16-43 | Botting Character Start Point

When the character's life reaches about one quarter remaining, click on the Heal 1 button to convert Mana into Life. Using the screenshot of the Attack scene, find a pixel on the life bar while about one quarter of the life bar is still red, as in Figure 16-44. My grid coordinates were 221x and 824y.

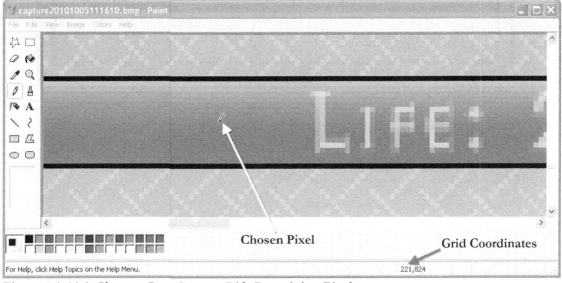

Figure 16-44 | Choose One Quarter Life Remaining Pixel

Enter in your specific grid coordinates into the Automation Tool Helper to get the color of the pixel, as in Figure 16-45. The color return for my pixel was FFBF4242.

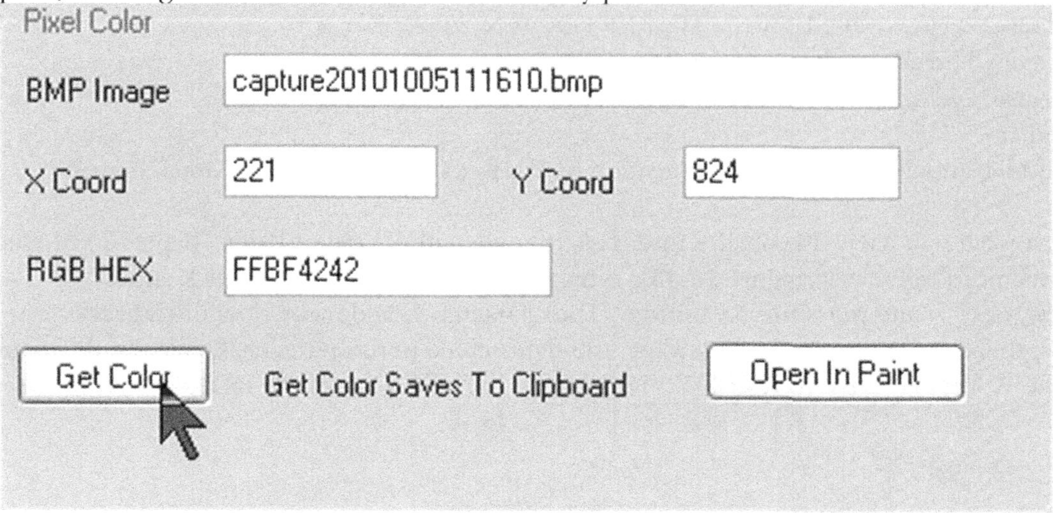

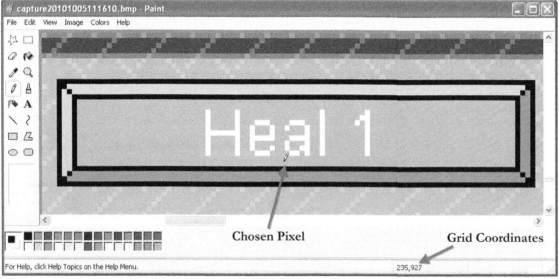

Figure 16-45 | Get Pixel Color

If the color is no longer reddish, then click on the *Heal 1* button. Find the middle of the *Heal 1* button using the screenshot from the Attack scene, as in Figure 16-46. My specific grid coordinates were 235x and 927y.

Figure 16-46 | Pixel In The Middle Of Heal 1 Button

The Bot will moniter the *Wait* button. When the *Wait* button has turned to ready, determine whether the character's life bar has dropped to less than one quarter. If the character's life is less than one quarter, then hit the *Heal 1* button, or else click the *Attack* button.   Below is a visual diagram of the logic, shown below in the example in Figure 16-47.

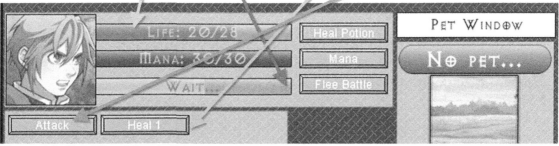

Figure 16-47 | Visual Logic Diagram

Add the code to determine whether the life bar is less than one-quarter and click *Heal 1* button, or else click the *Attack* button, as in Figure 16-48.

```
Else
  ' Fight Scene
  Dim lifeBar As Color = screenCapture.GetPixel(221, 829)
  Dim lifeBarColor As String = Hex(lifeBar.ToArgb)
  If (lifeBarColor <> "FFBF4242") Then
    'Heal 1
    Dim Prop As New RECT()
    GetWindowRect(p.MainWindowHandle.ToInt32, Prop)
    Dim xAppPos As Integer
    Dim yAppPos As Integer
    xAppPos = Prop.Left
    yAppPos = Prop.Top
    Dim xRel = 235 + xAppPos
    Dim yRel = 927 + yAppPos
    Cursor.Position = New Point(xRel, yRel)
    mouse_event(MOUSEEVENTF_LEFTDOWN, xRel, yRel, 0, 0)
    System.Threading.Thread.Sleep(50)
    mouse_event(MOUSEEVENTF_LEFTUP, xRel, yRel, 0, 0)
  Else
    'Attack
```

```
    Dim waitScreen As Color = screenCapture.GetPixel(394, 888)
    Dim waitScreenColor As String = Hex(waitScreen.ToArgb)
    If (waitScreenColor <> "FF899770") Then
      'get Window Position
      Dim Prop As New RECT()
      GetWindowRect(p.MainWindowHandle.ToInt32, Prop)
      Dim xAppPos As Integer
      Dim yAppPos As Integer
      xAppPos = Prop.Left
      yAppPos = Prop.Top
      Dim xRel = 140 + xAppPos
      Dim yRel = 927 + yAppPos
      Cursor.Position = New Point(xRel, yRel)
      mouse_event(MOUSEEVENTF_LEFTDOWN, xRel, yRel, 0, 0)
      System.Threading.Thread.Sleep(50)
      mouse_event(MOUSEEVENTF_LEFTUP, xRel, yRel, 0, 0)
    End If
  End If
End If
```

Figure 16-48 | Add Life Bar Check And Heal 1 Button Click

Now test what you have. Make sure Firefox is running with World of Pain: Chapter 2. Move the character to right, as in Figure 16-49. Now click the *Save All* button. Click either *Start Debugging*, or (F5) and press the *Bot* button. The character should move down for three seconds, then up for three seconds. When the fight screen pops up the character should attack when the WAIT bar turns to READY, and if the LIFE bar is less than one-quarter the *Heal 1* button is clicked. When finished hold down the CTRL key.

Figure 16-49 | Botting Character Start Point

Summary

In this Bot you show how to combine mouse clicks, keystroke sending, and pixel recognition.

Appendix A:
Bot Automation Tool Box Directory

Mouse Click At Current Location

```
Private Declare Sub mouse_event Lib "user32" (ByVal dwFlags As Integer, _
ByVal dx As Integer, ByVal dy As Integer, ByVal cButtons As Integer, _
ByVal dwExtraInfo As Integer)

Private Const MOUSEEVENTF_LEFTDOWN = &H2
Private Const MOUSEEVENTF_LEFTUP = &H4
Private Const MOUSEEVENTF_RIGHTDOWN = &H8
Private Const MOUSEEVENTF_RIGHTUP = &H10
```
Libraries

```
' Left Mouse Click
mouse_event(MOUSEEVENTF_LEFTDOWN, 0, 0, 0, 0)
System.Threading.Thread.Sleep(500)
mouse_event(MOUSEEVENTF_LEFTUP, 0, 0, 0, 0)

' Right Mouse Click
mouse_event(MOUSEEVENTF_RIGHTDOWN, 0, 0, 0, 0)
System.Threading.Thread.Sleep(1000)
mouse_event(MOUSEEVENTF_RIGHTUP, 0, 0, 0, 0)
```
Code

Set Focus On Remote Application

```
Private Declare Function SetForegroundWindow Lib "user32" _
    (ByVal handle As IntPtr) As Integer
```
Libraries

```
Dim ps() As Process = Process.GetProcessesByName("processName")

If ps.Length > 0 Then
   'Set Focus
   Dim p As Process = ps(0)
   Dim hWnd As IntPtr = p.MainWindowHandle
   SetForegroundWindow(hWnd)
End If
```
Code

Specific Key Automation With Control On Press And Release

```
Private Declare Sub keybd_event Lib "user32.dll" (ByVal bVk As Byte, _
    ByVal bScan As Byte, ByVal dwFlags As Integer, _
    ByVal dwExtraInfo As Integer)

Private Declare Function MapVirtualKey Lib "user32" Alias "MapVirtualKeyA" _
    (ByVal wCode As Integer, ByVal wMapType As Integer) As Integer
```
Libraries

```
'Press Spacebar
keybd_event(Keys.Space, MapVirtualKey(Keys.Space, 0), 0, 0)
' Wait 200 milliseconds
System.Threading.Thread.Sleep(200)
'Release Spacebar
keybd_event(Keys.Space, MapVirtualKey(Keys.Space, 0), 2, 0)
```
Code

Specific Multiple Key Press

```
Private Declare Sub keybd_event Lib "user32.dll" (ByVal bVk As Byte, _
    ByVal bScan As Byte, ByVal dwFlags As Integer, _
    ByVal dwExtraInfo As Integer)

Private Declare Function MapVirtualKey Lib "user32" Alias "MapVirtualKeyA" _
    (ByVal wCode As Integer, ByVal wMapType As Integer) As Integer
```
Libraries

```
keybd_event(Keys.M, MapVirtualKey(Keys.M, 0), 0, 0)
keybd_event(Keys.Z, MapVirtualKey(Keys.Z, 0), 0, 0)
System.Threading.Thread.Sleep(200)
keybd_event(Keys.M, MapVirtualKey(Keys.M, 0), 2, 0)
keybd_event(Keys.Z, MapVirtualKey(Keys.Z, 0), 2, 0)
```
Code

Using CTRL Key To Terminate Timer

```
If (My.Computer.Keyboard.CtrlKeyDown) Then
    ' Do Not Start
Else
    Timer1.Start()
End If
```
Code

Pause Or Sleep Between Clicks, Button Down/Up, And Or Calls

```
'Sleep for two seconds
System.Threading.Thread.Sleep(2000)
```
Code

Sending Keys Automation

```
' Send the keystrokes to the application.
SendKeys.SendWait("Please give me an F, because I deserve it!")
System.Threading.Thread.Sleep(1000)

' Send "Ctrl a"
SendKeys.SendWait("^a")
System.Threading.Thread.Sleep(1000)
```
Code

Determine Absolute Position Of An Application And Then Relative Within An Application And Application Width And Height.

```
Private Structure RECT
   Public Left As Int32
   Public Top As Int32
   Public Right As Int32
   Public Bottom As Int32
 End Structure

Private Declare Function GetWindowRect Lib "user32" Alias _
   "GetWindowRect" (ByVal hwnd As IntPtr, ByRef lpRect As RECT) As Integer
```
Libraries

```
Dim ps() As Process = Process.GetProcessesByName("calc")

If ps.Length > 0 Then
   'Set Focus
   Dim p As Process = ps(0)
   Dim hWnd As IntPtr = p.MainWindowHandle
   SetForegroundWindow(hWnd)

   'get Window Position
   Dim Prop As New RECT()
   GetWindowRect(p.MainWindowHandle.ToInt32, Prop)
   Dim xAppPos As Integer
```

```
    Dim yAppPos As Integer
    Dim appHeight As Integer
    Dim appWidth As Integer
    xAppPos = Prop.Left
    yAppPos = Prop.Top
    appHeight = Prop.Bottom - Prop.Top
    appWidth = Prop.Right - Prop.Left
End If
```

Code

Mouse Click On Specific Application

```
Private Declare Sub mouse_event Lib "user32" (ByVal dwFlags As Integer, _
ByVal dx As Integer, ByVal dy As Integer, ByVal cButtons As Integer, _
ByVal dwExtraInfo As Integer)

Private Const MOUSEEVENTF_LEFTDOWN = &H2
Private Const MOUSEEVENTF_LEFTUP = &H4
Private Const MOUSEEVENTF_RIGHTDOWN = &H8
Private Const MOUSEEVENTF_RIGHTUP = &H10
```

Libraries

```
Dim ps() As Process = Process.GetProcessesByName("firefox")
If ps.Length > 0 Then
    Dim p As Process = ps(0)
    Dim hWnd As IntPtr = p.MainWindowHandle
    SetForegroundWindow(hWnd)
    Dim Prop As New RECT()
    GetWindowRect(p.MainWindowHandle.ToInt32, Prop)
    Dim xAppPos As Integer
    Dim yAppPos As Integer
    xAppPos = Prop.Left
    yAppPos = Prop.Top
    Dim xRel = 140 + xAppPos
    Dim yRel = 927 + yAppPos
    Cursor.Position = New Point(xRel, yRel)
    mouse_event(MOUSEEVENTF_LEFTDOWN, xRel, yRel, 0, 0)
    System.Threading.Thread.Sleep(50)
    mouse_event(MOUSEEVENTF_LEFTUP, xRel, yRel, 0, 0)
End If
```

Code

Pixel Detection

```
SendKeys.SendWait("%{PRTSC}")
Dim clip As IDataObject = Clipboard.GetDataObject()
If clip.GetDataPresent(GetType(System.Drawing.Bitmap)) Then
   Dim screenCapture As Bitmap = _
      CType(clip.GetData(GetType(System.Drawing.Bitmap)), Bitmap)
   Dim heart As Color = screenCapture.GetPixel(106, 1003)
   Dim heartColor As String = Hex(heart.ToArgb)
   If (heartColor = "FFF85010") Then
      ' Desert Island Scene
   Else
      ' Fight Scene
   End If
End If
```
Code

Start Remote Application

```
Dim p As Process
 p = Process.Start("C:\Windows\system32\calc.exe")
 p.WaitForInputIdle()
System.Threading.Thread.Sleep(2000)
```
Code

Start Remote Application And Resize

```
Public Declare Function SetWindowPos Lib "user32" Alias _
   "SetWindowPos" (ByVal hwnd As IntPtr, _
      ByVal hWndInsertAfter As IntPtr, ByVal x As Integer, _
      ByVal y As Integer, ByVal cx As Integer, _
      ByVal cy As Integer, ByVal wFlags As Integer) As Integer

Public Const SWP_NOMOVE = &H2
```
Libraries

```
p = Process.Start("notepad.exe")
p.WaitForInputIdle()
System.Threading.Thread.Sleep(4000)

SetWindowPos(hWnd, IntPtr.Zero, 0, 0, _
   800, 600, SWP_NOMOVE)
```
Code

Start Remote Web Browser With URL

```
Dim p As Process
p = Process.Start("C:\Program Files\Mozilla Firefox\firefox.exe", "http://www.lulu.com")
p.WaitForInputIdle()

System.Threading.Thread.Sleep(2000)
```
Code

Start Remote Web Browser With URL And Resize

```
Public Declare Function SetWindowPos Lib "user32" Alias _
    "SetWindowPos" (ByVal hwnd As IntPtr, _
      ByVal hWndInsertAfter As IntPtr, ByVal x As Integer, _
      ByVal y As Integer, ByVal cx As Integer, _
      ByVal cy As Integer, ByVal wFlags As Integer) As Integer
```
Libraries

```
Dim p As Process
p = Process.Start("C:\Program Files\Mozilla Firefox\firefox.exe", "http://www.lulu.com")
p.WaitForInputIdle()

System.Threading.Thread.Sleep(2000)

Dim ps() As Process = Process.GetProcessesByName("firefox")
Dim pTemp As Process = ps(0)
Dim hWnd As IntPtr = pTemp.MainWindowHandle
SetWindowPos(hWnd, IntPtr.Zero, 0, 0, 200, 200, 0)
System.Threading.Thread.Sleep(2000)
```
Code – More Reliable

```
Dim p As Process
p = Process.Start("C:\Program Files\Mozilla Firefox\firefox.exe", "http://www.lulu.com")
p.WaitForInputIdle()

System.Threading.Thread.Sleep(2000)

'Resize Window
SetWindowPos(p.MainWindowHandle, IntPtr.Zero, 0, 0, 800, 400, 0)

System.Threading.Thread.Sleep(2000)
```
Code - Shorter

Using Findwindow To Detect Application Or Application Children By Title

```
Private Declare Function FindWindow Lib "user32.dll" Alias "FindWindowA" _
    (ByVal lpClassName As String, ByVal lpWindowName As String) As Integer
```

Libraries

```
Dim windowHandle As Integer
windowHandle = FindWindow(vbNullString, "High Scores")
If windowHandle <> 0 Then
    SetForegroundWindow(windowHandle)

End If
```

Code

Index

322

I hope you enjoyed the book. This book is dedicated to the memory of Stewart Miller, a great brother.

Sincerely,
Steven C. Miller Jr.

Made in the USA
Middletown, DE
24 August 2022

72153244R00183